DISCRIMINATION AND POPULAR CULTURE

Discrimination and Popular Culture

Edited by Denys Thompson

Second Edition

HEINEMANN
LONDON

Heinemann Educational Books Ltd

LONDON EDINBURGH MELBOURNE AUCKLAND TORONTO
HONG KONG SINGAPORE KUALA LUMPUR
IBADAN NAIROBI JOHANNESBURG
NEW DELHI

ISBN 0 435 18883 6

First published by Penguin Books Ltd, 1964
Second edition first published jointly by
Penguin Books Ltd and Heinemann Educational
Books Ltd, 1973

Published by
Heinemann Educational Books Ltd,
48 Charles Street, London W1X 8AH
Printed Offset Litho and bound in Great Britain by
Cox & Wyman Ltd, London, Fakenham and Reading

Contents

Foreword

The present book is a revised and for the most part re-written edition of the original volume, with an additional chapter by Fred Inglis and a new writer on 'The Film'. The first version was designed to follow up a Conference organized by the National Union of Teachers, with the title 'Popular Culture and Personal Responsibility'. It was attended by large numbers 'of those engaged in education together with parents, those concerned with the welfare of children and young people, and people involved in the mass media themselves'. The aim was 'to examine the impact of mass communications on present-day moral and cultural standards', and the purpose of the book was to develop the use for good of the mass media.

D.T.

1   Introduction

DENYS THOMPSON

This book is about the culture supplied to us by those who speak and write, design and compose, with large numbers of consumers in mind. Those numbers have increased enormously this century to the present figure for the world's population of 3,500,000,000, which is likely to double in the next thirty years. Many of our needs, our real ones as well as those constantly being thought up for us, are met by very large concerns, which will be larger and fewer if the present trend towards international combines continues. Imperial Chemical Industries for example has a capital of over £1,130 millions; Burmah Oil and Conoco together are capitalized at £1,200 millions; while the Ford Motor Company has assets of £2,140,000,000 and 317,000 employees. Such firms have a near-monopoly, and in the case of the public corporations of this country a complete monopoly, of the goods or services they are concerned with, or share it with a few other giants. So that it would be very difficult for instance to break into the markets for chemicals, cars, electrical goods . . . and impossible when the field is controlled by state businesses like the Coal Board and the C.E.G.B.

These large undertakings have a number of characteristics and aims in common. When they are manufacturers they exploit the advantages of mass-production – the breaking-down of a complicated process into a large number of small operations in which human labour is near-mechanical or unnecessary. The plant needed to produce the long runs that allow the end product to be sold profitably at a price within reach of the masses is complicated and expensive. Planning and setting-up may be a long job, and once the plant has started it must be kept going all day and every day if possible to recover the capital and keep the proportion of overheads low. The process may be so difficult to

9

restart that it pays to produce and throw away the product rather than stop, which is what happened when Courtaulds' Wolverhampton factory had a strike; yarn was made and then scrapped because it would have been more expensive to stop it. Consequently sales must be advanced all the time, and fresh uses and markets discovered, whatever the genuineness of the demand or the priority of the need. To keep the plant going as its nature demands the sales of mass-produced things must be everexpanding, and the market controlled as far as possible.

The large industry employs many professionals and experts. Fresh fields must be explored everywhere; diversification must always be in mind, as products go out of fashion or are superseded or, like tobacco, found to be lethal; human nature must be analysed with the possibility of fresh manipulations in view; points of design and technique and finance must be seen to. In this situation 'the professional ... tends to define his problems according to the technique that he has mastered, and has a natural desire to apply his skills'.* There is a lack of balance that favours technical advance for its own sake, whether it is good for humanity or not, and much ingenuity and energy are canalized to promote it. As Harold Agnew, Director of the Los Alamos Laboratories Weapons Division, so revealingly expressed it, 'The basis of advanced technology is innovation and nothing is more stifling to innovation than seeing one's product not used or ruled out of consideration on flimsy premises involving world opinion'.† Any technique that can be applied, is applied. Some of the results we have seen in Vietnam.

This restless process is rationalized, both by the businesses concerned through their many mouthpieces, controlled or subservient, and by mesmerized politicians. From their utterances, reported in almost any day's newspaper, we learn that we exist as a nation to produce more goods; the gross national product is the article of our faith and the measure of our well-being.

The industrial system was early condemned by Marx for its life-long cruelty to the children, women and men who worked it and for its inefficiency in failing equitably to distribute its needed

*Noam Chomsky in the *New York Review*, 2 January 1969.
†*Congressional Record*, 27 July 1967.

products. It is less criticized nowadays for exploitation and inefficiency, as a greater share for the workers appears to have been gained – though Professor J. E. Meade has shown that the rich are getting richer and the poor poorer. It is supposed too to have become less cyclical in its operation and to have banished the boom-slump sequence, though in 1973 it is impossible to believe this. What has happened is not that depressions have become a thing of the past, but that their worst effects are diminished by the welfare state.

Modern critics of the industrial system have been reiterating versions of the same main charge for forty years or more. That is: it does not provide a society in which people can flourish as human beings. It develops private affluence while maintaining public poverty, so that a majority have enough money to do their duty as consumers and tag after the leaders of the colour-supplement life, while hospitals, schools, housing, galleries, museums, the regeneration of towns and the conservation of the country are starved. Professor J. K. Galbraith described the plight of America in this respect in *The Affluent Society*; in this country we have more to be proud of, but not much, for essential services are short of resources, while unwanted products are over-supplied. Not because they are needed, but because, like imitation louvres to fix to your doors, they can be made vendible. When we come to goods that do fill a real need we find that they are of poorer quality than they should be, often because of built-in obsolescence and planned deterioration. Moreover a very great deal of what public spending there is runs on the wrong lines to meet no true need or public demand – such as large aircraft, large airfields, large roads, space ironmongery and a crippling armoury of weapons. Above all weapons, and more weapons – the mythical deterrent that implies 'as morally justifiable the obliteration of the world we know'* or, as Professor J. K. Galbraith put it in a recent talk, 'An economic system which addresses itself energetically to products that would destroy that system and all its participants does seem rather mindless'.†

*Professor D. M. Mackinnon, 'Ethical Problems of Nuclear Warfare' in *God, Sex and War*, Collins, 1963.

†'The Crisis of the Modern Industrial Society' – lecture delivered at Cambridge, 16 February 1971.

Two other criticisms of the industrial system receive a good deal of attention nowadays. First, the destruction of the earth's resources 'with a reckless prodigality which entails almost a certainty of hardship for future generations', prophesied by Bertrand Russell half a century ago,* is far advanced. These resources in this country include the natural beauty, natural life and the wonderfully satisfying rural landscape that are being insanely destroyed. A small example from America illustrates several points here: Suffolk county on the eastern sea-board has placed a total ban on the sale of detergents because they seep through septic tanks into the underground water supply, with the result that in some areas water comes foaming from the tap. The vast sums that we waste on the insecurity of armaments could be diverted into making industry innocuous, restoring the country, and making the towns fit to live in.

In addition the way of life that is prescribed by the industrial system is found wanting, when it is seen that our function as individuals is to consume its products and employ its services. In the words of Angus Maude, describing the cultural sterility of a society dedicated to consumption, 'It doesn't much matter what we consume, so long as we consume enough. What we *want* to consume matters even less; the producers will make whatever is most convenient and "efficient" for them, and then persuade us to want it'. Our 'standard of living' goes up; our sense of well-being goes down, and unhappiness, loneliness, strain and violence are measurably on the increase. The rootlessness and pressures of urban life produce, according to Christopher Mayhew, a psychological pollution that is 'as dangerous to the health of our minds as open sewers once were to our bodies'.† We suffer from being over-persuaded that we need the products of a busy technology, and from living in a state of over-population that is thought already to have entered the destructive phase.‡

The industrial society's own measure of its efficacy is the gross

*Quoted by Noam Chomsky in the second Bertrand Russell Memorial Lecture, 1971.

†At a conference of the National Association for Mental Health, 25 February 1971.

‡Professor Ivor H. Mills in *The Times*, 21 August 1970.

national product, though for many years it has been eroded by critics such as Veblen, Lawrence and Russell in their very different ways, and by their successors. Now it is toppling, especially since its inadequacy as a goal for planning has been made starkly clear by the failure of advanced industrial techniques when applied to developing countries, where they have resulted in 'social disruption, the aggravation of unemployment and little change in the majority's standard of living'.* Growth mania, according to René Dubos, is driving towards an unbelievable future – 'a dismal and grotesque magnification of the present state of affairs ... a world in which everything will move faster, grow larger, be mechanized, bacteriologically sterile, and emotionally safe'.† The dissatisfaction of many young people with the aims that society holds up for them is evidence of a spreading realization that the economy supplies not the goals and the life that people want, but what the most powerful wish them to want.

That last sentence points to one of the two ways in which the mass media are related to the industrial system. First, they are a part of it as large-scale buyers and spenders and makers of profits; secondly, they are the preachers of its theology and the mouthpiece of its gospel. When we look at the first connection – the entertainment industry as big business – it becomes more and more difficult to make dividing lines, so great has been the diversification and the empire-building of recent years. A newspaper proprietor on the other side of the world acquires control of a television or publishing company; a miller buys cinemas; a film magnate or a transport firm may turn to book publishing; and we may expect developments as the tobacco groups feel the impact of public concern about the danger of their products. The BBC spends £100 million a year, and even the decaying cinema, with attendances down to a tenth of what they were eighteen years ago, is still big business. There are about 1,600 cinemas, of which half belong to the Associated British Picture Corporation (owned by E.M.I.) and Rank; the two firms have recently spent between them £12,000,000 on modernizing their cinemas. Newspapers exist to make money out of advertising, and their colour

*Eric Wigham in *The Times Business News*, 15 September 1970.
†René Dubos, *So Human an Animal*, Scribner, 1968.

supplements were devised solely as vehicles for this; they are also tied up with forestry-owning and pulp mills. Sunday papers complete the needed seven-day week for expensive machinery.

When we turn to the media as mouthpiece of the industrial system, we shall not find them spending their time and our money on explicit praises of the gross national product. The method is less blatant, more compelling than that. The system is established as the basis of our lives by day-in, day-out assent – by being taken for granted, with never a mention of a serious alternative. The conventional view of the G N P is found among politicians, editors of newspapers and some academic economists, but for millions of us it is the dreary round of consumption and our duty as colour-supplement consumers that are glorified by a heavy weight of direct advertising, and more subtly by plays and films and much that passes for entertainment on television.

There is constant pressure to consume more and hence to produce more, to keep up with the neighbours at home and abroad. Though a majority of us have more than was enough for our grandparents, we are not to be allowed to enjoy the fruits of our labour in the form of leisure. For most the basic needs are fulfilled, though not always as well as they might be, but fresh ones are constantly being created, and leisure is a sort of extension of work, so that earnings can be spent on advertised goods and services. Living is distorted; as Professor Galbraith has written, the elaborate myth with which we surround the demand for goods 'has enabled us to become persuaded of the dire importance of the goods we have without our being in the slightest degree concerned about those we do not have'.* He develops the long-standing charge against advertising with a wealth of example; but views such as his are not heard as often and as clearly as they should be, for the media are part of the system which produces for the sake of production and fulfil their function of proclaiming the good life as a series of opportunities taken to spend and display. Pure entertainment on the mass media is hard to find; what happens is a conditioning of the viewer or listener or reader, who comes to accept with the offerings of the media the scheme of things which produces them.

*J. K. Galbraith, *The Affluent Society*, p. 120, Pelican edition, 1962.

When the controllers of the media are not providing a form of covert propaganda for the status quo – and they are not necessarily doing so consciously – they defend what they supply on the ground that they are giving the public what it wants. What happens is that they give the public what they wish it to want, and then interpret acquiescence as approval. But they do not really know; they have no vital contact with their audiences – the plural is important and tends to be deliberately neglected – and know little about them. The 'public', they say, wants only to be entertained; but the evidence is against this generalization, which is certainly unsupported by the vague tolerance felt by a number of people for the goods and entertainment they buy. As Lord Hailsham said of television:

> The T.A.M. rating can be, I think sometimes is, a melancholy record of third and fourth preferences – the maximum number of viewers who can be induced not to turn off, the highest common factor of endurance without enthusiasm.

Even if the controllers could establish in a particular case that there was a genuine preference for their offering, they would in many cases be found to have created the taste for it. What sells most is rarely the best line, more likely the most strenuously promoted, and need bear little or no relation to consumers' wishes. The controllers' measure of success is profit, and they arrange that what is sold is the most profitable, or what their tunnel vision envisages as the most profitable. The extent of their power should not be over-estimated, but in some fields it is considerable, as Mr H. Ratcliffe, of the Musicians' Union, records, in speaking of popular music and records:

> Any music publisher can tell you six months ahead which tune is going to be popular. The public does not make a tune popular. Subject to certain exceptions, some flukes here and there, we know in advance what is going to be popular six months ahead, and the publishing business makes sure a tune it wants to be popular is popular, by spending enough money to make it popular.

In these circumstances the individual does not matter, so long as the figures of people serving the system by consuming its products are high enough. He is thus part of a statistical nought,

15

and as such the object of the controllers' contempt. This emerges in the vocabulary of admen, when they discuss at their conferences the manipulation of human beings, and in what Cecil King, Chairman at the time of the *Daily Mirror* Newspapers, is reported to have said: 'In point of fact it is only the people who conduct newspapers and similar organizations who have any idea quite how indifferent, quite how stupid, quite how uninterested in education of any kind the great bulk of the British public are.' For comment, here is Arnold Wesker:

It is the age of the big insult – trivia pays larger dividends, therefore trivia must be what is wanted. Is this a deliberate policy to keep the nation cretinized by trivialities or does it stem from a profound belief that the people of this country are cretins from the start?

The cynical view of people is reflected in a no-choice policy, for choice involves some acquaintance with the possibilities, a more than superficial acquaintance. Such a knowledge of the range of things to choose from is just what the controllers in general are unable to supply. The hunt for mass audiences, needed to attract advertising and pay for it, causes the controllers to narrow the field of taste in which people can discriminate: 'they will be kept unaware of what lies beyond the average of experience.'

Considerations such as those above were in the minds of those, teachers and others concerned with teaching, who took part in the original conference that led to the writing of this book. They did not accept the contention that what is offered as entertainment is entertainment and nothing more; and the most noticeable thread running through the proceedings was a hostility towards the present misuse of the mass media. For example, Stuart Hall said, 'There is bound to be a very deep conflict between the task of education and the role of the media, which are still closely linked to securing profit and to the advertising industry.' The word 'medium' itself was clearly felt to be a misnomer, when those who operate the channels decide what shall flow through them in the way of selected views, filtered news and processed entertainment. They have by now stabilized the tastes they cater for.

They provide for these artificial tastes with a synthetic 'culture' that takes over and doctors any genuine preferences and desires. Together the media control the agenda, deciding what shall be in the forefront of our minds and at the centre of our hearts – a much more up-to-date means of manipulation than propaganda. That is basic. In addition a great deal of moral and aesthetic counter-education goes on, and a steady stream of attitude-forming entertainment is turned out. A small straw in the wind is the way in which accents and styles of speech thought to be demotic spread in the media themselves and then among young people, from children at school to college lecturers. In itself that is unimportant, but it is usually a sign that attitudes are being moulded. At the time of the original conference the *Year Book of Education* made the point:

> Faced with this kind of pressure the responsibility of the teacher becomes very great. Matched against the glib facility of a radio commentator supported by all the gimmicks and aids to presentation, the classroom teacher is gravely hampered in an age in which the titillation of public fancy has become a matter of professional expertise. His influence on adolescent minds has to be weighed against that of ephemeral stars of film or T.V. screen. The easy success of popular entertainers is in great contrast to the sustained effort needed to achieve anything worth while in other spheres – and especially in the school.

When the Education Act of 1871 began to provide free schooling for all, Matthew Arnold saw it as an advance towards the education of the working class as the future holders of political power. Now it looks as if all that happened was that business gained better clerks and Northcliffe found plenty of readers for his new-style daily paper. Too little was done for children as human beings. Things have improved since then, and in our particular field many schools help their pupils to understand the language of advertising, to read between the lines of their newspapers and to shop around on television. Radical critics describe this as mere guerrilla skirmishing – 'sporadic gunfights won't do'* – and they are probably right for most pupils, though one knows from experience that for some, not necessarily with high I.Q. labels, the stimulus even of such unmethodical forays can last a lifetime. At a good many other schools, however, nothing is

*Fred Inglis, *Literature and Environment*, p. 233.

17

done to prevent school-leavers being easy game for the media, and anything acquired at school in the way of moral and aesthetic training is shed when contradicted and attacked by the entertainment industry. As Sir J. L. Longland has noted, 'The functions which the community has entrusted (to teachers) are too often inhibited, frustrated or completely defeated because those they care for succumb to the attraction of other doctrines and values.' Young people are issued with a culture package that exploits any elements of genuinely popular music and poetry there may be.

Such manipulation ought to be prevented. Angus Maude, observing the extent to which immature tastes are exploited by 'the commercial greed of the producers of ephemeral trash' has made one proposal – for compulsory saving for teenagers, the money to be 'repaid, with interest, at whatever age is deemed to represent maturity.' The idea as he develops it is attractive, but does not seem likely to commend itself to politicians. Yet the principle whereby people are protected from themselves as well as from gross exploitation ought to be extended, if one takes the view that the twentieth century imposes a servile contentment of the mind as effectively as the nineteenth enslaved the worker's body. And just as the early Factory Acts were opposed for sapping the workers' independence, protective measures today will be criticized as paternalist. With physical drugs it is comparatively easy; their effects can be measured and recorded and their sale if necessary controlled, because all this is in the field of science, which commands respect and assent. Critics of the media are unlikely to carry such weight, since what they deal in cannot yet be as accurately tested as drugs, though it may be just as toxic. In addition to turning a cold eye on the offerings of the media they will certainly try to ensure that there is a range over which real choice can be exercised.

It is to education that we must look for the answer to some of the problems we are considering. It has had some successes, and will have others, if it is seen more clearly as a point at which the ideas and efforts of men and women of goodwill can be focused. It can be particularly effective in this country, because here as in no other education is independent of governmental and political pressures and is free to develop its own purposes. The field is

18

open, because many of the conventional leaders have vanished or betrayed their trust – the kind of society offered to us by politicians, for example, is inadequate. Other designs have been prepared by scientists, philosophical anarchists, psychologists, sociologists . . . but there is no need for those concerned with education to add more. There are several ways in which they can contribute. It is part of a teacher's interest to see that the soil is right for the plants he is tending, and this is where he must have some idea of a society that offers opportunities for human beings to develop properly; he will wish his plants to grow in accordance with their own best nature. And he will probably wish to equip his pupils to see the need for changes and to play their part in bringing them about; it would be obscurantist not to do so. None of this means that teachers should become politicians or narrow specialists on (say) the environment. Rather in an age of centrifugal specialisms they will be eclectic, using the specialists, assessing their offerings, providing a centre among eccentricities. Teachers, from primary to university stage, may come to be the only people who know where the real centre is, because they are daily concerned with the growth and welfare of human beings. Not that they are by any means the only people so engaged, of course, but they are the most numerous and the most involved in positive work. They have the greatest responsibility and the greatest opportunity. The original conference that led to the writing of this book produced a verbatim report, remarkable among such things for its incisiveness and the measure of agreement among the speakers reported; so that one would like to see further meetings of the kind, some of them with rather more representation of universities and colleges. The results would include further inquiry into the working of the mass media, into ways of using them positively and methods of combating them where necessary; and a fuller and more effective sense of their responsibilities in training departments and colleges of education.

Not that there is need to wait for research. The direct approach has been followed in schools for forty years – *Culture and Environment*, by F. R. Leavis assisted by the present writer, appeared in 1933 – in the forms of analysing advertisements, studying the Press, films, and so on, together with the quality of living

19

associated with them. Of such work Raymond Williams writes in his *Communications*:

The work ... is especially important in adolescence: in the leaving years especially, for it is then that the conflict between the values of school and the values of the adult world is most obvious. There is no need, however, for the work to be confined to schools. It should be a central part of the new liberal studies courses in technical colleges, and of apprentice courses. It should form a main part of informal work in the youth service, and it should be a normal subject ... in adult education.*

Obviously the schools can give only a start, but it is a start that teachers can give with confidence that there will be results from their prompting an awareness. That will be on the intellectual side. Perhaps emotional education is more important, achieved by bringing pupils into as much contact as possible with the best that they can take in the way of art and literature and drama and music. If standards are offered, starting with elementary points of design in housing, furnishing, hardware, cars, roads ... comparisons will be made. Other needs are really good school buildings – one of the best agents for humanizing and civilizing, as Arnold noted; a curriculum planned as a unity; training for survival as human beings in an overcrowded and distracting environment.

Further action is necessary. For example the power of advertising especially should be curtailed, hostile as it is to the education of the young and far too influential in agenda-making for adults, through its effects on films, television and the printed matter that carries it. It is the notion of the good life upheld, not just bad buys and convenience foods, that we damn it for. It is the means whereby the industrial society expresses its intolerance of individual taste and imposes conformity; as part of the manipulating that makes people behave as the system dictates, it is inimical to freedom; it blinds us all, including many of us who criticize some of its aspects, to the fact that 'the fundamental problem of Western European economy is and remains that of

*Raymond Williams, *Communications*, pp. 136–7, Pelican edition. The whole of chapter 5 is recommended, with its proposals for education, amending the institutions and changing the institutions.

achieving stabilization, of developing an economic system that will cease to worship a purely quantitative "standard of living" and foster, instead, the quality of life.' (E. F. Schumacher, in a paper on nuclear energy presented to a conference of the Federation of British Industries).

BOOKS

NOAM CHOMSKY, *American Power and the New Mandarins*, Penguin Books, 1969

J. K. GALBRAITH, *The New Industrial State*, Hamish Hamilton, 1967; Penguin Books, 1969

FRED INGLIS, *The Englishness of English Teaching*, Longmans, 1969

RAYMOND WILLIAMS, *Communications*, Chatto & Windus, 1966; Penguin Books, 1968

2   Townscape

FRED INGLIS

Any argument about culture must imply, or make explicit, a powerful political content. The people whose first business it is to think hard and truthfully about culture have come, over the past ten or fifteen years, to perceive and understand that content. It is no use pretending that students have often used that perception in such a way as to make their society see the gaps between what it does, and what it professes to value, but they have seen that culture reposes within the circuits of a living politics, and it is that politics which may explain how our culture moves and changes. For our culture is our way of life – its whole busy action, its values, its arts and symbols, structures and institutions. More than that, or rather, penetrating every corner of this giant and intricate organism, culture is the total, mobile body of feelings and beliefs, intentions and reasons (terms none of which are in the least synonymous) which inform that ceaseless action. Now when we talk about our culture we have learned to lift traditionally sanctioned areas out of the living totality and treat them separately. Culture then is literature – and within literature, novels, plays or poems – or it is music, painting, or individual buildings. In the unbroken reproductions of a technological culture it is harder to make the act of separation – to lift out T.V. or electronically stored music and to look at it hard. But whenever we do, it is vital to remember that we distort the body of beliefs and feelings carried by the form – T.V. or films or poems or whatever – and that we study an experience drawn out of the living culture which gives it meaning.

This warning is perhaps most needed when we report on the meanings and values carried by our townscape. For we can talk about an individual building: it is a traditional and precious activity. Besides, we know who designed it, and generally for

22

what purpose. We can walk round it and give it a date; we may place it in the continuity of a given style or a certain architect's work. But to read and understand the whole texture of a landscape is not only a much more recent endeavour, it is bafflingly complex. Such reading requires not only a careful defence against vulgar-minded generalization, either about the damnable decline of industrial culture or about its neon excitements, it also needs a readiness to launch upon generalizations which, without being blank or cruel to the human experience summarized, nonetheless grasp its central meanings. Such a readiness can only take off from 'an intelligent saturation' in the life which is to be analysed. Only as a consequence of such familiarity can a student of his culture get anywhere near the truth about it. For it is important to repeat the old bromide that judgements about popular culture will yield no truth if they are made out of any doctrinaire framework – either about the awfulness of pop, or about its sacredness.

An adequate reporter from an area of culture will need to work through three stages. He will first need to recognize not only what traditions his materials derive from, but something about the source of his own criteria and judgement. He will need, in the case of townscape, to know how he has learned to look at his environment. Secondly, he will need some theories to explain what has happened, why changes occurred and what order they may have. Again, in the case of townscape, he will need to construct some explanation, however reach-me-down, of why industry has arrived and what it has done. It is a measure of English queasiness about the word that one needs to point out at this stage that as a matter of logical necessity his explanation will have political bearings. Third and last, deriving from the first two stages as well as all such previous analytic experience, he will bring to bear his vivid sense of the human and moral meaning of what he sees – his sense of its deathliness or vitality, of its significance both for him and for the people who made it and use it, its religious power maybe, or its playfulness, its coarseness or its reassuring homeliness. And it is at this stage that the crucial decisions and judgements get made, and at this stage too that the painful strictures are passed on people, and their culture, with whom, for all that he may find intolerable, a man who studies his

23

culture cannot ever break off his human connection. Not only that: the final insult would be to mitigate a first censure for the sake of keeping in touch; such mitigation would (paradoxically) involve a drastic foreshortening of human possibility; as who should say 'I will tolerate your unspeakable Japanese garden, stained-glass leaded lights and Cotswold-stone-cottage slab chimney because (poor chap) you and I are both men'. There is something rank both in the pitying kindliness and the high euphoria with which the English liberal patronizes either pop or subtopian cultures. But then there is a no less disagreeable iciness breathed out by the disdain and weariness of the disapproving. There is a poise, there is a resistance which can speak cuttingly to its audience, both for it and with it; which can speak with warmth and largeness of temper without conceit or mock modesty. To write like this would be indeed to create a sociology with authentic powers. Such a sociology would make of our culture a map upon which it would be possible to find oneself; it would provide bearings as to scale and contour and direction; it would supply routes to the individual without sacrificing an independent authority, larger than individuals but containing them all. Of its nature it would sacrifice preposterous (in the exact sense of the word) claims to 'value freedom'.

What follows are some notes towards such an inquiry, based on the landscape which affects the lives and understanding of everyone of us profoundly. The approach I suggest could be taken up in part or in whole by groups of students in primary school or extra-mural classes or university. I know at first hand of examples of all three. The judgements I make are certainly intended to have a more than narrowly personal relevance; at the same time, like any idea of politics, they imply the chronicle of an autobiography, they grow from one man's life at a point where the roads cross: these books on one side, a life and a history on the other.

The warning shots against the onslaught of industry upon the English landscape were first fired with some telling power at the beginning of the nineteenth century. It was then that forward spirits began to notice the evils of industrialism. For we find, in

24

the works of the great romantic revolutionaries, in Blake, Words-worth, Byron, Cobbett, Shelley, Beethoven, Delacroix, Lamar-tine, a central contradiction. These men speak as the voices of the new populism; for the first time poets gave a voice to the whole inarticulate crowd, the men and women who entered European history for the first time. At the same time, in the magnificent works of the Romantic movement – in *The Prelude*, or the *Pastoral Symphony*, these same men damned the city, and got out of it. The history of nineteenth-century art, literature, and music and much of the past seventy years as well has been the history of a national imagination trying to keep faith with its rural memories and at the same time to make cities it can believe in. The experience of the city is the central source of energy in Dickens, in the Impressionists, in Proust, in the Cubists, in Stravinsky. Lawrence's novel *The Rainbow* is the great threnody in our language upon the ruin of the lovely English landscape; it closes with a vision of the hateful rash of little red houses creeping across the Nottinghamshire hills. In Eliot's poem *The Waste Land*, the city is the place of desolation, of restless, isolated strangers hurrying about their business.

> Unreal City,
> Under the brown fog of a winter dawn,
> A crowd flowed over London Bridge, so many,
> I had not thought death had undone so many.
> Sighs, short and infrequent, were exhaled,
> And each man fixed his eyes before his feet.
> Flowed up the hill and down King William Street,
> To where Saint Mary Woolnoth kept the hours
> With a dead sound on the final stroke of nine.

This is the imagery which a great many English people have absorbed. From dozens of reports, from diaries and letters and novels and bits of sociology early and late, there breathes out the sweet, musty and penetrating odour of a nostalgia which longs for the lost beauty of the English garden.

Nostalgia for the countryside even in Dickens is intolerably sweet and strong. At the end of *Our Mutual Friend*, of *Bleak House*, of *Martin Chuzzlewit*, as refuge in any of his other great books, the poet of the city invoked the great images of the English

25

garden, the man-made landscape which at its best probably held the loveliest balance between climate, topography, agriculture and human repose in European history. Those images penetrate our whole consciousness and our national imagination. From Spenser's *Prothalamion*

> Against the bridal day, which was not long,
> Sweet Thames! run softly, till I end my song...

to Keats's *Ode to a Nightingale* the antique images are called up tirelessly to dance to new measures. From Spenser to Keats and on to Yeats those images drift in plaintive cadences into the mythology of a nation.

> I cannot see what flowers are at my feet,
> Nor what soft incense hangs upon the boughs,
> But, in embalmed darkness, guess each sweet
> Wherewith the seasonable month endows
> The grass, the thicket, and the fruit-tree wild;
> White hawthorn, and the pastoral eglantine...

The landscape of these poets was man-made, slowly and as a matter of quite conscious vision for the future. The gardens left London for the country during the great boom of late Tudor and Elizabethan England. The castles turned their moats into ornamental water and became country houses. The infinitely shrewd and aesthetically faultless plunder of the New World and of the East began. The buccaneers did not only bring back the hauls of El Dorado; they planted the great gardens of Audley, Wilton, Burghley and Hardwick with cedars from Lebanon; they brought back fig-trees, grape-vines, apricots, peaches; they planted new flowers – clematis, wistaria, Dutch bulbs – to join the traditional dog-roses, speedwell and may of the madrigals. As the country houses became mansions and palaces, the gardens became parks. The enormous increase in flocks of sheep, deer and cattle cleared vast tracts of forest and the eighteenth century set to to make the picturesque landscape. The cultural contribution of this century is still robustly alive in a million Ideal Home gardens. For the eighteenth-century landowners, the country gentleman farmers, the landscape gardeners, painters and architects colluded to produce the main concepts of that exquisite landscape which today

26

we see in our imagination as typically English, which crops out in miniature versions in front of picture windows and spec. builders' neo-ranch-houses all over Britain, and which is kept alive in the offices of the British Tourist Association and shipped abroad, in the teeth of the truth, to the dollar-spending and hard currency nations. In the eighteenth century, the gentlemen devised the nooks, bowers, surprises and sudden prospects to which the small, changeable scale of English topography lends itself so easily, and at the same time they turned the common people off their own land and enclosed it. Now it is never easy weighing the suffering of the past in the scales of twentieth-century liberalism. There can be little doubt that the enclosures caused a great deal of immediate human misery; there is equally no doubt that they were a part of a revolution in agricultural method which transformed production and made, in the years up to the Corn Laws, an enormously larger quantity of food available, if only grudgingly. But the relevance of the Enclosure Act for our purposes is that it completed the colonization of the English landscape from the bleak, ungiving heath we find today in North Yorkshire or Cornwall into the subtle, rhythmic patterns of wall, copse, hedge, wagon ways, small fields and the connecting farmsteads and market towns, which we have learned by heart from the nineteenth-century novelists, poets, and painters. The enclosure confirmed the *scale* of the English country: the size of the fields, the generous placing of chestnut, ash, elm and oak, the permanence of the low hedges which gave both privacy and neighbourliness to the landscape, all this rich orchestration formed a style which still dominates much of our imagining about the communities we live in and try to plan for. The Englishness of the English landscape (and, necessarily, townscape) is one of the richest achievements of a popular culture.* No doubt the argument will be advanced (again) that this manifestation of culture was hardly 'popular' in the fullest sense, and that the men who have left their mark most visibly across the map of England were the grandees and seigneurs, or their helots, the hired landscape

*Its system of typical features has been classically described by Nikolaus Pevsner in *The Englishness of English Art*, Architectural Press, 1956; Penguin Books, 1963.

gardeners – the Kents, Reptons and Browns – whose only office was to do their master's pleasure; or that, again, the recorders of the masterpiece, the landscape painters from Morland and Gainsborough, through Constable and Cotman, to Palmer or Lear sentimentalized the life they recorded and only saw the squalor of the cottages from a long way off, the other side of Dedham Vale. Such a case makes a number of mistakes which it is important to get straight, if the study of culture really is to give us some idea of what meanings men have given to their lives in the past; if we are to learn from that past – and, futurology and tea leaf-reading apart, there is nowhere else we *can* learn from – then our understanding of culture must take in many more dimensions than the reflex class-consciousness and simple-minded social determinism, for example, which characterize most educational thought today. We shall need a reading of cultural conditions in a way which does justice to the density of life which they contain. But more than a full, imaginative saturation in the material, we need a grasp on the structure of feeling which provides the explanatory key to the cultural life we are studying. What would such a key be like which would explain the version of the English landscape which came into circulation about the beginning of the nineteenth century and exerts such a pull today?

I have described in a very compressed form the making of the English landscape up to 1800. It is about then that a few writers began to notice what the industrial and agricultural upheavals were doing to the landscape. At the same time they were able to draw on a tradition as ancient as the history of their own literature to confirm the opposition of town and country. From medieval courtly love stories through *As You Like It* and *The Winter's Tale* to the Pastoral eclogues in imitation of Virgil and Horace by Ben Jonson, Dryden and Pope, the poets had ample precedent for naming the city as the centre of grime and corruption and the country as the source of innocence, cleanliness and beauty. But the vision of the English landscape was not simply the product of its literature* nor indeed of a topography derived from pastoral poetry. Not only did Cobbett and Wordsworth

*I hope it is not immodest to draw attention to my anthology *The Scene*, Cambridge, 1972, which collects together some of the best-known poetic visions of the countryside since Spenser.

put the people of England squarely down on their own land, but the painters brought an entirely unidyllic attention to the people at work. The great line of English water-colourists, Crome, Cotman, Girtin, Cozens, the Varleys, not only introduced and confirmed a new imagery and gave a fresh, sparkling surface to the national imagination, they also peopled this world with men and women at work – ploughing, sailing, shepherding, feeding beasts.* The man who confirmed these tendencies and made them his own was Constable. The people of his pictures are building boats, drawing barges, driving wains, and all this rendered with what he himself saw as the scientific eye – the eye which had been taught by the giants of the eighteenth century that surface impressions are the source of all experience. Constable wrote:

Painting is a Science, and should be pursued as an inquiry into the laws of nature. Why, then, may not landscape painting be considered as a branch of natural philosophy of which pictures are but the experiments.†

The sedate, precise intention of this sorts well with his remark 'It cannot be too much to say, that the landscape is full of moral and religious feeling'. Constable gives us an insight into 'the structure of feeling' in his time, and a measure of its unity. The infinitely fine and delicate balance which then obtained between the state of technology, the systems of production and the moral perception of shape and tincture is fully realized in this part of its popular culture. Constable was a rich miller's son – as his brother said, 'When I look at a mill painted by John, I see that it will go *round*'. He knew the work at first hand, and the details of his pictures – the precise bevelling of the ancient wain, the newly planed wood just bent into shape for the boats – are the artistic equivalent of the actual wood, itself the product of what was a necessary morality of work and craftsmanship.‡ George Eliot

*The seminal record of their work, outside the galleries, is Martin Hardie's *Water Colour Painting in Britain*, 3 vols., Batsford, 1967.
†*C. R. Leslie's Memoirs*, ed. J. Mayne, London, 1951, p. 323.
‡In this argument I have been enormously helped by, and at moments am simply paraphrasing, an excellent essay 'Workmanship and Design' by Andor Gomme, *Delta*, Cambridge, 45, March 1969.

put it, for Adam Bede at work as a carpenter in 1799, like this:

His work ... had always been part of his religion, and from very early days he saw clearly that good carpentry was God's will – was that form of God's will that most immediately concerned him.*

We can see the same values carried by the lockgates to the canal which Constable painted, and in the thousands of lockgates all over the country. They testify in the most eloquent way possible to the presence of an authentic and common culture, and provide a point of comparison when we wish to know whether or not we may find another such point of vitality today. A canal junction gives us a rich quarry. We may see the accuracy with which the massive gates are matched, and the niceness of balance with which gear-wheels and handles are adjusted. We may note the closeness with which hand-planed timbers have been dovetailed and morticed, braced on the outside against the greater mass of water. But more than the details of an exact and efficient technology, we need to register the completeness with which a typical canal junction or a big sequence of locks is articulated. We can undoubtedly find more exquisite or more powerful forms of engineering, in ancient and modern cultures, but the canals may serve as examples of a high point in a culture of town or landscape. The lock-keeper's cottage, the short arc of the bridge over the canal, the parallel lines of path, grass, walls and hedge ensure that such places *are* places: their parts cohere in an order and rightness which is itself satisfying and the implicit morality of which makes a stand against the smooth and impassive surface of the intense inane.

> Oh! Blessed rage for order, pale Ramón,
> The maker's rage to order words of the sea,
> Words of the fragrant portals, dimly-starred,
> And of ourselves and of our origins,
> In ghostlier demarcations, keener sounds.†

The canal junction I am thinking of (and we would each take our own examples, some obviously more telling than others) is not

Adam Bede, Ch. 50.

†Wallace Stevens, 'The Idea of Order at Key West', *Selected Poems*, 1953, p. 79.

simply a satisfying pattern of grouped shapes. It is the difference between an abstract painting and a still-life. When all has been said about the tension generated by the painting of a Mondrian or a Ben Nicholson they are still fatally lacking in human content. Why this is so depends upon the history of the past two hundred years, and whatever it is that has driven all but the greatest painters and sculptors out of contact with the human and non-human world. A still-life possesses this advantage over Ben Nicholson: that the objects represented have absorbed something of the history of the people and the time which has worn, polished, scarred and fondled them.* In the same way the relation of cottage to lock to path and bridge, to coping-stones and the brick-laid platforms along the rim of whose arc the wooden beams turn give back the meanings of the lives which made them. The laying of the rounded bricks at the edge above the water is an example not only of comeliness and soundness but also of the judgement and care needed by the workman to fasten and align bricks of slightly varied sizes. The result is a floorscape† of much greater interest than a more developed technology could have shown. Its texture is more subtly varied, partly because the builders only used bricks for a limited area, partly because the bricks themselves are varied. And then the floorscape takes *its* place in the tessellation of the whole place; a rhythmic, varied and living statement about the lives and work of the men who used the place, about their relations to one another, to the materials with which they had built the place, both as home and point of transit, and to those mysterious Pleistocene forces which had given them their local geography.

It is these relations whose presence or absence will make a living townscape. There are very few examples of the small corners of the English landscape made between 1758 when the Bridgewater canal opened and about 1830 when the system was fairly complete, which fail to be as admirable as I have described. They represent – if we separate them for the moment from their

*cf. D. H. Lawrence in *The Rainbow*: 'The furniture was old and familiar as old people, the whole place seemed so kin to him, as if it partook of his being...'

†Gordon Cullen's word, from his fine primer *Townscape*, Architectural Press, 1961.

continuing history – a rich point in cultural history for which the inadequate metaphor can only be a balance, a delicate poise between the moving and changing forces of technology, moral and labouring energy, the landscape as a man-made and a natural presence, the relations of domestic and industrial economy, and the systems of production. Whatever the discrepancies in suffering and happiness in other parts of their lives, Constable and the watercolour painters, the canal-builders, the bargees and the entrepreneurs who hired them, the landowners of Claremont, Osterley Park, Twickenham gardens, Chatsworth, the speculative builders of Salisbury Cathedral Close bear their different witness in this area to a common and equal culture. They knew how to make a place.

We are heirs to that knowledge. The upheaval in social and moral thought on either side of 1800, the revolutions, the street fights and rural riots, the growth of cities and the many accounts of the salvation held out by a return to nature, all this still fills our minds and spirits with its old power. But history has moved on. We now need an account of that movement which will explain at least some of the things that have happened to our town– and landscapes since the greatest period of English painting coincided with the completion of England's greatest success in making a landscape.

There are first some obstacles to clear away. The report on the momentum of English townscaping as it accelerated on to the present day can only be desolate. The fine balance of reciprocal forces tilted and smashed. Another one, in another part of people's lives, held itself for a while. But no one with his sight and sensibility could now say that we share a proper culture for making towns and landscapes. Nonetheless, this does not mean that success is impossible. A sombre view is not necessarily a passive or fatalist one. First, no one can doubt some of our successes in, say, new town planning, roadscaping the motorways, rescuing old towns from the blitzkrieg of the juggernaut truck or, on a much smaller scale, in mending fences, making gardens, in building cupboards or a new henhouse; we can always find innumerable cases where the job has been prettily done. The spasmodic decline of a visual culture which, like any high point in cultural triumph, could only briefly sustain itself, is not evenly downhill. And the conditions for its recovery may always be dormant in any given society. The second point is a matter of insistent emphasis. What is lost is irrecoverable on its own terms. Constable's England has gone. If we re-make a healthy visual culture it must be on our own terms. And there is nothing predetermined about this. When we regret 'ah, it couldn't last – the Florentine Renaissance, Elizabethan literature, the eighteenth-century garden', no doubt we are right. The balance of forces changes. But it changes not under the impulse of blind, non-human forces; it changes as a result of the decisions of men. The recovery of a landscape is a matter of decision, and this is true of any cultural life. When I say decision I do not mean some act of the fixed, insensate will. I mean the vital movement of men's souls to what they most need. To know what you really want is the hardest thing in the world to know. But it can be known, if men make the creative effort. Only the knowledge is tied to a moral scale whose measurements can depend on some general recognition, and it is a notorious truism of the times that such recognition is impossible. We need now to consider how the disintegration came about and what the chances are for general repair and the resurrection of a common purpose in the future. What can we gather from history – from the irrecoverable world of John Constable, Wordsworth and Robert Owen – and put to our own purposes? And where shall we find the buds and shoots of life in the townscape of today? Where, too, shall we *not* find it – what in that townscape is dead and deathly?

It is a necessary piece of myth-making to say that at such-and-such a point the landscape was achieved and English towns were at their finest. The appalling jerry-built slums of Manchester had begun before Nash finished Bath. Yet we must have a point of comparison for the present, and it is certainly true that the men who built and maintained the mills of Dedham Vale, tended the oaks of the Test valley, or designed the canal village at Stoke Bruerne, who completed Marlborough, Lyme Regis, Stamford, Harrogate or Edinburgh – these men simply could not have committed some of the brutality done to the country since. It

33

absolutely won't do to point out* that the landowners ripped up the parterre to get at the coal as soon as they knew it was there, and would have done every bit as horribly as Peacehaven in Sussex or the brick moonlands of Bedfordshire if they had known how. That their technology was too elementary is a constituent fact of their culture and of their frame of mind.

The deep-rutted by-roads . . . and the winding lanes, preserve through years of neglect the traces of technique in their hedgerows . . . (and) in their ditches. On the old ruinous field gate, with its highly arched, tapering top bar rudely carved on the underside against the tenon, the grey mass cannot hide the signs of vitality more marvellous than its own – the intensified vitality of those skilled hands that shaped the timbers.†

This moving eloquence does not rest upon a myth. The evidence is there to check in just the places the writer names. During the hundred and fifty years (or so) since many of the gates, walls and ditches were made, that subtle combination of technology, technique, morality and working relations has utterly changed its grain.

In a very crude way the change was the result of those familiar entries in all off-the-peg formulas of social change: industrialization, democratization, secularization, and the growth of cities. Within this large grid, we can make some more particular guesses. First, it is clearer than ever today and cannot be said too often that the development of mass production systems in which the men and women ('operatives') had no interest beyond the wage they drew, drove a deep rift between a man and his work.‡ At the same time techniques of automation and assembly-line ensured that not only were more and more parts ready-made, they were produced in one place and put together in another. Across a century or so (there seems no reason why the process should take any longer: in some industries a couple of generations is enough) traditions of apprenticeship and patient indenture, of the steady and disciplined application of a learned judgement of

*cf. the straightfaced Wellsian J. H. Plumb in *Crisis in the Humanities*, Penguin Books, 1964.

†G. Sturt, *Change in the Village*, Duckworth, 1912, p. 138.

‡The history of the perception and consciousness of work remains to be written, though all diagnoses can only start from Marx and the Victorian novelists.

hand and eye, gave way to an altogether different training, often pleasanter and less strenuous, but necessarily acquired in the abstract and in another place. The training of engineer, architect, spiderman, forester, carpenter, shepherd, teacher, became adjusted to a special programme carried through in a special place. The materials of the craft became no longer known as from one place and for a lifetime. The profound experience of the individual trees shown by the men in Hardy's novel *The Woodlanders* (one of them knows his way in the pitch-dark by feeling the trees) was no longer possible. At the same time, that local inwardness is replaced by a more exact and confident knowledge of the behaviour of trees in all parts of the country. But all such knowledge became more generalized, known at a distance. Not that this alone would explain the disastrous loss of touch which our present treatment of the country betrays. We need also to invoke the distance placed between men and their work by the use of standardized and prefabricated materials. Instead of the 'workmanship of risk', in which the inherent unpredictability of the material ensures all sorts of working and visual interest, we find the dominance of 'the workmanship of certainty' in which such interest is deliberately eradicated in order to obtain a greater efficiency.* The danger then becomes that the repetition of perfect uniformity is dull and deadening. There are two solutions. The first is to maintain within the repetition of uniformity a random variety in inessential parts of the design. In townscape, especially on the vast scale of modern construction, this is easy. You plan the variety of texture which will give you the unplannable changes you need: the surface of water, the changing reflections thrown back by glass, the dappling of light by leaves, the living variety of gardens, of drying washing, of people's movement and adaptation. (Think of the variety of places where people will sit down and picnic.) The second is deliberately to abandon the workmanship of certainty (and the likely benefits of its greater cheapness) in the interests of a more risky variety. This latter solution makes for the incredibly busy trade of the present in Heal's and Habitat iconography – the *art paysan* glazeless pots, adzed tables,

*I take this pair of distinctions from David Pye's admirable book *The Nature and Art of Workmanship*, Cambridge, 1968.

35

rough-planed elm chairs, scrubbed pine and thick rugs of the high Hampstead style. These goods are the product of the still powerful Arts and Crafts and Garden City movements which took their energy both from the Romantics and from the picturesque tradition. I shall try to revalue that heritage in a moment. The point is this: as the technology and the systems of production changed, so did the workman's, designer's, planner's, and artist's relations with their materials. But changing technology and a consequent change in training and attitude to material do not in themselves account for the near-universal loss of touch. If a definition of idiocy is to insist on the validity of an utterly private, self-fulfilling and circular moral universe (circular because there is no chance of contradiction), then we are idiots of space and shape. What caused the idiocy?

It is already clear that no one demon can be arraigned as the agent. We have looked at the creation by Romantic and picturesque landscapes of a national imagination. We have further considered the changes in technology and its culture in the situations of work. Consciousness also changed. During the nineteenth century the individualist ethic won a unique dominance. Yet at the same time the socialist ethic struck its roots and expanded at a fabulous rate. An odd, striated mixture of the two produced the first criticisms of an industrialized townscape, left and right combining in blueprint for the future.

The first individualist was the businessman. The ethic of unregulated free enterprise without social controls and with a profound disregard for the human life which the enterprise employed produced the shocking wastes of early industrial England. There can be for us no complacent reading of this scenery. For the concentrations of capital which necessarily followed this investment programme generated a community of interests which in turn issued in the great civic building of the Victorians – in Leeds Town Hall, Bradford Exchange, Manchester Town Hall, Newcastle's Grey Street, Liverpool's St George's Hall, the Chamberlains' Birmingham – this solid, dignified, occasionally noble directory of its wealthy age.* The same age

*There is a racy and excellent brief review of these places in Ian Nairn, *Britain's Changing Towns*, B B C Publications, 1967.

built the Merseyside, Tyneside, Humberside waterfronts, together with the thrilling stations and landscape of the railways.
The daintiness and tiny scale of Yorkshire or Monmouthshire
dale stations together with Euston, St Pancras, and the big
northern terminus stations are statements of a once popular
culture, the moments of confidence which that culture permitted
in its own unrivalled expansion.

The giant size and intermittent splendour of Victorian capitalist or industrial building begins however to become a symptom
of a deep split in the consciousness. On the one hand, power,
capital, organization, the public world; on the other, individuals,
domestic living, powerlessness, poverty, fragmentation, the
private world. And a townscape grows up which expresses this
split. The corporate state comes into being, it follows the demise
of the public-spirited and philanthropic Victorian businessman.
The diffusion of responsibility throughout the giant institutions,
the need for capital to *increase* its surplus-values if it is to hold
on to the profits, the managed perpetuation of old social forms
and classes in unprecedented conditions for production and
labour, all this created a townscape in which the giant agencies
could place at will the cathedrals of their productivity, and
individuals did what they liked with the space that was left. The
unbelievable speed with which the industrial landscape covered
England, the abrupt change in the materials of building, the scale
of the new technology, the dominance of free enterprise and the
individualist ethic, and the absence of an adequate social and
moral economy, combined to devastate the brief, precarious and
lovely balance in the ecology discovered and held for different
decades in different places between about 1750 and 1939. Capital
and industry dominated the cities; beneath their vast walls
crept out the long lines of private dwellings whose response
to the smell, dirt, magnificence and brute size of the city was
to cherish the romantic dream of the countryside at its best.
The suburban garden becomes a central symbol of English
domestic living any time after 1830. Lawrence classically
diagnoses a continuing condition of the whole English
people – a shared and, in the imaginative sense anyway, equal
culture:

As a matter of fact, till 1800 the English people were strictly a rural people – very rural. England has had towns for centuries, but they have never been real towns, only clusters of village streets. The English character has failed to develop the real urban side of a man, the civic side. Siena is a bit of a place, but it is a real city, with citizens intimately connected with the city. Nottingham is a vast place sprawling towards a million, and it is nothing more than an amorphous agglomeration. There is no Nottingham, in the sense that there is Siena. The Englishman is stupidly undeveloped, as a citizen. And it is partly due to his 'little home' stunt, and partly to his acceptance of hopeless paltriness in his surroundings. The new cities of America are much more genuine cities, in the Roman sense, than is London or Manchester. Even Edinburgh used to be more of a true city than any town England ever produced.

That silly little individualism of 'the Englishman's home is his castle' and 'my own little home' is out of date. It would work almost up to 1800, when every Englishman was still a villager, and a cottager. But the industrial system has brought a great change. The Englishman still likes to think of himself as a 'cottager' – 'my home, my garden'. But it is puerile. Even the farm-labourer today is psychologically a town-bird. The English are town-birds through and through, today, as the inevitable result of their complete industrialization. Yet they don't know how to build a city, how to think of one, or how to live in one. They are all suburban, pseudo-cottagy, and not one of them knows how to be truly urban – the citizen as the Romans were citizens – or the Athenians – or even the Parisians, till the war came.*

I am sure that this diagnosis is right, though there may be slightly more to be said for it than Lawrence says. For (in F. R. Leavis's phrase) 'the inevitable creativeness of everyday human life' manifests itself in robust and admirable ways as well as in sickening sentimentality in the English suburban townscape.

Now no one who has eyes to see can doubt that our townscape is predominantly awful. The domestic and private ethic which has so deeply penetrated the English spirit transpires in the revolting details of gnome and barrowland, in sham Cotswold stone-facing and Lego roofscapes; in fat and folksy chimneys and in the ample, exotic rollcall of English house-names, the whimsies and the cosiness of 'Silver Whispers', 'Dreamcote',

*'Nottingham and the Mining Countryside', *Phoenix*, 1931, reissued Heinemann, 1961, p. 139.

'Kosy Kottage', 'The Old Shack', 'Rose Retreat', 'Braemar', 'Burnside', 'Thatcher's Croft', 'Meadow Memories' (*sic*). It is not enough to call them dreadful and to add new ones to this anthropologist's bestiary. These names testify to the enduring power of the myth of rural idylls. They pay debased tribute to that myth, and to the assertion by the householder that here he is, and he is not to be budged. In the face of the omnipotence of cash and society, he can at least see his home and garden in his own terms. This assertion is an important factor in catching for a moment the spirit of English popular culture. It is certainly alive in its horticulture and in the astonishing busyness of its domestic activities. The crude assertion that we are a nation of Bingo-players and television-watchers does not square with the un-quenchable flow of energy plain to see in the gardens and do-it-yourself machinery of every housing estate in England. It is a natural part of most men's education, in and out of school, that they can and do build their own cupboards, draining-boards, greenhouses and pigeon-lofts; mend and maintain their own vehicles and – by the hour – tend and shape their gardens. On any fine evening between May and September, you will find at least one person of a household out in the garden from seven till ten. The strips of land running back parallel behind the gaunt council estates of the forties and fifties will turn in a wide arc of floribunda from spring to autumn; from daffodils and tulips to petunias, sweet peas, pansies, peonies, begonias, and on to phlox, dahlias and chrysanthemums, commanded for almost the whole time by the multitudes of official English roses, and flanked by a crowded greenhouse. The same flowers fill the Dream-land Ideal Home estates and the showgardens of the stately houses. Here, I think, we find – along, say, with national sport – one of the expressive centres of our popular culture. It fulfils many conditions of a culture; it defines and expresses real moral aspirations for beauty and order, it provides a language within which friendships may be made and sustained for a lifetime, and within which a man's identity may be confirmed. It may also provide what is still rare in our culture – a meeting ground for both men and women. In their gardens Englishmen make fewer mistakes than they do in their handiwork: on the whole they

39

do not betray the loss of touch which marks so many failures in the use of building materials, the placing of houses and the growth of townscapes, and which leaves acres of half-rural or village hillsides blitzed by selfishly placed bungalows, by the harsh angles of off-the-peg greenhouses, or the earnest obtrusiveness of the public lav.

The success of English gardens is not at all unmixed with sugariness and whimsicality. We have goblins, barrows, kidney ponds, stippled-pastel flags and sanipak urns to contend with. Nor is it only that queer mixture of superstition and infantilism. There is also the cloyed English taste for candy-floss blossomers at the expense of nobler trees like chestnut or beech even in city squares and in the arabesque of motorway intersections. There is an unmanly preference for the dainty and pretty at the expense of boldness. There are sham rustic boarding and trellises, and coy little swoops to garden paths, instead of the sensible patterns of older gardens. But the sugar blossom and the rustic seats are (again) payment in a debased coinage to the old dream of a perfect ecology. In a fine poem, Charles Tomlinson takes the measure of the gap between dream and present reality:

> Ranges
>   of clinker heaps
>   go orange now:
> through cooler air
>   an acrid drift
>   seeps upwards
> from the valley mills;
>   the spoiled and staled
>   distances invade
> these closer comities
>   of vegetable shade,
>   glass-houses, rows
> and trellises of red-
>   ly flowering beans.
>   This
> is a paradise
>   where you may smell
>   the cinders
> of quotidian hell beneath you;

        here grow
            their green reprieves
    for those
        who labour, linger in
            their watch-chained waistcoats
    rolled-back sleeves –
        the ineradicable
            peasant in the dispossessed
    and half-tamed Englishman.
        By day, he makes
            a burrow of necessity
    from which
        at evening, he emerges
            here.
    A thoughtful yet unthinking man,
        John Maydew,
            memory stagnates
    in you and breeds
        a bitterness.*

The dream in the garden has had a larger effect than the patterns of fading allotments. Ebenezer Howard in the late 1890s, solidly at one with that vigorous, dissident conscience spoken for by Pugin, Ruskin, Morris and the much underpraised Rossetti, produced perhaps the most influential version in his *Garden Cities of Tomorrow*. Even people who have never been near Letchworth and Welwyn, Howard's two working models, know at least a rudimentary version of his ideas: that a city should have space and grass, and that it should give large, dirty, industrial plant a special place of its own; that it shouldn't be too big; that it should have ready access to the refreshments and surprises of open countryside. Howard created the image, 'green belt'. Once again, crude cultural statements do not meet the historical situation. Early in its expansion, Howard called a halt to the unregulated imperialism of giant corporations. He worked steadily through to 1939 and the stream of his influence collided with and flowed powerfully into that of the Bauhaus prophets of a new architectural environment as well as that of the acolytes of

*'John Maydew, or, The Allotment' in *A Peopled Landscape*, Oxford, 1963.

Le Corbusier, 'La Ville Radieuse' and the new machine age. Howard's ideas and those of his often influential disciples – men like Patrick Geddes, Raymond Unwin, William Holford, Leslie Martin,* and Thomas Sharp – struck strong chords in English culture. The 'green belt' appealed to that essential industrial notion, a day in the country. The provision of grass and trees and open space was a generous response to the dead-ends, the revolting shut streets and Tom-All-Alones of industrial ghettoes. The idea spoke eloquently to the eternal dream living out its time in the saccharine reproductions of *The Haywain* (Constable's blustery wind toned nicely down) in Boots' and a thousand calendar photographs. But then Howard and the others, softening Corbusier's brutalism and the elegant forms and surfaces of the Bauhaus, reverted to their historical and cultural traditions and produced the new industrial townscape-with-grass-verges at Harlow, Hatfield, Basildon, Stevenage. The gentle liberal herbivores of the gently reforming socialist government presented the Town and Country Planning Act of 1947 and the New Towns Act of the same year. The acts spoke, as they say, to the English temperament. The town plans – and those that followed at Aycliffe, Peterlee, Hook (never built), Telford, Runcorn, Milton Keynes and a dozen others – are less the triumphs of modern rationalization techniques and hierarchies of criteria than of the ruminant English imagination. The towns are decent, cleanly, a bit bloodless, sadly lacking in civic sense or community, in political richness; they are at their very best in local sectors, corners of towns where kids play and pram-pushers can chat. Their schools and colleges are the best things about them. The classic Hertfordshire primary schools designed by the Smithsons in the fifties offer perhaps the most positive contribution in a single design to the national townscape. They present a world on the five-year-old's scale: she can see out of the window, she can move around as she must; classroom, working area and corridor interpenetrate one another *and* the garden outside. The lessons of Frank Lloyd Wright come solidly

*There is a useful brief history in Lewis Mumford's essay 'Old Forms for New Towns' in *The Highway and the City*, Secker & Warburg, 1964, pp. 35–44.

home to the integrated day: 'bring the outside in'. Such schools are wholesome, homely, and endlessly varied. They are both a living-room and a tiny town. Finally, they reflect the best part of a big change: the arrival of natural rights for children. However we convict our progressive selves of sentimentality, it is a happier affair being an English child these days than ever before. 'Life, liberty and the pursuit of happiness . . .' is an honourable trinity for primary schools. But once outside its educational efforts (and what I have said can be strongly applied to the plateglass and country garden universities) the herbivorous planner-architect's nerve has too often wilted or borne up only feebly against the roar of the man-eaters.

For the man-eaters *are* winning. We pay our modest homage to the successes won under the banner (Le Corbusier's in the first place) 'Espace, Soleil, Verdure'. Perhaps even more important, we have learned better to see what we have got. The prompting of such a man as Nikolaus Pevsner* and many men after him have emphasized the dazzling variety and plenitude of native domestic architecture. Not only the masterpieces among the country houses, but also the dignity and power of Victorian industry and town-planning,† the charm and good manners of seaside Queen Anne, all gables and bargeboarding,‡ the energy of many modern buildings, odd structures like gas-holders, steelworks, a row of shops or council offices which would not appear on conventional tourist routes.§ The tiny few who are interested enough to think about such matters know now that

* Whose mammoth series for Penguin, *The Buildings of England*, has surely been one of the great cultural achievements since 1945, matching in stamina, range, humanity and humour the giants of the past – Mills, Macaulays, Sidgwicks, over whom we shake our heads and say 'they don't come like that anymore'.

†In assorted publications, e.g. Quentin Hughes, *Seaport*, Lund Humphries, 1964; Andor Gomme and David Walker, *The Architecture of Glasgow*, Lund Humphries, 1968; J. M. Richards, *The Functional Tradition in Early Industrial Buildings*, Architectural Press, second edition 1967.

‡Mark Girouard, 'Queen Anne', *Listener*, May 1971; Roy Worskett, *The Character of Towns*, Architectural Press, 1968.

§ Sylvia Crowe, *The Landscape of Power*, Architectural Press, 1958; Gordon Cullen's classic primer *Townscape*, Architectural Press, 1961.

43

the source of its distinction is the close-packed variety of the English town and landscape. There is no one perfect model. So that even as sensitive a man as Thomas Sharp (in *English Panorama*, Architectural Press, 1936; *Town and Townscape*, John Murray, 1968) can sometimes sound prissy when objecting to the jostle and vulgarity of big city building. A city is not a town, and neither place is a village. In the 'man-sized'* scale of the English landscape the environment alters radically within a few miles: from giant cooling towers and heavy industrial plant to farmland and on to the wide, birch-lined avenues of quiet suburbs.

We see this landscape from the motor car and the lorry; they are now the measurers of scale for our landscape. It may be that the rapidity and insulation of travel by car has been one cause of our insensitivity. The vulgar surrender to speed implicit in the vast demolition which accompanies motorway constructions is a key symptom of a nation which does not know what to do with its own land.† No doubt the motorways too have known their successes‡ but the primacy of the road-building programme, the huge and terrible ruin which it has already caused, and its onward thrust is at once the symbolic and actual vivisection of the last hopes we have of making a decent modern environment. And what does that last, frail phrase portend? What homeland is thinkable for the next few decades?

First things first. It is no longer possible to plan and debate at the pace of the eighteenth-century landscapers and their patrons. We cannot, in the teeth of genocide, war, poverty, and global poisoning, see our landscape as avenues and obelisks on a permanent social way. If we do – and there is every sign that is how planners *do* think – then the man-eaters, the giant corporations

*The metaphor is Eric Lyons', who has applied it most rewardingly to his architectural work for Span Housing. See particularly the remarkable venture of the new village at New Ash Green in Kent.

†cf. Lewis Mumford, *The Urban Prospect*, Secker & Warburg, 1968, p. 106: 'Speed is the vulgar objective of a life devoid of any more significant kind of aesthetic interest.'

‡Nan Fairbrother makes some excellent suggestions in *New Lives, New Landscapes*, especially 'Roads as a New Environment', p. 271 ff.

who would rip up Snowdonia for copper,* put juggernaut trucks through Bath, Chester and Canterbury, motorways through the Chilterns and airports in Buckinghamshire, will simply destroy England for returns in sterling. Arguments about the landscape turn upon our intentions now, and it is no use pretending that the orotund phrases of industrial relations will do anything to resolve the conflicts. Getting ourselves around a table, meeting each other halfway and negotiating settlements which are acceptable to both sides is flapdoodle (cf. the Duke of Edinburgh's Commission Report, *Countryside in 1970*). There are hard, sharp, and bitter disagreements about which there is *no* compromise. We shall do better to see where we are. For as I have said, a popular culture is the product of human decisions. An adequate description of what we have now is necessarily a matter of choosing, of saying 'here, this is dead; there, that's what we must nourish'. Such choice is therefore a part of a continuing historical action. Now in very large areas our culture is brutal and indifferent to its landscape. Largely, the people do not care if, as is the case, one historic building per day is, against national laws, being knocked down. They see themselves as helpless to prevent a hotel being built at the head of Clifton Gorge† but they also see capital and private enterprise as in any case having *the greater right* over natural beauty. They accept a mindless version of 'progress' which permits the destruction of York as somehow the product of destiny when it is indeed the project of the juggernaut owners to smash down any obstacle between them and the dividend. They simply have not noticed the extinction of butterflies, the ripped-out hedges (11,000 miles per year; 117,000 since 1956), the blasted dereliction of huge areas of England and Wales, and the squalid imperialism of the Army, which now appropriates *two and a half times* as much land for its out-of-date and preposterous weaponry as it had during wartime.‡ They are numb to their disinheritance: the slaughter of the nightingale, the wren,

*Rio Tinto Zinc, in fact: see Paul West's excellent study of this firm's piracy, *Tears of the Earth*, Earth Island, London, 1972.

†cf. *Private Eye*, No. 245; *Guardian*, 24 May 1971. But, temporarily at least, the guerrilla groups have sabotaged this plan, at the public inquiry in November 1971.

‡See *Hansard*, 20 March 1971; *Private Eye*, No. 242.

and the skylark; the dying oaks of Southern England, starved to death upon a dried-up water table punctured by hasty building; the wild flowers which have vanished under strychnine sprays and the tidy, tungsten-lighted mind of the county council highways department. When you have said all you may about the mobility and magnitude of an industrial landscape, you are left with the world we have lost,* and the smashed, littered contours of modern England.

And yet. And yet. I have said that any cultural argument is political. We are at a point in history when the evils of industrialism are seen to be declaring themselves most obviously. More people than ever before have noticed. Under the relentless onslaught of industrial expansions, we have seen the earth and sea move in outrage. It is probably essential for survival that the drive for economic growth is reversed.† When these changes press home upon people's immediate lives then some minorities have reacted reasonably. They have rediscovered a reasonableness which correctly rejects the criteria of the cost-benefit analysis. For it is not reasonable that ordinary human living shall become wretched and intolerable because of noise; the protesters' victories at Stansted and Cublington against the third London airport were local victories for reason. At the moment it is not clear whether the last reasonable decision – not to build an airport at all – can be taken by the helots of productivity. But the Cublington victory was a political one; it underlined what could happen to the landscape in the next thirty years, and it reminds us that

*I am trying to describe a change in consciousness, as much as anything. Peter Laslett's book *The World We Have Lost*, Methuen, 1965, is an essential aid. 'The time was when the whole of life went forward in the family, in a circle of loved familiar faces, known and fondled objects, all to human size. That time has gone for ever. It makes us very different from our ancestors.' p. 21.

†It is worth notice that the last Labour Minister for the environment, Anthony Crosland, is still genially reproving 'middle-class defenders of their privileges' for trying to turn the tide of the motor-car back from the countryside. His bluff philistinism of course (one has to keep one's eye on the electorate) is not in a position to imagine that the actions of eleven million people might still be wrong, nor indeed that they might not rather walk if anyone had built a landscape in which that was still possible. See C. A. R. Crosland, *A Social Democratic Britain*, Fabian Society, 1971.

in that short term we remain still our own men. It further reminds us that in the ambit of modern technology our back garden is larger than we thought. In spite of our cedarwood fences, we cannot keep out Concorde, the M4, and the liner lorry. For it is not merely gunslinging to see the lines of the modern townscape which have become so much clearer in the past twenty-five years as battle lines. Over there, the predators of capital, the corporations, the cost-benefit analysts and system rationalizers. Their weapons: the juggernaut truck (see tables at end of chapter), the sales graph (especially of cars), vast and heavy plant, motorways, the wreckers' ball and chain, the unspeakable power of cash. Over here, the private life and house, the garden, the local industry, the shop, quiet, the pedestrian scale. The battlefield is no doubt too simple. Many men stand with a foot in both camps. But we shall have to choose between them, on many occasions and in different places. What is now clear for the first time is that groups of local people are prepared to choose. The politics of the seventies are short term: stop the motorway, resist the airport, close the bombing range, clean up the slurry, pedestrians only, mind our kids, this beach is ours, hands off our village, save the trees. Though there is no likelihood that the hundreds of amenity groups will come together for long years yet, this new, noisy crowd is the most positive point of hope for our landscape we are likely to find. The groups are minorities. Very well. We mostly live in our minorities. But (for example) the entrepreneurs and shopkeepers who turned down Lionel Brett's plan for York* are also a minority. They have more power than the people. They do not have more sense. They insult the people in the people's name. The sting of that insult is at last being felt by the so-called minorities. They too have their power. Their different claims – for space to play, for quiet, for room to walk, for controlling the size and speed of traffic, for trees, or simply for homes of their own – speak up for long-silent centres in our feelings. The action groups are helping men and women to a sense of their public selves. Not in the interests of public living, but so that private

*I would like space to treat this whole scandal as a case-history. See *York: A Study in Conservation*, Viscount Esher, H.M.S.O., 1968, for which the York Council has substituted a scheme of epic destructiveness.

47

from: *Heavy Lorries: A Memorandum to the Minister of Transport*, October 1970, Civic Trust, 18 Carlton House Terrace, London S.W.1.

Increase in the number of heavy goods vehicles on the roads In the period between 1956 and 1968 there was a big increase in the number of heavy goods vehicles on the roads. The number of vehicles between 5 and 8 tons increased by 293 per cent, that of vehicles over 8 tons by 567 per cent. In both cases the rate of increase was higher than that of private cars (178 per cent). Full details are given in the table below.

TABLE 1 : Increase/decrease of road goods vehicles (by unladen weight) and cars, 1956/1968

	under 2 tons	2–3 tons	3–5 tons	5–8 tons	over 8 tons	cars
1956	673,000	322,000	103,000	28,000	6,000	3,888,000
1957	711,000	309,000	114,000	30,000	7,000	4,193,000
1958	754,000	293,000	135,000	33,000	8,000	4,555,000
1959	796,000	279,000	157,000	37,000	9,000	4,972,000
1960	844,000	266,000	186,000	41,000	11,000	5,532,000
1961	881,000	248,000	212,000	47,000	13,000	5,983,000
1962	894,000	230,000	226,000	53,000	15,000	6,560,000
1963	925,000	224,000	244,000	61,000	19,000	7,380,000
1964	957,000	212,000	260,000	70,000	21,000	8,252,000
1965	946,000	194,000	269,000	76,000	25,000	8,922,000
1966	920,000	176,000	271,000	88,000	29,000	9,522,000
1967	915,000	169,000	274,000	99,000	34,000	10,312,000
1968	914,000	153,000	263,000	110,000	40,000	10,816,000
% increase or decrease	+ 36	− 52	+ 135	+ 293	+ 567	+ 178

TABLE 2: Goods transport in Great Britain by mode, 1956/1968 by total ton miles (thousand million)

	Total	Road	Rail	Coastal Shipping	Inland Waterways	Pipelines
1956	54·9	23·3	21·5	9·9	0·2	0·1
1957	53·9	22·9	20·9	9·8	0·2	0·1
1958	53·6	25·2	18·4	9·7	0·2	0·1
1959	55·6	28·1	17·7	9·5	0·2	0·1
1960	58·7	30·1	18·7	9·5	0·2	0·2
1961	60·5	32·3	17·6	10·1	0·2	0·3
1962	61·1	33·6	16·1	10·8	0·2	0·4
1963	61·6	35·0	15·4	10·6	0·1	0·5
1964	66·6	39·0	16·1	10·7	0·1	0·7
1965	68·2	41·0	15·4	10·9	0·1	0·8
1966	67·9	41·5	14·8	10·6	0·1	0·9
1967	73·2	43·0	13·6	15·5	0·1	1·0
1968	75·5	44·0	14·7	15·3	0·1	1·4

living shall be tolerable again. If, in the end, we can get beyond the short term goal and see the land as having its own, non-human life and shape, we might recover some of the dignity which goes with the knowledge that we live in a geography larger than we are ourselves.

BOOKS

GORDON CULLEN, *Townscape*, Architectural Press, 1961
   Tenterden: a report on townscape presented to Kent County Council, H.M.S.O., 1968
NAN FAIRBROTHER, *New Lives, New Landscapes*, Architectural Press, 1970; Penguin Books, 1972
LIONEL BRETT, *Landscape in Distress*, Architectural Press, 1965
   York, A Study in Conservation, H.M.S.O., 1968
ROY WORSKETT, *The Character of Towns*, Architectural Press, 1969
THE CIVIC TRUST, *Heavy Lorries: a Memorandum to the Minister of Transport*, 1970 (Civic Trust, 18 Carlton House Terrace, London S.W.1)
IAN NAIRN, *Outrage*, Architectural Press, 1955
   Counter-Attack, Architectural Press, 1957
KENNETH BROWNE, *Studies in the City*, Architectural Press, 1972
F. and E. INGLIS, *Your England: Blotscape*, Chatto & Windus, 1967
G. BELL and J. TYRWHITT (eds), *Human Identity in the Urban Environment*, Penguin Books, 1972
   Traffic in Towns (the Buchanan Report), Penguin specially shortened edition, 1964

3   Advertising

FRANK WHITEHEAD

Advertising slogans can range all the way from the trite ('Why don't we do this more often?') through the vulgarly inane ('I'm Debbie. Fly me to the moon over Miami') to the idiotically bizarre ('I dreamed I made sweet music in my Maidenform bra'). For the advertising executive there is only one criterion to be applied to all of them: will they induce people to buy more of the article in question, more Brand A,' more beer, more soap, more brassières? Any effect that advertising has upon our culture or values or language is thus unintended and (from the copywriter's point of view) strictly irrelevant – but that doesn't make the influence any less potent or less far-reaching. Indeed if culture is 'the whole way of life of a community' there is a case for saying that the cultural kingpin of twentieth-century Britain is the advertising industry. Certainly no one today can escape continual assault by advertisements in one form or another. (Can *you* remember a day this year when no advertiser's message reached you – not even a hoarding, a shop-window display, a phrase on a cereal packet?) And in 1971 direct expenditure on advertising in the United Kingdom amounted, according to the advertising industry's own estimates, to £591 million – a figure which does not take into account the very large sums spent on packaging, much of which is very closely geared to advertising and sales promotion.

These vast sums are spent by business firms in the expectation of specific economic advantages, and the exponents of advertising (usually employees of advertising agencies) who are so assiduous in writing letters to the Press usually base their defence on the claim that a modern industrial economy 'cannot exist without advertising'. The economic case for advertising must be examined later. The main concern of this essay is

51

with its unplanned yet pervasive influence upon the quality of our thinking and feeling, and upon the goals towards which we strive both in our individual lives and in the network of social relationships which make up our civilization. There are two main questions to be asked here. First, what kinds of emotional appeal do advertisers find it profitable to play upon, and what is the effect on our sensibilities of the copywriter's persistent harping upon these feelings? Second, in what ways does financial dependence upon advertisements affect the quality, content, and availability of the media (newspapers, magazines, television, and radio programmes) through which advertising is disseminated?

Before we consider these issues, however, it must be made clear that there is a great deal of advertising which we can safely ignore because it confines itself, unexceptionally, to providing information about goods and services for sale. Broadly speaking, the classified advertisements, in small print, in a news-paper fall under this heading; as do the majority of advertisements in trade and technical journals which are directed at other manufacturers or traders; together with a certain number of the display advertisements for local shop-keepers which appear in local daily or weekly papers. At the opposite pole are almost all television commercials and most of the display advertisements in national daily and Sunday papers and large-circulation magazines – a very high proportion, in fact, of all the nation-wide advertising which is addressed to the ordinary purchaser or final consumer. These advertisements contain a minimum of informational content and set out primarily to work upon our feelings and half-conscious attitudes by non-rational suggestion. This distinction between 'informational advertising' and 'advertising by psychological manipulation' is admittedly a rough and ready one, and there are many dubious cases in the border-land between the two. Thus 'Asphalting contractor: drives and paths re-surfaced from 50p square yard; phone —' falls clearly enough in the one category; while 'It's smart to drink Port' belongs unmistakably to the other. We might find it harder to agree on a classification for the single-line advertisement which appeared in the *New Statesman*'s Personal Column for many years: 'French taught by Parisienne; Results guaranteed'.

STRATEGIES OF PERSUASION

To persuade people to a course of action by reasoned argument would seem to be a perfectly legitimate procedure for the propagandist, whether political or commercial. The advertising 'profession' has long been of the opinion, however, that human beings in the mass are more malleable if you address your appeal not to their intelligence, but to their private fears, anxieties, prejudices, and day-dreams. The strategy employed has been aptly characterized by Aldous Huxley:

> Find some common desire, some widespread unconscious fear or anxiety; think out some way to relate this wish or fear to the product you have to sell; then, build a bridge of verbal or pictorial symbols over which your customer can pass from fact to compensatory dream, and from the dream to the illusion that your product, when purchased, will make the dream come true.

The method can be studied at its crudest in the picture-strips which tell the predictable story of the housewife whose marriage was nearly wrecked because she failed to drink the right brand of night-time beverage or the courier who nearly missed promotion because he had omitted to protect himself against B.O. by using one particular brand of toilet soap.

Reliance upon such appeals (what Thorstein Veblen called 'a trading on the range of human infirmities') tends to breed a peculiarly distasteful form of contempt for human nature. The attitude can be studied in these off-the-cuff observations from the Vice-President of one of the world's largest advertising agencies (quoted by Martin Mayer in *Madison Avenue U.S.A.*):

> People are very much alike the world over. You try to take something away from them, they resist. They all want some security. They're all a little lazy. And there isn't a housewife anywhere who doesn't want to look presentable – or wants to hear the truth about how she really looks.

The same outlook was given more guarded expression in an advertisement for a leading British advertising agency which appeared in a quality daily newspaper:

53

PEOPLE ARE ONLY HUMAN

Let's keep them that way. Let's resist any suggestion that they are statistics or cardboard cut-outs or unseen unknowns. People are people.

Oh yes, men are sometimes the smiling, extrovert athletes who look out on us from hoardings and cathode screens. But mostly, remember, men are home lovers and gardeners; they visit their parents and they play with their children; they sing sentimental songs in the pub, and they know the taste of fear.

Oh yes, women are sometimes the smiling, porcelain figures who look out on us from beside the athletes. But mostly, remember, women are mothers and housewives; they visit the shops and they play with their children; they sing sentimental songs at the sink, and they know the taste of tears.

These are the people (there are no others!) we must needs reach with our products, our services, our ideas.

There's nothing unreal or unfathomable about people. They're only human.

This is in itself an intriguing example of the copywriter's craft; it leads off with an incontrovertible platitude (carefully designed to suggest a community of fellow-feeling between writer and reader), and then keeps our attention with a button-holing insistence thinly overlaid by a beguilingly near-conversational intimacy of tone. Flattery is an indispensable weapon in the persuader's armoury, so a little uplift is thrown in for good measure; but the most perfunctory of pseudo-poetic echoes ('know the taste of fear', 'know the taste of tears', 'must needs') are evidently all you need in this line, even for an intellectual *élite* (in this case the *Guardian* readership). There must be a certain defensiveness of stance behind the desire to dissociate *this* agency from the irritated disbelief aroused by the glossy stereotypes who figure in T.V. commercials; but the allegedly more 'real' alternative is presented with a revealingly cynical condescension. One might know that it would be *sentimental* songs which 'they' sing in pubs and at sinks. And the keynote of the whole ethos is surely contained in the words 'nothing unfathomable'; this is the aspect of our common humanity which the adman will do his utmost to perpetuate.

In recent years the advertising world has turned increasingly to the twin techniques of market research and motivational research, in order to make more efficient its empirically-gained knowledge of how best to work upon human frailty. Market research uses sampling methods borrowed from sociology in order to find out who buys a particular article and its rival brands, and then to classify the purchasers or potential purchasers in terms of age, sex, locality, income-level, and social status; the advertising agency can then select the appeal judged most appropriate for members of this social grouping, and place its advertisements in the media which are most likely to reach them. Motivational research is linked in many people's minds with the name of its most aggressive propagandist, the American Dr Ernest Dichter; it uses a somewhat dubious version of depth psychology to establish, by a paraphernalia of 'depth interviews', psychodrama, and projective tests, the unconscious significance which any commodity has for its purchasers. Thus Unilever's agency Lintas a few years ago 'wrung from forty women the surprising information that soap is subconsciously viewed as something potentially harmful: the ideal soap is not the one that does most good but the one that does least harm'; this provided the rationale for an advertising campaign in which Astral cream soap was claimed to be 'less drying' to the skin and 'baby mild'. Similarly the Maidenform Bra series of advertisements ('I Dreamed I Stopped Traffic in my Maidenform Bra') in which a young woman walked about in her brassière among normally dressed people were said to be justified because of the exhibitionist tendency in all of us which makes us wish to appear naked or scantily dressed in a crowd.

In spite of these pseudo-scientific refinements the main types of appeal in use today remain very much the same as those which were anatomized by F. R. Leavis and Denys Thompson in *Culture and Environment* (1933). There is still much exploitation of fear in various forms – fear of losing one's job, fear of failure in courtship or marriage or parenthood, fear of what the neighbours will think if the clothes on your washing-line are only white and not 'dazzling-white' or of what the shopkeeper must think when you ask for 'inferior toilet-paper'. The fear of social inferiority figured not long ago in a series of advertisements for one of the 'Big Five' banks, in which a

55

young woman realizes that she is getting less courteous attention in a department store than the other customers because she pays cash for her purchases instead of paying by cheque. (An unlikely situation, one would have thought, in real life, but perhaps such advertisements may yet succeed in bringing it about.) Carrying the same implication that the all-important issue is not what you are but what other people think of you, are the numerous advertisements which sell us clothes, furniture, motor-cars, refrigerators as status-symbols – an opportunity for conspicuous expenditure which will impress the Joneses next door as evidence of our opulence and refinement. (Currently cigarette advertisements use the word 'taste' with carefully calculated ambiguity, while a stereo record system is advertised as 'for people who have come to expect a beautiful sound from beautiful things'.) Such claims for exclusiveness are often of course addled from the start, since the advertisements are in reality directed not at a minority but at the self-deluding majority. However, the advertiser can always try the alternative approach of tapping our innate impulse towards unthinking conformity ('millions' smoke this cigarette, 'everyone' enjoys this ice-cream); we are all inclined to feel safer if we know we are only doing what other people do, and it's no concern of the adman if, in thus eroding a little more of our belief in the importance of individual judgement, he carries us a step farther along the road towards 'other-directed' living (David Riesman's phrase) as opposed to the 'inner-directed' morality which has been the mainspring for all the major cultural achievements of Western civilization.

Another well-tried appeal still much in vogue is that which trades upon our superstitious faith in 'scientific' authority. In advertisements for toothpaste, disinfectants, patent medicines, beauty preparations, and the like, a young man in a white coat (it may not be explicitly stated that he is a doctor or research scientist) dispenses polysyllabic mumbo-jumbo which is all the more impressive because we don't in the least understand it. Recently this exploitation of hypochondria has been extended to our pets, so that we are exhorted nowadays to make sure that our budgerigar doesn't go short on vitamins, and that our cat gets its full quota of minerals and marrowbone jelly. Working in a similar way in a different field is the claim that 'No other *soap-filled* pad works like a Trojan because now it contains a Foam-Booster'. We might reasonably ask whether foam is either necessary or helpful to the cleaning-action of wire wool, since consumer reports have revealed that some synthetic detergents can work perfectly well with little or no foam, and that manufacturers add a foaming agent (usually alkylolamide) not to improve the efficiency of their product but to induce a feeling of confidence in housewives who associate plentiful lather, in soap, with cleaning power. The copywriter, however, is relying upon the loaded word ('Foam-Booster') to head us off from making any such inquiry. If we refuse to be lulled (or battered) into acquiescence we usually find that any statement that may be wrapped up inside the hypnotic slogan is either tautologous or too vague for verification to be possible. Just what kind of 'degree' is it, for that matter, that millions of Aspro-users keep finding themselves 'one under'?

It can be argued that the constant appeal to discreditable impulses of this kind is unlikely to have much effect except on those who are already abnormally susceptible. We may agree that it is the self-indulgent who will respond with most alacrity to slogans about chocolates with 'less-fattening centres', or to the stomach-powder manufacturer's encouragement to 'Eat what you like – without suffering for it'. On the other hand advertising agents are united in their conviction that sheer weight of repetition can be amazingly effective (hence the remarkably long life meted out to such slogans as 'Players Please' or 'Guinness is Good for You'); and it should be remembered that what we are exposed to is a combined assault by many different advertisers, all converging to direct their appeal to a small number of well-proved human weaknesses. Thus although it may be only the exceptional motorist who falls in at all fully with the implications of the invitation to 'Put a Tiger in your Tank', nevertheless this particular extreme example works in consort with a host of other advertisements for petrols, cars, and motoring accessories to establish an unquestioned assumption that what every motorist longs for above all (on our overcrowded roads) is speed, engine-power, and acceleration. Road safety was not until recently considered a strong selling-point for motor-cars.

This is perhaps a convenient opportunity to note that advertising agencies seem to be, in private, distinctly cautious in their estimate of their own persuasive power, preferring usually to follow the line of least resistance rather than seek to challenge or work against existing tendencies at all directly.* Thus motivational research revealed a few years ago that most people brush their teeth only once a day, before breakfast and therefore 'at the most pointless moment possible in the entire twenty-four-hour day from the dental hygiene standpoint.'† The reaction of the advertising agencies, however, was not to undertake a campaign to persuade the public of the importance of brushing one's teeth after meals in order to minimize dental caries. Instead they accepted that the operative motive in using toothpaste is the desire to give a pleasant taste to one's mouth first thing in the morning, and therefore made flavour the selling-point in their advertising. Hence, the emphasis in much subsequent toothpaste advertising on 'clean mouth' and 'tingling taste'; later Colgates ('Children love its minty flavour') made even more irrational play with the same motivation in their slogan 'Brush before breakfast ... destroy bad breath ... fight tooth decay ... *all day*!'

For the most part, therefore, advertising acts (and is content to act) as a reinforcement of already existing tendencies, but even so it seems likely that the multiplicity of small pressures work together to effect significant shifts in the total pattern of

*It is difficult to know to what extent advertising should take the credit (or the blame) for the vast changes in consumer behaviour which have occurred over the past century or so, since advertising is never the only causal factor at work, and it seems virtually impossible to isolate its influence from that of other social forces. However its real yet limited effectiveness can perhaps be illustrated by one case-study cited in *Advertising in Action* by Ralph Harris and Arthur Seldon. The Milk Marketing Board campaign associated with the slogan 'Drinka Pinta Milka Day' was accompanied by an increase in advertising expenditure from £390,000 in 1956–7 to £1,315,000 in 1960–61. Over this period the decline in milk sales was halted, and consumption moved upwards from the relatively low point of 1,337 million gallons per year to a record 1,409 million gallons.

†Vance Packard, *The Hidden Persuaders*, p. 21.

socially-accepted values. In countless ways often unnoticed we are led to accept as common ground a world in which the key to happiness is the possession of the newest model of car, dining-room suite, refrigerator, and television set, in which any malaise can be neutralized by recourse to a branded anodyne or laxative, and in which the chosen reward for a hard day's work is to 'treat yourself' to a luxury you can't afford because you feel you 'deserve' it – or even 'owe it to yourself'. The picture of the good life thus built up is as notable for its omissions as for what it contains; books, symphony concerts, and art exhibitions, for instance, command no advertising budget. In general terms the verdict of the Pilkington Committee cannot be seriously questioned:

Since they [television advertisements] sell goods by holding up certain attitudes as admirable, it seems obvious that they are at the same time and to some degree 'selling' the attitudes also. Although there is no compelling statistical or quantitative proof of this, failing such proof the responsible course must be to assume that the attitudes and values which act as vehicles for the sale of goods are themselves also being 'sold'.*

The tendency to reinforce impulses which are socially undesirable is only part of the problem. Even more insidious may be the advertiser's growing ingenuity in linking his product with ideas and images which are in themselves innocuous, pleasurable, even commendable. In consequence of this the concepts of sexual love, manliness, femininity, maternal feeling are steadily devalued for us by their mercenary association with a brand-name – as though the real human values they represent can be purchased by rushing out and buying a new shaving lotion, a new deodorant, even a new washing-machine. Mother-love seems to be the target most favoured by practitioners of this tactic, and the following example is only a little more nauseating than most of its kind:

When there's love at home, it shows. It shows in the smile of the mother who gives it. It shows in the happiness of her family who are secure in it... It shows in the fact that she chooses Persil for their clothes.

*Report of the Committee on Broadcasting, p. 80.

59

Children are notoriously photogenic, and the calculation is, presumably, that the smiling face of a toddler (preferably in colour) will generate enough initial goodwill to outlast the impact of such a punch-line as: 'Mother can you be sure? Can you be sure your children are getting enough body-building goodness?' – or even of so embarrassingly Barrie-esque a piece of dialogue as:

> Mummy, who do you love best?
> What a funny question!
> Well, you don't give *me* that nice soap.
> But baby's skin is very delicate...
> So is *mine*, Mummy!
> All right, darling, you shall have Johnson's too...

A similar estimate of our willingness to tolerate commercial intrusion into intimate corners of our personal lives is manifest in the glamorous photographs of young lovers with heads together in happy harmony over glasses of stout ('Jennie shared Neil's love of walking ... and his choice of drink'), or stretched out on a grassy bank to enjoy, in the intervals of courtship, a puff at their favourite brand of cigarette. In the following example, taken from a woman's magazine, the reader's eye is to be riveted first by the large and romantically-composed photograph and then led, by carefully selected typography and layout, through the skilfully-contrived verbal daydream to the final goal of the brand-name.

> That magical summer,
> he found love in a soft glance...
> a radiant complexion

Lovers Meeting

It began long ago ... with a letter in Sue's childish hand to her penfriend Kim in California. She had quite forgotten Kim when years later a letter brought news of her and went on ... 'This is really to introduce my brother Pete. He's won a scholarship to study in your country and knows just no one there. Then I thought of you ...' and not long after, Sue heard, for the first time, Pete's deep slow voice on the telephone asking for a date. They met – and then again. His gentle manner, his disarming grin, soon made him a favourite with her set. Then, more and more, it was just she and Pete ... alone even in a crowd, in their own private world. One golden day by the river Pete

60

asked Sue to be his wife. Close to her, Pete felt Sue's cheek, warm and soft against his. 'My, you're beautiful,' he whispered. 'When they see that English complexion back home . . .' Sue is still as fresh and lovely as she was that day – thanks to Knight's Castile. . .

Obviously an important human emotion is trivialized when it is thus reduced to a single commercially-manipulable aspect. (In this case the aspect chosen is that of simple physical attraction; a comparable effect can be studied elsewhere in the salesmanship which seizes on 'Entice' as the name for a perfume or which recommends chocolates through the medium of a slinky vamp thinking – or saying – 'I like a man who likes me enough to buy me Cadbury's Contrast'). Over and above this, however, we can observe the inherent compulsion to stereotype experience on a level which is rapidly and universally communicable, and hence to congeal the capacity for emotional response in forms which are even more standardized and constricting than the magazine fiction from which they derive. Here are feelings which have indeed been 'processed' to the uniform consistency and flavourlessness of a cheese spread.

After the advent of television advertising in September 1955 the main weight of mass advertising was transferred increasingly from the Press to the television screen. Expenditure on television commercials climbed rapidly, reaching a total of £106 million in 1965; and although there has since been some reduction in television's share of total advertising expenditure, nevertheless in 1971 expenditure on television advertising was £143 million (24 per cent of total advertising expenditure for that year). A high proportion of this is spent by the manufacturers of a small number of highly advertised commodities such as soaps and detergents, polishes, toothpastes, soft drinks, sweets and chocolates. Thus in 1960 tobacco manufacturers spent nearly £4½ million on television advertising as opposed to about £3,800,000 on Press display advertising. The specially-formed companies which make most television commercials can command lavish resources – the budget for a hundred feet of advertising film is reported to be higher than that available for making even entertainment feature films. They are able to call too upon the talents of many of the country's outstanding technicians and film-directors:

witness the work of Lindsay Anderson for Rowntree's, of Karel Reisz for Persil, and of Joseph Losey for Nimble Bread. To analyse the methods used by advertisers in this evanescent medium is peculiarly difficult; words are no longer the main channel of appeal, but have become only one adjunct among many – the visual setting, the personality of the actors, the camera angles and cutting, the background music, the catchy singing-jingle, the appeal of the puppet figures or the amusement contributed by the animated cartoon. There can be no doubt that the combined effect of these multiple resources makes an exceptionally powerful impact. Moreover they blare out upon the viewer at a time when he is sitting at his own hearthside, comfortable, relaxed, almost defenceless; since they often appear unpredictably in the middle of a programme, the only way to escape them is to refuse resolutely to turn the knob of one's set to the commercial frequency. It is rash to generalize, since the medium makes it possible to combine a remarkable variety of different appeals within the space of a single forty-five-second commercial; but it would seem that the aggressive hectoring approach is giving way increasingly to more subtle forms of blandishment. The preferred aim nowadays is to associate the product with pleasurable screen images and personalities rather than harp on fears and anxieties that may introduce a jarring note into the family viewing. Soap or beer brands are linked, by the most tenuous of connections, with idyllic rural or sporting scenes, photographed in sunlight which is unfailingly benign; while a bedtime drink has to be extolled to us, in rapt tones, because it provides 'a *happy* flavour at the end of each day'. An unbridled euphoria must surely overtake any viewer who watches for long enough the succession of eupeptic faces smiling forth from spotless kitchens whence all effort has been banished and in which every mouthful that is tasted calls for an ecstatic coining of superlatives.

In recent years there has also been a marked stepping-up of the advertiser's traditional reliance upon appeals to irrationality; and this seems to be due at least in part to the nature of the television medium itself, where the director's multiple resources for influencing mood and atmosphere make it far easier to sidestep the sceptical reaction and to exploit to the full the power of unconscious and semi-conscious association. There is, however, a further important factor which has worked in the same direction. The standardization made inevitable by modern mass-production methods has meant that increasingly the most heavily advertised products are indistinguishable from their nearest competitors – apart from their brand-name. Few smokers, for example, can tell one make of cigarette from another by taste alone; while consumer reports have revealed little significant difference between the various brands of detergent, either in efficacy or in chemical composition. In this situation advertising agencies are led to concentrate above all on the emotional aura they can attach to their client's 'brand-image', whether by finding a new brand name, by giving a new colour to the package, or by exploiting some wholly irrelevant association which has been proposed by the motivational-research analyst. To the logical mind it may seem a doubtful recommendation for a breakfast cereal that it provides 'the fastest breakfast ever'; nor would any reasonable person choose one tin of soup in preference to another on the grounds that it had been 'tested' at ten o'clock rather than eleven. Nevertheless it seems that if such a claim is insisted on with apparent seriousness often enough, many people can be hoodwinked into overlooking the absurdity of it; the indirect effect of this in reducing our capacity for rational choice in matters of more moment for us than soup-buying will surely bear thinking about.

Brief mention should be made here of some other ways in which advertising has lately adapted its methods of approach in response to changing patterns in the social environment. First, the insistent stress on 'newness' in current advertising. 'What's new in Colgate Dental Cream that's MISSING – MISSING – MISSING in every other leading toothpaste?', screamed one (American) advertising agency a few years ago; and today we are constantly invited to be all agog at a 'new' soap, a 'new' detergent, an 'enticingly spicy new flavour' in a soup, 'an absolutely new kind of softness' in a toilet roll. 'Now – superb *New* packs' proclaims an advertisement for Wills's Whiffs – as though *this* was just what we had all been waiting for. This

63

line of attack makes capital out of our layman's awareness that technological change in industry is going ahead today at an unprecedented rate. There are, indeed, genuinely advantageous new techniques for constructing automobiles, preserving food, synthesizing fibres, and so forth – though sometimes these advances have, in their early stages of development, attendant snags which are very little publicized. But much of the advertising that hammers away most noisily at this theme of 'newness' is concerned with modifications which are of very slight or even doubtful benefit to the consumer. Thus it seems, oddly enough, that the composition of a toilet soap may be modified from time to time in ways which are *not* widely publicized, after which the manufacturer will go to town in his advertising with an eye-catching but essentially non-significant variation which can only be described as a gimmick (the introduction, for example, of Lux in four pastel colours 'To mix! To match! To have fun with!'). In some cases the advertiser's obsession with 'newness' can be related also to an industry's decision to keep its mass-production assembly-lines flowing at a constant rate either by making the product less durable than it need be ('built-in obsolescence') or by continually changing its outward appearance so that last year's model soon looks old-fashioned ('annual styling').

The appeal of fashion is of course the favoured theme of much advertising directed particularly towards teenagers and young adults. Two recent examples will suffice: one for a face-powder – 'The IN look is pearled translucence' (here a dash of pseudo-science has been added to the mixture); the other the slogan, linked with a series of photographs of well-known jazz performers, which informs us that PEOPLE WHO SET TODAY'S TRENDS DRINK Long Life CANNED BEER (an interesting example this of the way in which changing patterns of social prestige have installed the television or entertainment-world personality as the contemporary inheritor of the snob-appeal formerly wielded by a testimonial from the Countess of X). It should be noted that marketing studies carried out in the past decade have revealed that young people between the ages of fifteen and twenty-five dispose of a remarkably high spending-power. According to Dr Mark Abrams, Britain's five million teenagers

spent in 1959 no less than £830 millions, the average boy spending
£3.57 a week, and the average girl £2.70. A high proportion of
this money goes on a fairly narrow range of consumer goods
(particularly clothing and footwear, tobacco, drinks, sweets,
cosmetics, records, magazines); and in consequence some manufacturers have seen an advantage in angling their advertising to
catch this teenage market. (Notable examples at different times
have been Rowntrees, Skol Lager, Babycham, and Players,
Strand, and Bristol cigarettes; some of the collective advertising
of the Brewers' Society has also had the evident intention of
rehabilitating both beer and pubs in the eyes of young people,
though not specifically of teenagers.) One motive for spending
big money on advertising for this age-group is the hope, often
justified, that 'brand-loyalty' once established may last for life;
and the same argument applies with even more force to advertising directed at children. Understandably enough most parents
would prefer to be able to choose their breakfast cereal on its
own merits and not on account of the balloon or toy bullet
inserted inside the packet; and they are inclined to feel some
resentment at the attempt to put pressure on them indirectly
through such slogans as 'Don't Forget the Fruit Gums, Mum!'
Moreover it seems wrong, to many adults, that immature minds
should be subjected to unscrupulous psychological manipulation
for commercial ends. There may be little reason to believe that
children are notably more susceptible than their elders to direct
pressure from the admen; but since their attitudes and outlook
are still in process of formation, there seems little doubt that
they are exceptionally vulnerable to the indirect influence upon
values and standards discussed above, and the massive weight of
persuasive advertising to which they are at present exposed seems
bound in the long run to stereotype and debase the quality of
living of future generations.

'PAY THE PIPER, CALL THE TUNE'

Propagandists for advertising make much of the fact that advertising revenue enables us to watch television free of charge
and to buy newspapers and magazines at a price considerably

below the sum which they have cost to produce. The 'fact' is itself slightly mis-stated. We do, of course, have to pay the full price, in the end, for our papers and television programmes – by means of a small impost every time we buy detergents, cigarettes, petrol, or toothpaste. Moreover, this indirect form of compulsory levy reduces the power of each one of us to decide what he will pay for, and how much he will pay for it. I can choose whether or not to subscribe towards the cost of the BBC's programmes through the purchase of a television licence; but we all have to contribute our annual quota to finance the 'Independent' Television channel, whether we possess a television set or not.

These subsidies which advertising pays on our behalf add up to vast amounts. In 1971 the television programme companies received from advertising revenue some £128 million net. In the same year about £418 million was spent on all forms of press advertising, of which some £108 million went to national newspapers, £152 million to regional newspapers, £54 million to magazines and periodicals, and £52 million to trade and technical journals. It is more difficult to estimate the net financial gain to the Press, since a newspaper has to pay for the paper and ink needed to print the advertisement, and also to staff and maintain its own advertising department; but it seems safe to say that at least half the total advertising revenue can be regarded as a net subsidy. If there were no advertising it is likely that we would have to pay nearly double its present selling-price for a popular paper, and more than double for a quality paper.

The main effect of this dependence on advertising can be stated very simply. Advertisers want their advertisements to reach as many people as possible; they pay for space in newspapers at the rate of so much per column-inch per thousand readers, and they pay for time on commercial television according to the number of captive viewers they can count on having delivered to them. (In 1970 a full-page advertisement cost £5,500 in the *Daily Express*, or £4,390 in the *Daily Mirror*, while London Weekend Television charged £620 for 7 seconds of advertising at a peak viewing-time.) The overriding aim of the media-owner must therefore be to secure for his advertisers a guaranteed mass-audience. Newspapers, magazines, television programmes are in any case already fantastically expensive to produce; the initial outlay (on equipment, machinery, personnel) has to be spread over a very large number of readers or viewers if there is to be any possibility of profit. The influence of the advertiser steps up a little farther the already-compulsive drive towards a mass-audience – an audience numbered not in thousands, or hundreds of thousands, but in millions.

Where numbers are what really count, the inevitable tendency is to pull them in by playing safe; by sticking to tried and tested formulas which appeal to the lowest common factor in every one of us; in general, in fact, by concentrating on those forms of entertainment or items of news which promise the maximum immediate titillation in return for the minimum effort. Unless it be very late at night, when the audience will be relatively small anyway, no commercial television programme can afford to appeal to a minority – not even to those sizeable minorities which care for opera or ballet or Beethoven or Shakespeare. The fate of the *News Chronicle* in 1960 showed that nowadays even a million readers are not enough to keep a daily newspaper alive.*

The snag in all this is that universality of appeal is not quite the same thing as popularity. A newspaper or magazine which 'has something for everyone' may be bought by millions and yet give little real satisfaction to any of its readers; the television programme which fewest people switch off may yet be keenly enjoyed by no one. The need to approach us all as units in a mass involves inevitably a levelling-down in the general standard of taste – a studied avoidance of the areas of experience in which we live most fully, either as individuals or as members of a group sharing a common passion or enthusiasm; a drift instead towards

---

*Exceptions to this are the handful of quality papers which get by with a circulation of only a few hundred thousand. Because they have a high proportion of middle-class readers with above-average purchasing-power they are able to charge above-average rates for advertising space. For the most part only a limited range of advertisers find it worthwhile to pay these rates – manufacturers of luxury cars and central heating equipment, for example; there is also a certain amount of prestige advertising designed to keep a firm's name in front of the directors and executives of other firms.

the inertly conventional triviality which is utterly without character but for that very reason antagonizes no one.

Dependence on advertising moreover implies a subtle distortion of purpose, in that the paramount need is to please the advertiser rather than to satisfy the reader or viewer. The entertainment or the page of print comes to be judged in part as a setting for the advertisements which border it (*they* after all are what bring in the profits). This consideration certainly determines presentation, as one may know when trailing a magazine-story through its devious trickle, flanked all the way by brand-names, from page seven to page seventy. It may also influence content, though the relationship is necessarily more elusive in this country than it has sometimes been in the United States, where commercial sponsors have been known to abandon a programme series because it provoked too much suspense or too much laughter for their purpose. (One can see that it might be better business to frame one's sales-talk with a mildly hypnotic panel-game rather than have it drowned by amused comment on the vagaries of 'I Love Lucy'.) Even here where direct sponsorship has been excluded, one may doubt whether the advertisers would remain content for long if the entertainment provided by the programme companies were markedly more absorbing than the commercials which punctuate it every thirteen minutes. Certainly one often has the impression that the advertisements and the bait which accompany them are remarkably similar both in ethos and in surface appearance. In particular, one may suspect an ulterior motive behind the prevalent bonhomous atmosphere of synthetic optimism; isn't this the mood in which the advertisers think we're most likely to part with our money? One recalls the sponsor who once told a leading American television impresario* 'in a wonderful phrase delivered with a completely straight face that what he wanted was "happy shows about happy people with happy problems".'

Easier to illustrate, of course, are the more trivial manifestations of the power of the advertising manager – the editorial puff for the advertised product, the special supplement concerned with holiday travel or with some particular industry, the colour

*David Susskind, quoted in *Power Behind the Screen*, by Clive Jenkins.

section shrewdly constructed according to the space salesman's specification in order to tap for the *Sunday Times* certain new sources of advertising revenue. And deference to the susceptibilities of advertisers also shows itself in two negative respects, which are rather more important. It inhibits most newspapers from any attempt to review critically ordinary commercial products in the same way that they review books or films. And it ensures that one will never hear, from either Press or commercial television, any radical criticism of the advertising industry itself, however much this might be in the public interest.

THE ECONOMIC ARGUMENT

In 1938 two per cent of our national income was spent on advertising. This proportion dropped sharply during the war, but has risen steadily in the post-war period to over 2·1 per cent in 1963. European countries spend less proportionately on advertising than we do, but the comparable figure for the United States is considerably higher (2·7 per cent in 1963). Another interesting way of looking at these figures is to compare the annual amount each country spends on advertising for each member of its population. A 1970 survey estimated this at 89.56 dollars per head in the United States, as compared with 21.31 dollars or £8.90 per head in the United Kingdom. The indications are that the more prosperous a country becomes the more it spends proportionately on advertising, though which is cause and which effect is a moot question. The probability is that the proportion of our national resources which we in Great Britain devote to advertising (already high comparatively) will continue to increase in the future.

It is obvious that the individual manufacturers who allocate resources to advertising believe that this improves their sales and increases their profits, although their grounds for this belief can seldom be of a kind which would satisfy a social scientist seeking meticulous proof. (Advertising agents are inclined to claim any increase in sales as evidence for the efficiency of their advertising campaign, although in reality advertising is only one among a large number of factors that may have been at work. It

69

is significant that a recent study by an economist reported that: 'The attempt to discover the reasons why firms spend particular amounts on advertising proved fruitless... Most firms which expressed an opinion thought that they were spending too much on advertising but had to do so because their competitors did so.'*) The question we need to ask, however, is: 'What are the social benefits which accrue from the expenditure to society at large?' One claim customarily advanced is that advertising reduces prices to the consumer because it makes possible the economies resulting from mass production. Here too it is very hard to isolate the influence of advertising as such; but some instances can be cited which disprove the general contention. Thus *Shoppers' Guide*, Number 9, p. 19, reported the case of a kettle, the price of which had been raised from 23s. 1d. to 37s. 6d.; when questioned, the manufacturer wrote: 'An extensive national advertising campaign is being conducted on it... This increase in price is mainly due to the advertising charges.' In the same year a manufacturer of raincoats gave an account in a letter to the *Guardian* of discussions he had had with an advertising firm with a view to entering the field of branded goods. If the proposal had gone through, the cost of advertising would have meant an increase in price to the consumer of nearly £1 (about fifteen per cent), whereas the maximum possible saving by way of reduced overheads as a result of increased production would have been a matter of coppers. Some multiple stores have shown that it is perfectly possible to achieve mass-production economy with either negligible or very moderate advertising, and at the same time to sell a thoroughly sound product (e.g. Boots' Anti-Freeze) at a price much below that of expensively-advertised competitors.

Certainly it may be true that when a genuinely new product is launched (ball-point pens and synthetic detergents are often cited as examples), heavy initial advertising is necessary in order to build up a mass market quickly. Detergents, however, have continued to carry massive advertising long after the point at which they became fully accepted by the housewife; and in this case at least a reduction in the advertising budget, reported to

*T. Barna, *Investment and Growth Policies in British Industrial Firms*, 1962, p. 24.

have amounted at times to as much as a quarter of the selling-price of every packet, could have resulted in a useful price-cut to the consumer.

In the case of washing-powders, heavy advertising has been the main weapon in a prolonged trade-war in the course of which the two giants, Unilevers and Hedleys, have virtually carved up the market between them. A number of studies have shown the extremely wide variation between different products in the amount of advertising they carry. Thus the ratio of advertising expenditure to turn-over may be as much as twenty-two per cent for patent medicines and cosmetics (1958 estimate). On the other hand, although expenditure on advertising all alcoholic drinks reached in 1959 the vast total of £16–18 millions, the turn-over was also so large that this represented only three per cent of total sales. Kaldor and Silverman in their thorough study of British advertising in the year 1935 concluded* that the extent of advertising was related not so much to the nature of the commodity as to the number of manufacturers competing for the market, advertising being heaviest where there was fierce competition between a fairly small number of large advertisers. There are grounds for thinking that this analysis could be shown to be equally valid in relation to advertising today. Toilet soap, toothpaste, sweets and chocolates, breakfast cereals, ice-creams, refrigerators are all heavily advertised products, the market for which is divided between a handful of very large firms. In such cases high advertising costs tend to act as a barrier against the entry into the field of new competitors and at the same time to enable the existing firms to maintain both prices and profits at a high level. When a new competitor has enough capital to pay the heavy entrance-fee, advertising expenditure may soar even higher for a time. Thus, a few years ago the British soup market, then dominated by Heinz, Crosse & Blackwell, and Batchelor, was invaded first by Knorr-Swiss (later bought up by an American firm, Corn Products) and then by the American giant, Campbell Soups; and advertising expenditure rose rapidly to over £2 million a year. In such conditions it is hard to see how advertising

*N. Kaldor and R. Silverman, *A Statistical Analysis of Advertising Expenditure and of the Revenue of the Press*, C.U.P., 1948.

can bring any price benefit to the consumer, either during the fiercely competitive 'oligopolistic' phase or at the later stage when one firm has succeeded in establishing a near-monopoly.

More plausible superficially is the argument that we live in a large-scale industrial society which is subject to constant technological change and in which mass-produced articles have to be brought to the consumer through increasingly impersonal channels of distribution. In such a society advertising is necessary in order to keep the consumer informed about new materials, new gadgets, new ways of living (some apologists would even say 'to create new wants', though it is hard to see how a want can be very important if it has to be persuaded into existence). Certainly there is much we need to know when we set out to buy a drip-dry shirt or have to make up our mind between linoleum and vinyl for our flooring; and we commonly find that, even when we keep away from the self-service shelves, the shop assistant is in no position to help us since the only thing he knows about his wares is whether or not they have been advertised on the telly. The information we require is often complicated; even the lucidly-presented pages of *Which?* do not always make it easy to master. By contrast the information contained in advertisements is minimal, and what there is is suspect. *Suggestio falsi* is regarded as a legitimate device, and we are in for disillusionment if we suppose that a statement that 'Bakers eat it' (a branded loaf) means that someone has conducted a survey of bakers' bread-eating habits. Brand advertising as we know it today is, in fact, geared not to rational decision but to impulse-buying in the supermarket.

A further argument advanced for advertising is that it increases total consumer spending, and thereby helps to create a high level of employment and general prosperity. In so far as this is true (and most economists would regard the case as 'not proven') the effect is accompanied by a distortion in the *pattern* of spending which goes far to nullify any benefit which you or I might feel in our own living. This can be seen particularly clearly in relation to the free gifts and 'premium offers' which have proliferated so enormously in recent decades, largely under American influence. Apart from the illusion of having obtained something for nothing, are you really any 'better-off' when you have received a plastic rose attached to your detergent packet, or have purchased a wobbly ball at a cut-rate by sending a postal order accompanied by two packet-tops? The 'premium offers' are sometimes (though not invariably) good value for money, since direct buying in large quantities enables the manufacturer to offer his silver-plated teaspoons at a price lower than that in the retail shops, yet without much cost to himself. (Many of the offers are, in fact, 'self-liquidating', and cost the manufacturer nothing so long as they sell out.) But clearly these offers, particularly when directed at children, must tempt many families to divert money away from a genuine need to the purchase of an article which is not much wanted and may in the event be little used. Similarly with the national budget, since it is often inessential goods (confectionery, cosmetics, cigarettes) which are the most heavily advertised, and in any case the incidence of advertising is determined not by any criterion of public good, but by the state of competition existing within the various industries.

Professor J. K. Galbraith has pointed out that in the United States 'advertising operates exclusively . . . on behalf of privately produced goods and services'; the result is a social imbalance between privately-produced goods and publicly-supplied services which he has trenchantly characterized as a contrast between 'private wealth' and 'public squalor'. In Great Britain the dichotomy is less obvious, since the nationalized industries do advertise to a moderate extent (both for directly commercial and for prestige reasons), and there is also a small amount of 'educative' advertising on behalf of public health and accident prevention. Nevertheless the trend over the past decade has undoubtedly carried us some way towards a reduplication of the American pattern. Our eyes and our ears are constantly assailed on behalf of more beer but not more schools, more laxatives but not more hospitals, more sweets to be eaten between meals but not a more adequately staffed school dental service. And although Government policy has been the main culprit, the pattern of advertising has surely done much already to accentuate the currently-alarming 'imbalance' between private and public forms of transport.

73

WHAT REMEDIES?

The increased volume of advertising in the post-war years, and in particular the licensed appearance after 1955 of fireside hucksters in every home, produced an unmistakable upsurge of public irritation and uneasiness. One public opinion poll for instance showed that sixty-one per cent of those interviewed were 'annoyed a lot' by commercials in the middle of television programmes; and other research studies have shown that many people have developed quite elaborate avoidance techniques to shield themselves from paying attention to either television or newspaper advertisements. Public resentment found one form of expression in the foundation in 1959 of the Advertising Inquiry Council, an unofficial non-party body which set out to represent the interests of the consumer in advertising. The A.I.C. published invaluable reports on the advertising of tobacco and of alcohol, and acted usefully for some years as a watchdog on guard against specific abuses by advertisers; its campaigning probably contributed something to the Labour government's decision in 1966 to ban cigarette advertising on television. Extreme cases of misrepresentation in advertisements are in any case subject to restriction in certain fields by legislation, while the Trades Description Act of 1968 should, in theory, have extended considerably the legal protection accorded to the consumer at large. Mention must be made also of the 'self-policing' of British advertising by the advertising industry itself. The Advertising Association and the Institute of Advertising Practitioners had developed over the years a voluntary 'code' operated by their own members; and in 1962 the Advertising Association decided to extend this voluntary system by setting up an Advertising Standards Authority with 'full powers of enforcement'. The A.S.A. is financed by the Advertising Association, but has an independent chairman and fifty per cent lay membership. The adequacy of this form of voluntary control has been widely questioned, particularly by the Consumer Council. In addition, the Independent Television Companies Association have their own regulations for television advertising, and it is claimed that this control has become more stringent in recent years. Now,

74

however, the Advertising Inquiry Council has become inactive (its work was always constricted by its shoe-string budget), and the Consumer Council has been abolished by the Conservative government (even though it was a former Conservative government which first set it up in 1963). As a result the only organized body capable of representing the interests of the consumer is now the Consumer's Association.

In relation to the wider issues it is tempting to put one's faith in education, and to hope that as fresh generations grow up to be more discriminating and critically-minded in their reading, viewing, and spending, the mass-persuaders will be compelled to raise their sights and to reduce their reliance upon cheap emotional manipulation. Certainly there would be more chance of this happening if time could be found before they leave school to alert all teenagers to the nature of the appeals which will be played upon in order to wheedle their first earnings away from them. And from one point of view, the need for some inoculation of this kind has become the more urgent now that the techniques of commercial advertising are being used increasingly to mould public opinion by pressure groups of all kinds, not excluding political parties and even governments.

It is sometimes suggested that, if only it could be sterilized, as it were, by the need to woo a more critically-minded audience, advertising might develop into a beneficial cultural agency disseminating to a wider public the visual idiom of the modern artist and designer. There is scant substance to this myth, and precious little that one could point to as supporting evidence. In the early days of colour-lithography some artists of distinction (notably Toulouse-Lautrec and the Beggarstaff Brothers) were sufficiently excited by the new medium to design some highly attractive theatre posters; more recently London Transport has sponsored underground posters which are not at all bad to look at, and which may have had some effect in enticing travellers to visit places of interest near tube stations. But apart from a few highly untypical instances of this kind, advertising makes contact with significant movements in visual (and cinematic) art only to the extent that it extracts, for its own purpose, elements and motifs which have already degenerated into clichés. Moreover its

75

purposes are such that, in thus following a 'movement' at several removes, it also inevitably debases and vulgarizes it even further. There are no 'good' advertisements, only 'effective' ones. In this field, in fact, education must always be negative ('education *against*'); and in these circumstances we must not expect too much from it, or be surprised if its results are slow to show themselves.

In the meantime there is one other approach which ought to be explored. Far too much money is lavished at present on consumer advertising – far more than any economic argument could justify, even if the indirect damage to our cultural life is left out of the calculation. Much of it is spent, moreover, by a limited number of large manufacturers: the *Financial Times* reported in 1960 that half the advertising time on television was taken up by no more than twenty companies. Part of the trouble is that the whole of a firm's expenditure on advertising can be deducted as an allowable expense before computing the company profits which are liable to income tax. There seems to be no valid reason why a ceiling should not be set to this allowance, in rather the same way that an individual is limited to claiming two fifths of his life insurance premiums as an allowance against income. If firms had to bear a proportion of the expense of their advertising out of profits, they would be inclined to scrutinize their budgets more carefully; and some might find it would pay them better to put money into improving their product rather than into buying goodwill for their brand-name. It may be that as an indirect consequence the profits of the television companies would diminish, and we would find ourselves paying a more nearly-economic price for our newspapers and magazines – but even then how many people outside the advertising industry would feel moved to complain?

BOOKS

DENYS THOMPSON, *Voice of Civilisation*, Muller, 1943

VANCE PACKARD, *The Hidden Persuaders*, Penguin Books, 1960

MARTIN MAYER, *Madison Avenue U.S.A.*, Penguin Books, 1961

JEREMY TUNSTALL, *The Advertising Man in London Advertising Agencies*, Chapman & Hall, 1964

E. S. TURNER, *The Shocking History of Advertising*, Penguin Books, 1965

FRED INGLIS, *The Imagery of Power*, Heinemann, 1971

4   The Press

GRAHAM MARTIN

Plenty of people will try to give the masses, as they call them, an intellectual food prepared and adapted in the way they think proper for the actual condition of the masses. The ordinary popular literature is an example of this way of working on the masses.... But culture ... seeks to make all men live in an atmosphere ... where they may use ideas, as it uses them itself, freely, – nourished and not bound by them. This is the *social idea*; and the men of culture are the true apostles of equality.

MATTHEW ARNOLD

1

The Press* is by far the oldest of the mass media, and a compressed survey of its modern workings ought to find this maturity useful. The size and complexity of each medium, and above all, their elusiveness as a subject-matter make short treatment particularly hard. The Press is a subject neither small nor simple, yet its age ought to have given it shape and definition, to have familiarized both the problems and sensible ways of discussing them. Nevertheless, the Press cannot, in fact, be separated from the flux of popular culture any more easily than the other media. The fact of its history has not protected it from the contemporary pressures everywhere else in evidence – from changes silently imposed by the multiplying alternative ways of transmission, by the fact of these, as well as by the new styles and conventions which disseminate from them. Thus – is it any longer useful to talk in the old way about the Press in 'its political role' without taking in the contribution of radio and television news programmes? Or is it really worth while saying anything about the

*Defined in the Oxford English Dictionary as 'periodical literature generally', a useful reminder of the variety of publications that could here be dealt with; but the term will be confined to its usual compass – daily and weekly newspapers and journals.

Press 'as an entertainer' without grouping it with modern magazines, with the general increase of visual over verbal contents accelerated by the growth of photographic art, by the growth of films, and, again, of television? It is not only economically that the Press is now intimate with other media. Indeed, from the cultural point of view, the continuity it seems to keep with its dignified past can be misleading and though we may still hear about the 'liberty of the Press' – the famous slogan on the famous banner – the people now waving this are very unlike the radicals of the 1790s. Many of these changes and most of this inter-action with the other media have occurred within the last thirty years, some within the last fifteen. Should not precisely these ramifications into the media as a whole be the theme of this chapter?

As a subject-matter, then, the Press is just as elusive as the other media. But what of the methods which have become the established ways of treading the maze? Do they provide a framework within which the proportions of the subject can be fairly measured? It would be comforting to think so. Two standard, and nearly exclusive, approaches have emerged which can be called, shortly, 'historical' and 'literary'. Historical treatments conceive the Press as a quasi-political institution. From its beginnings in the Civil War (Milton the tutelary god), they trace its battles with government in the eighteenth century, its full emergence on the political stage in the nineteenth and certain degenerations from this ideal condition during the twentieth. The literary treatment, on the other hand, though it often depends on this history for some of its conclusions, starts from a different point. It sees the Press as part of a whole cultural condition, quite often as a symptom of a cultural disease. (Arnold's phrase for journalism 'literature in a hurry' stands for an attitude that preceded and has survived him.) The contents of newspapers are held to wield the same kind of influence over mind and imagination as literature itself. The analytic and judicial skills of the literary critic therefore apply, and a discussion of the Press becomes an analysis of representative pieces of writing, of their likely effects, or of what they tell about the state of mind of their writers or readers. Why will one or other of these well-tried approaches not serve here?

79

Partly because one needs both, and partly because of certain shortcomings each has shown. As usually practised, historical discussions have three disadvantages: they treat only certain kinds of publication and so are factually incomplete; they tend, like much 'institutional' history, to narrate a too-simple progress, as if the Press had somehow enjoyed substantial autonomy from other relevant social processes and conditions; and the controlling definition of the Press as adjunct of the developing political structure is too narrow. (These points have been compellingly brought home by Raymond Williams in *The Long Revolution*.) The result is that a sound historical perspective on the present scene is not so much difficult as impossible. The usual literary analysis is affected by this, since it always presumes some history, but it has two further disadvantages of its own, particularly relevant to the discussion of popular culture. First, it simplifies the relationship that exists between the contents of the Press and the readers. Its model is the relationship between serious literature and equipped readers, with all that this implies of attentive open-mindedness and readiness of response. While this may hold approximately at some levels, it is more and more misleading in these quarters where the issue of popular culture is most urgent. Second, it tends to identify the whole state of a reader's mind with what he reads, to allow only this reading as evidence. Certainly, it *always* matters what people read, but the written word is not the only, or even the main determinant of attitudes and values in most lives. The contents of newspapers do not impinge upon passive minds – we should be able to say this even without the supporting evidence about the complex ways people are in fact known to assimilate, select from, and reject 'communications' from the media. Finally, there is one objection to both approaches: they are apt to abstract the modern situation from the determining political and social context, as if – to cite one important result – real changes could come about within the Press alone. Yet even the partial history we have shows how close is the link between developments in the nature of the Press and in society as a whole. There is no reason to suppose that the future will be different.

The following discussion attempts therefore, though sketchily, to relate the styles and contents of the different products of the

Press to their social role; and to bear particularly in mind that the society itself has ways of preparing its members for a certain kind of newspaper. If our newspapers fail to discharge their traditional function, or if they indicate a cultural wound, the key to this lies not only, or even primarily, in the newspapers, but in the society which makes use of them. (Any changes would of course come up against the fact that much of the modern Press is a reactionary social force – and in a much more stubborn way than is indicated by citing the predominance of 'conservative' opinion.) How, then (to begin with theory), is the social responsibility of the Press, or 'Presses', conceived? Everything depends here on who provides the definitions, but the main division of opinion is firmly established. On the other hand, there is the 1949 Royal Commission's well-known judgement that 'in our opinion the newspapers, with a few exceptions, fail to supply the electorate with adequate materials for sound political judgement'. It is here taken for granted that the main business of the Press is political, and that it carries out its duties by disseminating information about appropriate events, and by sustaining regular debate on their meaning. In direct contrast: 'surely the amount of uplift you can fit into any popular medium has got to be kept pretty low.' The speaker is Cecil King at the N U T Conference – the sentence is typical of his style of mind – and the clear assumption is that the main business of the Press is not to 'uplift', but to 'entertain' its readers in ways they are known to enjoy: melodrama, gossip, sport (a kind of melodrama), exoticisms, 'titbits'. Neither of these definitions mentions money, yet a newspaper's attitude towards this is always illuminating. Political papers, which try to meet the requirements of the Royal Commission, want to make money in order to survive as political papers. 'Entertainment' papers, on the other hand, entertain in order to make money. This is to describe ideal types, to which few newspapers wholly correspond, but they provide a frame for analysis, and most papers recognizably tend one way or the other.

2

The political role of newspapers is the best known. Most judgements of newspapers take this as their starting point. It dominates the Press histories, and as a tradition claims the famous names. The newspaper as 'entertainer' is nearly as old, but it is less well known, and a good deal less approved. The history of the newspaper as a commodity is much shorter than these, and is only beginning to be recognized as a distinct phase that needs to be explored in detail. This is not, of course, because money-making played no part in the earlier phases. It did, but in a subordinate position. The aim of the early 'entertainers' was as much to achieve cultural recognition as to make money. Similarly, when Thomas Barnes' *Times* supported political reform in the 1820s, it grew in circulation, increased its advertising revenue, and became commandingly prosperous. But its political role remained vital, and it was the mid-Victorian editor, J. T. Delane, who gave this role its classic definition. In contrast, Northcliffe's *Daily Mail* of the 1890s was not directed at readers with political sentiments needing a public voice, but at a newly-arrived market of consumers ready for the appropriate cultural commodity. Northcliffe's ambition was to make money, and to do it he had to attract advertising. He therefore aimed at a large circulation, at the earliest possible moment, which he regularly announced. The politics of his paper, like the style and other contents (for 'tomorrow's £1000 a year man, so he hopes and thinks'), were those that would sell; or more exactly, and bearing in mind a modern case of the newspaper as a commodity, those that would not obstruct selling. ('We do not sell any copies of our politics' – Cecil King, speaking of the *Daily Mirror*.) The interplay of these different purposes – serious politics, entertainment, money-making – tells a good deal about any newspaper. If primarily a money-maker, we should ask why a paper's readers seem not to worry about politics. If primarily a political paper, we should look at the sources of its income, or lack of income. This usually shows why the paper can or does concentrate on the political role. It can also tell something about the actual politics: today's *Guardian* on the one hand, and *Tribune* on the other; or the post-1832 *Times* in contrast with Hetherington's *Poor Man's Guardian*, '... a weekly newspaper for the people, established contrary to the law to try the power of Right against Might'.

'A People are free in proportion as they form their own opinions', wrote Coleridge in 1796; and 'In an enslaved state, the Rulers form and supply the opinions of the people'. The political role of newspapers developed from an attempt to free (some of) the people from having their opinions formed and supplied by their rulers. In practice, this came to mean three things: accurate, independent, and timely reporting; sustained commentary and debate which, in given papers, followed a consistent political direction; and the strict separation of the one from the other. This is the tradition most people think of when they talk about 'a serious newspaper', and modern examples are usually discussed in intellectual or moral terms – balanced, discriminating, accurate, principled. But these qualities still take their energy from the political context in which they began, and they may be usefully conceived as laying down certain rules of communication between a paper and its readers which permit the latter to form – in a meaningful sense – *their own* opinions. When the rules are broken, the newspapers, like the rulers they originally displaced, begin to 'form and supply the opinions of the people'; (and in the modern situation, Coleridge's *supply* is prophetic). There is no need, in this discussion, to understand 'political' too narrowly. 'I regard the newspaper as a service ... for people whose obligations extend beyond their immediate circle' stated Roy Shaw at the N U T Conference, a definition which usefully shifts the emphasis from 'freedom' – the standard nineteenth-century goal – to 'obligation'. But even obligations to one's immediate circle – food, health, housing, education, play – are inextricably political today; quite apart from those that go beyond it.

Ideally then, and to some extent in practice, serious newspapers exist in a continued tension with government. They seek out and publicize facts government may prefer to hide; they explore muddles and injustices; they analyse events and government actions independently of the pressure of intrigue or expediency, though usually from a particular point of view. This commentary may be offensive to reigning governments, and is always likely to disturb them. Some material may seem concerned with questions of no immediately-recognizable bearing on politics. But inspection usually reveals potential or long-distance political import. Much contemporary scientific reporting comes

83

under this head. The political effectiveness of a newspaper depends on conditions that it may influence but does not directly control: notably a certain political structure. Where this structure is imperfect, a serious newspaper's operations are hampered: censorship, confiscation, fines, imprisonment of editors follow as a matter of course. Without going into the details of this structure (it is hardly enough to transcribe the magical sign 'Democratic'), two things are important. One is political rights like those of assembly, and of the ballot-box. The other concerns the readers, and is best approached by way of that common description of serious newspapers as 'responsible'. This, despite the portentous stereotype it probably evokes, contains an important truth. A 'responsible paper' will address itself to 'responsible readers'. What does this mean? A responsible person is one who is answerable for his decisions and acts, either directly to others, or if to himself, then on behalf of others whose claim upon him he fully recognizes. Responsible government is similarly answerable for its record. A 'responsible' newspaper is rightly so called because it associates itself with government by seeking to influence the decisions government takes. Its readers are 'responsible' in the same way: they identify themselves, albeit critically, with the process of government. The education of the readers – an education of the emotions as much as of the mind – must fit them for this part. The most radical *criticism* of government is as 'responsible' as the most zealous support, because it invites readers to think of themselves as being, or as intelligently supporting, an alternative government. The only 'irresponsible' criticism a paper can offer is one that ignores the need in any collective for taking and holding by decisions, and answering for them. 'Responsible' has collected several other meanings, but this is the important one, and the habit of making it synonymous with 'preserving the *status quo*' should be resisted. As applied to readers, it should be taken to refer not to mental or emotional make-up, but to their relation to government; above all, to the fact that they have, or feel themselves to have, a significant relation to government. It follows from this that 'irresponsible' readers lack this relationship.

This throws some light on the traditional practice of a serious newspaper: true facts, reasoned commentary, distinct from each other. From these it follows that newspapers, readers (and even if only formally, governments) recognize that certain intellectual and moral rules are necessary to political health. 'Responsible' derives its subsidiary meanings from these rules. But the root meaning of 'answerability' explains the peculiar stress laid on the separation of fact and comment. It is not simply that 'responsible' readers like to see the evidence from which comment is being drawn. The facts must be true and distinct because, quite apart from any editorial comment they may get, they are in themselves significant. To the 'responsible' reader, these facts indicate a reality with which he feels himself to be related. He can understand it, initiate further exploration of it, put the various bits together in his mind. He can – and this is crucial – act upon it as a result of what he has been told. Whether he will act, or when, and what the action will be (voting is not the only possibility) are of course questions which cannot be generally answered. What 'responsible' readers share, however, and it is this that makes them 'responsible', is a disposition to act upon information of this kind.

The history of serious newspapers shows this relationship between readers and the political world of relevant happenings which the paper mediates. The early and mid-Victorian *Times* is the best known case. Similarly the rise of the *Manchester Guardian* at the end of the nineteenth century was closely associated with the social groups who were asserting their claim to 'responsibility' through the Liberal Party. In the 1950s circulation increases in the daily and Sunday 'qualities' testify not simply to the spread of higher education within the middle class (and to a smaller extent, its increased penetration amongst the working class) but to the increased *political* relevance of education. An advanced industrial economy needs highly-trained specialists at many levels. The (late) political recognition of this was interestingly prefigured in the social prestige which some advertising stereotypes began to confer on education in the fifties. (The old anti-highbrow appeal has almost disappeared.) The very advertising campaigns of 'quality' newspapers address themselves to 'bright lively minds', 'top people' (i.e. non-top people pursuing the career of the talents). In the Meritocracy, 'responsible' readers are all educated. Even the old *Daily Mail* began to look out for 'busy *thinkers*'.

Nor is this just a matter of external catchwords. A commonplace of the economics of today's serious newspaper is the degree of its dependence on advertising revenue. (The 1962 Royal Commission calculated that in 1960, for national morning papers the proportion of income from sales and from advertising was 25 per cent and 75 per cent respectively for 'qualities', and 45 per cent and 55 per cent for 'populars'; for national Sundays the proportions were 21 per cent and 79 per cent as against 51 per cent and 49 per cent.) And this dependence is more than economic. Modern advertising works by manipulating various symbols so as to confer social prestige on the things it tries to sell. These symbols are very largely drawn from the language of class-discrimination. Clearly, the readers of the 'quality' Press, no less than the readers of the 'populars', respond to this language, otherwise the advertisers would find another. The claim of the *Sunday Express* to be, with the *Observer*, the *Sunday Times*, and the *Sunday Telegraph*, a 'quality' paper, throws a usefully harsh light on the ambiguity of this term. Why do 'responsible' readers react to such advertising? Because one way of associating yourself with government is by acquiring a life-style symbolically associated with older 'responsible' classes. The advertising in the serious Press helps to provide the emotional education which its readers require for their (partly fictional) 'responsible' role. It further provides emotional consolation for the consciousness that this role *is* partly fictional, and there is a link here with the advertising in some 'populars' where the rhetoric of compensation is brasher and shriller – more obviously compensatory, in fact. If advertising in the serious Press is much more prominent than fifty years ago, then that is partly because earlier serious newspapers could depend on their 'responsible' readers being subject to useful rhetorics elsewhere; from the pulpit, or in much literature. Tennyson, one of the masters of Victorian social rhetoric, rose to the peak of his fame during the decade in which Delane wrote his famous editorial.

To say this is not to depreciate the intellectual and moral values which ideally, and to some extent in practice, the serious

86

Press embodies. But to forget it is to subscribe to the notion that these values exist in a political and social vacuum. The tone of the serious Press often suggests that it grossly overrates its own detachment from the social–political context within which it operates. This position leads also to a serious failure to understand the 'emotionalism' of the 'popular' Press, or to conceive of any real alternative to the present state of affairs. The more complex picture of the serious Press and its readers also makes sense of certain recent developments, not conformable to the traditional ideal. There is the magazine tendency where, as in an earlier phase of 'popular' journalism, the varied contents of the Sunday papers have been imitated in the comparable dailies: articles on fashion, 'business', books, science, travel, cultural, and hobby pursuits interleaved with the customary political fare. Why have these subjects migrated from their own specialist journals (losing, it should be added, much of their indigenous plumage on the way)? If we think of the serious Press as *ritualizing a way of life* as well as fulfilling a political role, heterogeneity of content is only to be expected. The magazine tendency as a whole merges with the advertising in its role of emotional confirmation, and in answering the reader's search for identity. In fact, as has often been pointed out, there is sometimes little to choose between advertisements and feature articles. Another recent development, reinforced by the magazine tendency if not actually part of it, is the multiplication of feature articles on political subjects, of personalized reporting, and interpretation intended to do the reader's thinking for him in an idiom which for various reasons he finds satisfying. On their own, facts have to be understood and interpreted; and leader arguments are in a tradition and language which invite conscious assent or disagreement. But the reassuring caption 'From Our Industrial Correspondent' lulls the energies invoked by straight reporting and straight commentary, and half-authorizes selective reporting and unargued views. This is not necessarily a bad thing despite its undermining of the traditional dogma: styles and conventions develop with all genuine communication, and many topics gain from a condensed, and so selective, presentation. But it is worth being clear about it: the 'responsible' reader takes a great deal on trust; he likes the

87

world to be presented to him in a certain way; even the political relationship between him and his paper has its rituals. Serious political papers are usually classified in terms of express political affiliation. An equally, if not more, illuminating description would emerge from a study of the different rituals with which they familiarize the world for their readers. It would lead at least to a less rationalistic account of the Press as a whole.

3

What distinguishes the serious Press, filling with varied success the political role, from other newspapers? The latter will usually point to their larger circulations; the advertiser will underline contrasts in the wealth of the readership; the serious Press itself could divide the remainder into two groups: those attempting the political role in an illegitimate spirit, and those that largely ignore it. Both latter types have, in fact, much in common: notably a primary interest in money-making, and a shared method of attaining it.

In a classic denunciation of the Press in its illegitimate political role, Stanley Baldwin described two papers, Beaverbrook's *Daily Express* and Rothermere's *Daily Mail*, in these terms: '... not newspapers in the ordinary acceptation of the term ...' but '... engines of propaganda for the constantly changing policies, desires, personal wishes, personal likes and dislikes of [their owners]'; employing methods of '... direct falsehood, misrepresentation, half-truths ... suppression and editorial criticism of speeches which are not reported ...' in the furtherance of the owners' aims. The two Lords had been trying to exert direct political pressure on Baldwin's position within his own party. Baldwin's criticism usefully underlines the link between their pursuit of direct political power and the newspapers' defiance of the rules which characterize the legitimate political role. The procedure he describes permits an editor to mould reality into a shape suitably docile to the propaganda of the owner whom he serves. What, formally, such a newspaper offers as 'facts' are really arguments in disguise 'proving' the arguments that are explicit. It is as necessary to preserve the *formula* of true-facts-distinct-from-free-comment – simple advocacy is less effective, and not what people buy newspapers for – as it is to destroy the substance, the real tension between commentary and report which always guarantees the good faith of a newspaper. But the moulding of reality need not take this extreme form. There are subtler methods, harder to controvert because no longer aiming at direct power, but having political effect not less important because indirect. This effect stems less from the espousing of views – a vendetta against the British Council, or the United Nations – as from the picture of the world which selection and emphasis, rather than downright untruth, builds up in the reports. When this is created primarily for its psychological effect on the reader, it supports not so much a particular range of formulated opinions as the less-consciously held attitudes from which opinions emerge; and most notably, the kind of relationship which the reader feels himself to have with the reported world. In practice, this means two things: sensationalism and triviality. Important political events are treated as sources of fear, excitement, exultation, alarm; or curiosity, 'human interest', 'warmth'. Other events – disaster, gossip, domestic incidents, crimes, 'titbits' – are offered as of equal interest with the political events. Typographical devices intertwine the sets of occurrences: headlining, position on page, photographs. From whatever source, each event is presented in terms of some attitude which the reader will find it emotionally satisfying to adopt. (There is a certain analogy here with some personalized reporting in the serious Press). Like salesmen with a difficult product, these newspapers concentrate all their energy on the emotional make-up of their readers. This may seem (so certainly it is claimed) to offer a more generous attitude towards people than the 'dull rationalism' of the serious Press – a defence that would be more convincing if it were less obviously self-interested. It is more plausibly maintained that all reporting, page-making, and sub-editing, that the very process of communication in any medium, involves selection and emphasis, and that the 'popular' presentation of the world in some large circulation dailies is no more than a style among others, chosen in relation to a particular audience. This is to an extent true: the serious Press has its own varied conventions and procedures

89

which can be seen to correspond to different groups of 'responsible' readers. But the difference lies in the spirit in which each 'style' is set to work. No newspaper can present an objective world, but the scrupulous ones, recognizing this, say in effect: 'though this is how the world seems to me today, my own values necessarily enter into the presentation.' The unscrupulous paper says: 'this is a true picture of the world – ignore other versions as false, irrelevant, or boring.' Nothing is easier than to couple this message, daily dramatized in the whole typographical and verbal structure of the paper, with hearty declarations about freedom of comment. Unrelated to a world of events in which both reader and opinion have a significant role, this freedom is meaningless. In this context, opinions are never 'relevant', 'convincing', 'well or badly supported', but 'fearless', 'provocative', 'challenging', which, having nothing to do with *action*, they can well afford to be.

The real key to the political influence of such papers lies neither in the opinions which they propagate, nor in the attitudes which, in their preoccupation with 'human interest', they endorse or actively feed. It lies in the implication that without their colourful intervention there is no meaningful relationship between the events which they dramatize and the readers for whom the show goes on. In this respect, their 'style' has a hidden content. It speaks for readers whom it takes to be politically disenfranchised, for whom the news of political events is not about a world in which they feel they can meaningfully act. This is the more subtle form of political manipulation since it imposes on the reader an assumption of which he remains unaware. It also makes it easier to speak on his behalf. It is, in sum, the modern way of 'forming and supplying the opinions of the people'.

Between the illegitimate politics of the 'populars' and the newspaper whose primary function is to 'entertain', there are certain differences. If the political manipulator entertains, this is always less for its own sake than as a tacit bribe to the reader for allowing himself now and again to be violently jerked in a definite political direction. But when 'entertainment' (i.e. profit) is the goal, political material is both reduced in quantity, and subordinate in place. Typographical devices often submerge what there is into other material; or separate it off altogether from the major interests of sport, gossip, and crime. In the tabloid presentation, 'entertainment' assimilates everything into a fictional melodrama. Symbolized in the paper's 'personality', the reader becomes the hero of an endless tale, subjecting the world of 'them' (i.e. everything which the rhetoric cannot reduce) to magical defeats and rejections. What the defenders of the tabloid manner seem incapable of understanding is that theirs is not 'just a way of putting it' – a real victory for the newspaper's political role under unrewarding circumstances. (cf. Arnold's remark at the head of this chapter, and see the moving story told by Collins and King in the record of the N U T conference.) Whatever the nobly-educative intentions of the speaker, if *this* is his idiom then the effective content of his message shrinks and coarsens accordingly. Few issues, at any level, can survive this. Is it not better in this situation to abandon the pretence at anything resembling the political role, and admit to the guiding assumption that the audience in question finds the world of serious politics meaningless because it has no direct *continuous* participation? In effect, of course, precisely this admission gets made when apologists answer critics by denying the relevance of extensive political reporting to this audience. On the other hand, with issues that engage the direct interest of the owner (like the Pilkington Report) the 'tabloid' handling becomes indistinguishable from that of the political manipulator.

For different reasons then, or with different emphases, both categories of newspaper look on their readers as 'irresponsible'– open to manipulation, looking mainly to be amused, not intelligently related to the reported world, as politically disenfranchised.* Before proceeding then to the customary denunciation, it seems worthwhile asking whether there is not a very substantial social and political reality which partly justifies this assumption. Like the serious newspapers, the 'popular' and 'tabloid' function

*The social distribution of the different categories shows that readers like this are widely diffused through the whole society. (See *The Long Revolution*, pp. 211–13.) One of the strong motives such papers play on is the temptation we all share to lapse into effective disenfranchisement, to accept a passive role. In this, of course, they cooperate with tendencies in the political structure.

within a whole cultural context. If they represent something of what 'the public wants', there are likely to be good reasons for the public's taste; reasons beyond the common interest in the immediately striking, in the superficial, in the melodramatic. If there is fiction in the assumption of the serious Press that its readers are wholly 'responsible' about what they read – able to interpret, ready to act – then there is a corresponding reality in the assumptions of the large-circulation dailies. Seen in this light, we can explain the 'popular' presentation of serious politics as one result of the gap between the political forms and the political reality. That politics is treated at all corresponds to the theoretical expectations of a democratic structure. The treatment it actually gets – the myth-making, the idiom which calls every difference of opinion a 'row', and turns every issue into 'personal' terms, the sloganized parody that passes for debate, the daily processing* of political experience – all these show the reality. For this state of affairs, the responsibility of the newspaper owners is certainly great. Their barbarian misuse of these profoundly needed social institutions is still one of the scandals of our century. Nevertheless, any major change in these 'communication' styles necessarily implies equally major changes in the relationship which readers both have and feel themselves to have towards the world of decision and government. This awkward truth cannot be bypassed by grumbling about the stupidity and laziness of the readers of the large-circulation dailies. The numbers of people involved are simply too large for judgements like that to have any meaning; and the individuals who make up these numbers

*A. R. Crosland thinks use of the term *processing* betrays deep intellectual snobbery. (See his 'The Mass Media' in *Encounter*, November 1962.) So I had better explain my own, and indeed what I take to be the usual meaning. *Processing* means re-stating something within a set of conventions which transfer interest from the thing transmitted to the experience of transmission. Mr Crosland draws an astounding analogy between teaching and 'popular' styles of transmission: each involves simplification and dilution, he says, each is a kind of 'processing'. But there is this difference: a teacher aims to build a relationship between his subject-matter and his pupils *independent of himself*, while mass media 'processing' imposes upon *all* subject-matters a prior relationship between medium and audience. The nature of this relationship is such as to reduce most subject-matters. Needless to say, not all mass-media transmission is 'processing'.

are, in other areas of their experience, capable, and sane. A main accusation against the purveyors of the large circulation dailies is certainly that they build and maintain a major barrier to change and growth – for without the fuller and more continuous participation in the processes of government by real (and not formal) majorities of people this growth will not come. But in this accusation must be included the submerged assumptions of a good deal of 'responsible' criticism of their products.

It remains to say something explicit about 'entertainment' as such, since the attack on this from 'responsible' quarters is sometimes misconceived. All contemporary newspapers 'entertain', and in doing so follow a tradition as old as the more celebrated political role. Coleridge, who has been quoted in connection with the political role, himself contributed serious journalism on contemporary affairs when he wrote for the *Morning Post*. Yet it was the same paper which published his (amongst others') poems, claiming that some relief was due to its readers from 'ferocious politics'. Again, in the Victorian period, 'entertaining' Sunday papers largely devoted to crime-reporting achieved very large circulations. Northcliffe's 'revolution', seen not in its crucial economic aspect, but stylistically, was an adaptation of the human-interest of these Victorian Sundays for the new daily audience. In our century, the new development has been, in some quarters, the dissolution of the old barrier between politics and other material, so that, in the words of the song, 'The world is a show,/ The show is a world/ Of entertainment.' Most recently, the spread of 'entertainment' into the serious dailies has made it more difficult to see that lure alone as the fault of 'populars' and 'tabloids'. But what, exactly, is 'entertainment' in its modern sense? As far as the Press goes (and even further – the areas colonized by much television, most magazines, many films), its main function can be described as one of attitude-propping. At many levels, 'entertainment' supplies a cultural and moral rhetoric, an easy confirmation of group-feeling, a temporary but repeated answer to the demand for reassurance and approval. Despite the appearance of abundance and variety, 'entertainment' turns out to be remarkably uniform. For a given audience, sport, fashion,

93

intellectual and cultural news, fantasy, gossip, disguised gossip – i.e. chatty surveys of complex social phenomena – are all rendered in a common idiom, whose aim is to reassure the reader that all these matters are easily accessible, or reducible, within his scheme of values. Like a drug, this is, at any level, both addictive and enervating, and in particular cases (book reviewing is probably the best known) becomes more satisfying than the material it reduces. Like the selling of political news in 'human interest' and other wrappers, 'entertainment' reveals a deep nervousness about the unaided relevance and value of what it is dealing with. There is a constant tendency to humorous and witty treatment, of the imposition of a reducing tone of voice. The diffusion of this through the media is perhaps the most striking demonstration of the essential unity of function of 'entertainment' at all levels, in every context. (For a pertinent discussion of the style of some radio news presentation, see Stuart Hall's 'A World At One With Itself', *New Society*, 18 June 1970, pp. 1056–8.)

What this indicates is a much closer relation between the 'popular' and 'serious' Press than their different handlings of political material would suggest. The 'homely' personality of the tabloid paper, and to a lesser extent but with other additions, of the 'popular' daily, derives primarily from a need for a large amorphous undifferentiated audience. It must be large, because its individual members are not especially rich, and the advertising rates it can command not high. The existence of an audience like this depends on a fictional sense of identity provided in the style of the paper. Only a national diffusion of the audience will ensure a large enough sale, and this has to be created by excluding the differentiae of the regional and other minority groups which compose this audience. 'Entertainment' plays the key part in maintaining this fiction. It evokes from any given subject-matter the particular range of attitudes which make up the paper's personality. Features contribute a great deal to this process. ('In the *Mirror* the letters to the Editor get up to fifty-nine per cent [of the readership]' reports John Beaven in *The Press & The Public*, Fabian Tract 338 (1962). These letters are evidently picked for their display of 'attitude'. The next highest percentage, fifty-eight per cent, is for sport.) This same close

94

connection between newspaper-economics and entertainment-style exists in the serious Press, especially the Sundays, where again the advertising revenue depends on keeping readers with a certain income. To hold this audience the relevant 'attitude-propping' develops both in the formal contents – tone of voice, and range of topics – and in advertising style.

It is easier to describe than to make any general assessment of 'entertainment', and of the magazine influence. Defenders can always claim that newspapers are now more varied; critics that this, precisely, is what is wrong. Clearly, there are good things – which would at the 'popular' level especially be better if they were not styled and shaped by rigid conventions – and there is a great deal of the trivial and boring, at every level. Two points, however, widely apply. The source of feature writing is very often specialist books and journals – 'entertainment' feeds on these too often parasitically, returning nothing to the stock of original knowledge and work on which its own life depends. The serious Press might well consider subsidizing or contributing to specialist periodicals instead of continuously expanding their review pages and multiplying their feature articles. At the same time, they might set a general example as to tone by discouraging the baseless judicial pretensions of the people who do the feature writing. Is it too much to hope that 'entertainment' might make more use of the simple unopinion-ated report? (Not that there is anything simple about reporting.) But even if it did, the reader's thirst for social magic, spelling out the imaginary group-identities, would no doubt remain. With 'entertainment' above all, the larger social context has its relevance.

4

Concrete proposals for the reform of the contemporary Press fall into two categories: educational procedures, and institutional changes. The educationist hopes that if enough people learn to read a newspaper critically, the owners will have to change their ways. He would like to make the critical assessment of newspaper-contents a regular part of general education, and one of the lettered skills which the G.C.E. recognizes and tests. Valuable work has for some years been done on these lines, and the new liberal arts courses for students at technical colleges, the day-release courses and the teacher's training certificate offer scope for its extension. Analysis like this need not be confined to news-papers only, but can link with discussions of television and film in one way, and with literature and art in another. There is, though, one problem about these schemes: the skills in question cannot be taught as mere skills. They involve complex processes of judgement which can only be truly exercised by direct ex-perience of another kind of communication than that practised in the national dailies. How, within the educational structure, can this be achieved? It seems reasonable to ask whether, with the best will and the finest training, the teacher/pupil relationship with its own necessary conventions and perspective is an al-together adequate model. Fuller, more flexible practice in communication might arise from the actual use of the media by the pupils – newspaper, television, radio, and film – not for 'educational purposes', but for the direct exploration and inter-change of their own experience of their own world. The com-parative study of different reports of the same event would be more effectively illustrated if the event fell within the range of the child's (preferably passionate) experiences and interests; and would provide a more dramatic and telling illustration of the relativity of all reporting than any material to be found in a newspaper. It is this fact that makes tentativeness and good faith so crucial in all human communication, and the bad faith of the contemporary newspaper practice would be more meaningful. How real, even to a sixteen-year-old child, is the world which his study of the Press will lead him to suspect? For all but the bright students (whose other studies will in any case equip them with some of the relevant skills) is the material of the Press near enough to direct experience to yield the freshness of response without which the most compelling analysis of value is useless? The same arguments hold, in fact, for the study of newspapers as for literature: more writing and less discussion. The problems of page-making, headlining, paragraphing, typography, the effect of reporting in different styles and from different premises would

96

all be natural developments from a school newspaper working within the educational structure (and not, of course, used as a prestige bulletin, or for the handing down of adult guidance). The mechanics of printing would give direct knowledge of the influence wielded by technical factors. Large comprehensive schools would gain in real identity by possessing such a medium for inter-communication between the various age-groups and specialisms. There are obvious dangers but if the main goal is kept in mind – that communication should become a 'natural' part of human life – none that could not be surmounted. The critical counter-pressure that could develop against the contemporary 'popular' Press would not only be armed with analytic weapons, but propelled by a substantially different assumption about the use of language.

The other category of reforms concerns the structure of the Press itself, and the possibility of building institutional checks and safeguards against the more familiar shortcomings: pressure from advertisers, unscrupulous behaviour by journalists, inaccuracies, and sensationalism. Currently, the immediate need is to adopt the recommendation of the 1949 Royal Commission that the Press Council should include a number of lay members. The 1962 Commission has repeated this proposal.* Despite some good work, the Council has repeatedly failed to show that its professional ethic is adequate to the tasks of effective self-criticism. A professional group can only claim to regulate its own social responsibility if it acts upon standards which satisfy the lay public (e.g. medicine, and law). Sir Norman Angell proposed the setting up of a panel of highly experienced journalists who would write and edit a special newspaper, maintaining the most scrupulous standards in relation to facts, alleged facts, inferences from facts, and rumours. Such a publication might not be widely read, and would have to be subsidized, but it would act as a standard, with a general bracing effect. Other suggestions are the compulsory correction of mistakes (with fines for failure) in prominent type and place; and compulsory space for the views of opponents to the paper's general policy. But all these proposals, and especially the latter group, fail to touch the inner problem

*Which has now been put into practice.

of the 'popular' and 'tabloid' Press. There can never be laws against 'entertainment'. The standards of the serious Press at its best only become relevant if there is felt relationship between the reader and the news he is offered. This relationship cannot be created by adjustments within the current structure, dominated as it is by the newspaper owners from whose imperatives so many of the difficulties flow. The key to the problem lies in the economic and not in the institutional structure. As long as a major section of the Press can be treated as a commodity, primarily subject like other market products to the demand for profitable returns on the heavy capital investment needed by the modern printing industry, there is little room for movement except along the road which the Press is now travelling: mergers, concentration of resources in fewer and fewer hands, homogeneity in the product plus marginal differentiation (like the soap powders). The serious Press can resist to an extent (though as its magazine-tendency shows, much less powerfully than it imagines) because of the greater advertising revenues it can command. Change of another kind can only come from another source: the Press has no way of resisting or checking the energy of its own dynamic. This, indeed, is one of the depressing aspects of the current scene; the needed major criticisms do not come from within the profession.

There is no space here to develop the full argument for other kinds of proposal, but a sketch may indicate a more fruitful line of thinking. The search for profit leads to the Press's major dependence on advertising, and this in its turn dominates the style and content of what is published. If it were not for the artificially created national 'popular' audience, the conventions of 'entertainment' could be less strict, the need to 'sell' the news less pressing, the possibility of a genuine relationship between paper and readers more likely. The circulation of the national dailies was built up by destroying a flourishing independent local Press. Is it possible to reverse this process? Not in any simple way, of course, but the model is a valuable guide. If we had instead of one or two papers with a 3–4 million circulation, six or seven with a circulation of about 900,000–1,000,000 based largely on the major regions of the country, the 'popular' Press would present a much less depressing sight. One of the powerful impulses which the conventions of the national Press mobilize is the need for group-identities (cf. the use made of regional voices on radio and television for their 'warmth' and 'popular' quality). A reconstructed Press could find in this a more genuine tone which, far from being parochial, would be the right medium for communicating between the local and regional audience and the national and international scene. The only national dailies that are really *needed* are those which communicate news in which readers genuinely participate as members of the larger community. One would, in fact, hope to see the assimilation of the 'serious' Press to such dailies, or alternatively, a cut-down and amalgamated serious Press for professionals and specialists – subsidized if necessary.

It is difficult to see how this could come about, except from a decision to subsidize from public funds for a substantial period, perhaps ten years, the costs of printing and distributing at least two new papers, regionally based. These would not be 'official' sheets, but be run by practising journalists in an initially exploratory spirit, building perhaps from a surviving local weekly, a genuine paper of its community.* They would compete with the national dailies by providing much more truly 'what the public wants', because they would be in a position to take this more seriously than the 'popular' Press does. The aim would be to reduce the circulation of national dailies by offering readers a genuine identity, instead of the bullying rhetoric of the current fiction. They would not, one hopes, set out to be regional 'qualities', but more like regional 'populars' released from the exigencies of owner's politics *and* profits. They could be much more miscellaneous, less uniform in tone and manner. They could develop natural connections with local school newspapers which would provide continuity for each. They would, if successful, begin to attract advertising from the national dailies, the effect of which could only be to raise the prices of the latter, and so eventually depress their circulations. If this pressure were maintained, the nationals would have to adjust to the different

*cf. the argument for the protection and development of regional economies by the central government.

sort of audience which was being created. At the end of ten years, the position could be surveyed with a view to seeing whether decreasing the subsidy and raising the price would enable them to continue on a more permanent basis.

There seems to be no other way of breaking the hegemony of the advertising revenue but by this deliberate creation of a real alternative to it. In the long run, no change could, of course, be permanent without both major assistance from the educational structure, and major changes in the degree of participation in government. But such changes could not come about by educational pressure alone, because in this field a main 'educational' force is the current situation, and not the formal training given in schools. One need not, of course, underrate the opposition that other than educational proposals would arouse. As Raymond Williams has said, '... it is necessary to break through to the central fact that most of our cultural institutions are in the hands of speculators, interested not in the health and growth of the society, but in the quick profits that can be made by exploiting inexperience.' (*The Long Revolution*, p. 338.) To appeal from profit to the health of the society has never been a simple matter, but the longer the appeal is delayed the more difficult it becomes to formulate, the vaguer and stranger to the imagination the values it depends on. The speculation, meanwhile, will go on.

Note to the Revised Edition

Since this essay was first written, two institutions have been set up for the study of the mass media: the Centre for Mass Communications Research at the University of Leicester, and the Centre for Contemporary Cultural Studies at the University of Birmingham. Each has recently completed a full-scale project on the British Press, which will put all future discussion of the subject on a firmer basis both of evidence and of method. *Demonstrations and Commitment: A Case Study* (1970), from the Leicester Centre, analyses the Press and television coverage of the demonstration against the Vietnam war which took place on 28 October 1968. Two of its general conclusions are of particular interest here: the role of the expectations and latent assumptions of journalists in defining the news-value of a complex event like a

large, serious demonstration (in this instance, the selection of
'violence' as the crucial theme); and the fundamental *similarity*
of treatment of the event in both Press and television. The second
point raises again the question whether the news-gathering
function of the Press can now be fruitfully studied in isolation
from the other media. The study from the Birmingham Centre,
as yet unpublished, is entitled *The Popular Press and Social
Change, 1935–1961*. It is a comprehensive analysis of the *Daily
Mirror* and the *Daily Express* in their broader cultural function,
discussed briefly in these pages as 'entertainment'. The authors
concentrate on the different ways in which each newspaper
interpreted for its readers the major social changes of the period.
An introductory chapter, written by Stuart Hall, explains the
principal, and pioneering, method of analysis in which the tone
and diction of representative writing is seen to be the index to
the paper's conception of its ideal reader. As the first full-length
study of the British popular Press as a cultural, as distinct from a
political, institution, the importance of this study can hardly be
over-emphasized.

BOOKS

NORMAN ANGELL, *The Press and the Organization of Society*, Heffer,
1932

FRANCIS WILLIAMS, *Dangerous Estate*, Longmans, 1957

RICHARD HOGGART, 'Mass Communications in Britain' in *The
Modern Age*, ed. B. Ford, Penguin Books, 1961

BRIAN GROOMBRIDGE, *Popular Culture and Personal Responsibility:
A Study Outline*, NUT, 1961

RICHARD HOGGART, (ed.), *Your Sunday Paper*, University of London
Press, 1967

RAYMOND WILLIAMS, *Communications*, Penguin Books, revised
edition 1968

JAMES D. HALLORAN, PHILIP ELLIOTT, GRAHAM MURDOCK,
Demonstrations and Communication: A Case Study, Penguin
Books, 1970

A. C. H. SMITH, ELIZABETH IMMIRZI, TREVOR BLACKWELL, *The
Popular Press and Social Change, 1935–1965* (in preparation)

5 Television and Radio

PHILIP ABRAMS

When Denys Thompson asked me to revise this chapter for the new edition of *Discrimination and Popular Culture* I felt for a long time that the job was almost impossible. Since 1963 when it was first written there have been enormous changes in broadcasting. There is a great deal more of it for one thing. And it looks as though there is a great deal more variety within it. There are many more channels. Much more attention is paid to local and regional matters – especially by radio. Educational broadcasting has expanded enormously. Colour television has arrived. Both media have become almost painfully self-conscious about their social functions and about the 'problem of standards' in broadcasting; the serious discussion on television about the nature of television is now almost a regular weekly event. There has been a general shake-up of awareness about broadcasting – thanks in large part to the discovery in the mid-sixties of the works of Marshall McLuhan. Most of us would be hard-pressed to say just exactly what McLuhan's message about the media was but he did bomb a lot of conventional thinking about broadcasting to bits. He showed us television as *the* central agency, creative and expressive, of our culture and not just, as it had been before, one among many mildly problematic aspects of it.

In the face of all this could one just revise a piece that had been written in 1963? Wasn't it necessary to start again in order to do justice to the new media that had emerged in the interval? As I thought about this and watched and listened to broadcasting as carefully as I could, a general pattern of the broadcasting of 1971 began to take shape for me. It was on the whole a richer, more detailed pattern than one could have found in 1963 but to my surprise its basic shapes were pretty much the same. It was in July 1971 that an I T V showing of Hamlet allowed that moment

102

of pain and moral confusion when Claudius tries and fails to pray, 'My words fly up, my thoughts remain below', to be followed without punctuation by an advertisement for Playtex Longline Bras. There are if anything more mediocre old films shown now than then. A lot of what looks like enormously increased sophistication in the camera-work and in the packaging and presentation of programmes – the way a programme like 'The Persuaders' is dressed up for example – is really nothing more than an assimilation of the idiom of drama to what has long been the idiom of the advertisement. I concluded that the problem of discrimination in the face of broadcasting media was a lot more complicated now than it had been ten years ago, that one would need to make a lot more qualifications to get it right, but that it was at bottom the same problem.

One way in which it has become more complicated is that the media have largely succeeded (or perhaps they have just been lucky) in defusing the moral atmosphere in which they exist. In the early sixties it was still possible to apply simple old-fashioned value judgements to the media. One sounded a bit pompous and school-masterly but not utterly implausible. In the cool atmosphere of the seventies that way of talking about the media is just not on. I think what has happened here is that the media have created a climate of judgement in which it simply won't do to be terribly serious. After all, it is only television. Lots of nice well-known media personalities – Joan Bakewell for example – have written books or articles worrying in a nice moderate way about the role of television in society. Extreme positions can't be argued convincingly (even the one about media violence encouraging aggression in children has vanished into a morass of minute, contradictory and oh, so boring, research), and the extremists become figures of fun. And then we are all compromised. I like to be settled down soon after ten on a Saturday night for 'Match of the Day'; other members of the family want life to stop in our living-room whenever Morecambe and Wise are on. Of course all this is passive and without much positive value; but isn't it also normal and harmless? There can't be many of us who could get on the old kind of 'drugging the masses' high horse without hypocrisy. On the one hand the media are seen to be trying to do

103

their best. On the other hand we have all welcomed the media into our lives. Of course detailed criticism of particular programmes, and even major rows about whole styles of broadcasting (such as the one over 'Sesame Street') are still possible: but for most purposes we have bought the idea, which those who speak about the media from within mostly favour these days, that the media, being only media, come to us on a plane of moral and aesthetic indifference – to use an old theologian's word. It is simply not relevant or appropriate to get very worked up about them. Like parents and schoolteachers and supermarkets, broadcasting is simply there, a bit of the 'given' environment. We learn to live with it. You can always switch off.

The whole point of a book like this is to pull broadcasting out of the taken-for-granted environment, to look at it with surprise and to ask questions about it which call for answers in the language of hot value judgements as well as of cool evaluation; not just questions about what the media seem to be doing but about whether we ought to like what they seem to be doing, and about how we can make a case for their *not* doing what we dislike. Since it can be said that the broadcasting media do everything, this is a delicate as well as an unfashionable exercise. So we might as well go in at the deep end and start by stating some possible standards of judgement.

For all that has been written about the media in the last ten years, the Pilkington Report (the *Report of the Committee on Broadcasting*) which came out in 1960 still seems to me to put the problem of standards in broadcasting (the problem of the criteria in terms of which one could discriminate), most clearly. It was in the idea of 'trivialization' that the Committee which wrote the Report found the key to a critical perspective on broadcasting. Trivialization, they saw as a simple failure to treat the subject one is handling, whatever it may be, with the respect it deserves. A programme is not trivial because its matter is light or unimportant; it is trivial if its content is devalued in the process of communication. The passage where the Committee develop this point is worth quoting at length:

Triviality resides in the way the subject matter is approached and the manner in which it is presented. A trivial approach can consist in a failure to respect the potentialities of the subject matter no matter what it be, or in a too ready reliance on well-tried themes, or in a habit of conforming to established patterns or in a reluctance to be imaginatively adventurous ... in a failure to take full and disciplined advantage of the artistic and technical facilities which are relevant to a particular subject, or in an excessive interest in smart packaging at the expense of the contents of the package, or in a reliance on gimmicks so as to give a spurious interest to a programme at the cost of its imaginative integrity, or in too great a dependence on hackneyed devices for creating suspense or raising a laugh or evoking tears.

What I want to argue here is that tendencies to trivialization are rampant in British broadcasting now just as they were a decade ago, not because broadcasters are irresponsible people, but because the technical and social character of the situation in which these media communicate makes trivialization almost unavoidable. There is, as it were, a logic of broadcasting as a social process which makes trivialization very probable – something it will take more than a sense of responsibility to resist. It is against the background, and recognizing the force of this logic that one has to try to evaluate 'good' and 'bad' programmes. In any medium one can judge quality only in terms of the technical constraints and possibilities of the particular form of communication in question. In the case of broadcasting I would argue that the process of trivialization, or what we might call the 'law of optimum inoffensiveness', is to a large extent integral to the technical nature of the media and not something that needs to be explained in terms of the wickedness, bad taste, or financial greed of particular men who happen to be in charge of the media.

But to say that in British conditions the tendency towards trivialization is virtually a technical fact of life for radio and television is to state a problem, not to solve one. Within the limits set by the law of optimum inoffensiveness better and worse programmes are still possible; it is necessary to ask what, given those limits, broadcasters can do well and what they ought to leave alone. And here we at once come upon a peculiar characteristic of broadcasting among the mass media – the belief of

105

broadcasters that they can do everything, that theirs is a medium supremely suited to *all* forms of communication, and consequently that they should do everything. In fact there is a direct relationship, or so it seems to me, between the excessive pretensions of broadcasters and the trivializing effects of broadcasting. 'It's all the same, I don't enjoy it any more; it's boring' was the way one viewer described his experience of television to one investigator. If this seems a sad comment on a medium of which the proudest boast is that it brings 'Life' to the people, it is perhaps worth asking whether it is not the undiscriminating attempt to transmit 'Life' as a whole that is responsible for the blurring of identities and differences that such comments betray. Might it not be that just because these media try to do everything, try to 'hold a mirror up to society', try to compete with all other forms of communication, broadcasters lay themselves open to charges of triviality and that they themselves find it so difficult to realize their other professed aim, the aim of 'raising' standards of public taste?

This, essentially, is the problem I want to explore. It can be reduced to three main questions. How far and in what ways are tendencies towards trivialization an intrinsic part of what we might call the working logic of these media? Should and can radio and television cope equally well with all forms of communication, and if not for what sorts of communication are they best suited? Within these limits what ought we to mean by 'good' and 'bad' and the other evaluative noises we apply to radio and television programmes of different sorts?

The simplest description of the broadcasting media makes plain the nature of their working logic. Radio and television have four properties which distinguish them as media from all others. They are, too, peculiarly 'mass' properties – predisposing the communicators to treat their audiences as masses, that is. Broadcasting is universal, it is continuous, it is domestic and it is respectable. Each of these points needs to be qualified but each characteristic still has powerful consequences for what broadcasters do and have to do and hence for the content of the programmes they provide.

The universality of broadcasting has two aspects. Programmes

106

are as a matter of fact available to everyone, anyone can listen
or view. And this fact is subtly transmuted into a practice in
which as a matter of policy programmes are addressed to everyone; everyone, it is assumed, will listen or view – or at least
should be able to. In the earliest days of British broadcasting
these ideas were acknowledged explicitly and applied in a simple
form. Broadcasting, in the words of the Crawford Committee in
1926, was to be 'conducted by a public corporation acting as a
trustee for the national interest'. This notion of a national interest
in broadcasting has persisted (it was put to the Pilkington Committee by many witnesses for example) and has continuously
shaped the broadcaster's own sense of his role in society. The
BBC Handbook for 1971 says that the object of the Corporation
is 'to provide a public service of broadcasting for general recep-
tion at home and overseas'. Lord Hill, the Chairman of the
BBC, filled out that idea when he said that the BBC must be
'comprehensive enough not to exclude any taste', must 'think in
terms of serving the *whole* public'. The Television Act of 1964
which now governs the workings of independent television, and
the various policy statements made from time to time by the
ITA, offer a watered down and suitably commercialized but
essentially similar idea of the social function of broadcasting.
ITV is required to disseminate information, education and
entertainment 'of a high general standard' and to do so without
offending 'public taste' – it is in the notion of public taste that
the universalistic illusion slips in. Who is the public? In practice,
as many people as possible but all assimilated to the one mode.
Admittedly, the ITV *Guide to Independent Television* for 1971
dismisses the question whether broadcasting is or is not a public
service as 'increasingly out of date'.* But the same publication
reveals a very emphatic, almost strident, concern with the popularity of programmes, ratings, the size of audiences, the *quantity* of
appeal, which really is little more than a commercial version of
the BBC idea of reaching everyone as a matter of service. By
either standard good programmes are inclusive programmes –

*But there is a revealing value judgement here; up-to-date becomes a
synonym for good. Here again, the quiet influence of advertising values
(newness really is goodness in the market) on media values is apparent.

programmes everyone could enjoy. The ITV 'Top Twenty' are not programmes that anyone in particular has judged to be particularly good by any explicit standard of evaluation: they are just those programmes which are watched in six million homes.

This is the catch, and the *non sequitur*, of course. Audience size is *not* the only possible yardstick for judging whether one is serving the public or even being popular. It is a measure of tolerance, not a measure of taste. But given the way the broadcasting media define service, taste and the public, it tends to become the decisive yardstick. The idea of public taste and the idea of a very large audience act on one another in a peculiar alchemy which produces in turn that ideal of balance to which both main broadcasting agencies subscribe and which means in practice a determined pursuit of maximum inoffensiveness in broadcasting.

Once, about ten years ago, there was a programme called 'That Was The Week That Was'. It was vigorous, funny and rude, probably the nearest thing this country has seen to an engaged political cabaret. It was strongly objected to by many civic figures. It was widely attacked as tasteless. A small (only a few hundred thousand) minority were devoted to it, cheered and stimulated by it. Slowly, the tough edges of the programme were softened. The harsher moments of satire (when you felt that someone really disliked something) became fewer and more relaxed. After a season or two the format of the programme was changed. Pope's 'strong Antipathy of good to bad' showed signs of giving way to a more genial 'good for a giggle' view of life; the technique of Swift who 'lashed the vice but spar'd the name', gave way to the technique of Frost who, as it were, 'dropped the name but spar'd the vice'. The heirs of 'That Was The Week' were progressively less offensive to taste; and increasingly indistinguishable from every other variety show.

This true story is a sad epitome of what broadcasting, with its special criteria of taste and of the public, tends to do. Policy decisions about programmes incline towards a 'highest common factor', towards standardizing the content of the media at a level of maximum acceptability, towards treating as potentially homogeneous what is in fact an immensely varied and detailed

108

tangle of interests, expectations and tastes. Success, related to the notion of radio and television as universal media, means a minimum range of styles each of maximum inoffensiveness. It means what one critic has called 'computer programmes' – formula broadcasting, a search for sets of standard recipes for programmes that will 'work' in the sense of holding very large audiences with minimal and standard variations of character, sequence and situation. Many of these recipes are now so well-defined that the programmes they produce, not just serials and variety programmes but drama and documentaries as well, could well be written by machines.* The packages become steadily more predictable. A similar result of the same tendencies can be seen in the creation of a handful of contrived media languages. BBC 'standard English' is the most famous of these, the characterless, formal, entirely correct and socially unspecific usage in which the intention of the first Director General of the BBC to 'promulgate definite standards' was embodied. More pervasive now is the rival language cultivated especially by the independent companies, 'mid-Atlantic', the brisk idiom of the disc-jockey, the pop singer and the advertiser, equally unspecific, equally unrooted in English usage. Then, too, we have media working class, a strange mix of Barnsley, Birkenhead and Bethnal Green which, although not actually spoken by anyone, has the great advantage that it can be understood by everyone. These languages could simply not have come into currency as viable modes of communication without the broadcasting media. They are a striking example of the way in which these media *make* culture – and make it in the image, which is itself their own creation, of a society of masses. To my mind not one of these languages will stand comparison, for richness, impact or range, with the non-mass languages they are displacing. They reveal very clearly the price we, and broadcasting, pay for the commitment to universality

*Perhaps they are: 'We have brought in computers to help us, and this on a massive scale', Huw Weldon, Managing Director, BBC Television. Seriously, the sheer scale of the technology which broadcasting now presupposes makes a very high degree of predictability necessary at all stages of the broadcasting process – consider Mr Weldon's comments on the inconvenience caused for the BBC by the unscheduled occurrence of a General Election in June 1970 (*BBC Handbook 1971*, p. 15).

109

of communication. They were, however, justified before the Pilkington Committee in terms of an ideal of cultural democracy.

The desire to be democratic within the technical framework set by the media – very wide coverage and fairly few channels – does raise real dilemmas, of course. The problem is often presented as a choice between minority and majority interests. It can also be seen as a choice between standards of authenticity on the one hand and of acceptability on the other, between programmes that seek out and respect felt boundaries of taste and discrimination between audiences and programmes that ignore such boundaries for the sake of a larger, albeit less satisfied, audience. The democratic course, it is often argued, is obviously the latter. As a result very few people get programmes that are perfect for them but everyone gets programmes that are more or less bearable. My own feeling is rather that in matters of culture and communication the only meaning one can give to the idea of democracy is authenticity. The notion of a homogeneous mass audience which can be given what 'it' wants is, in broadcasting, thoroughly misleading. Democracy in a one-way structure of communication can only mean respect by the communicator, first for existing differences of group idiom, culture and interest within his audience, and second for the integrity of the material being communicated, for its intrinsic limitations, for the intractable *lack* of universality of most of what is worth communicating. But to interpret democracy in this way is, of course, to say that only some few sorts of programmes can be given anything like universal appeal without seriously diluting or compromising their subject-matter. This does seem to be the case and I shall argue later that it is only in the context of documentary broadcasting (using the term in a fairly wide sense) that these media can hope to combine authenticity and acceptability in any easy way. For the rest the broadcaster is likely to find himself in a situation where he can achieve one only at the expense of the other. He has to choose, and we may reasonably judge his programmes in the light of the sort of choices or compromises they suggest he has made.

Since 1963 the pressure on broadcasters to make this sort of choice in almost impossible situations has relaxed a good deal.

110

The introduction of BBC 2, the restructuring of the independent television companies with a much stronger regional emphasis, the reorganization of radio broadcasting in four semi-specialized channels, the setting up of twenty regional radio stations by the BBC (and the introduction of commercial local radio), the rapid growth of educational broadcasting, especially in connection with the Open University, have created great areas of broadcasting where the pressure of universality, the need to appeal to everyone in each moment of communication, is hardly felt. And yet in a curious way all this activity has remained on the fringe of broadcasting proper. The real thing, broadcasting as it hits the culture hardest, happens from 6.30 to 11.00 at night on BBC 1, BBC 2, and whichever ITV channel you receive and on Radios 1 and 2 on Saturday and Sunday mornings. And here the impact of all the innovations of the last ten years has been very slight. We are talking about a block of viewing and listening in which 'Show of the Week', 'Softly, Softly', 'Coronation Street', 'Opportunity Knocks', 'Oh Brother', 'Top of the Pops', 'Family Favourites', 'Z Cars', 'Tony Blackburn' and the 'News' constitute the basic pattern. It is not a pattern which has been much affected by the experiments and diversifications of the past decade. What has happened is that the media have created special viewing and listening enclaves for a number of special minority audiences – e.g., Radio 3 for the hundred thousand or so devotees of 'serious' music – and thereafter have gone on treating us as a mass.

A few facts and figures may be helpful here. Of twenty-three and a half thousand hours of radio broadcasting by the BBC in 1969–70 just over ten thousand were taken up by 'light' music. The average audience for 'Family Favourites' in that period is calculated as ten million, six hundred thousand; the average audience for the most popular programme on Radio 3 was one hundred and fifty thousand. Or contrast the cosmopolitan, entertainment-dominated programme output of a company like Thames Television which provides so much of ITV's peak-time broadcasting ('Callan', 'For the Love of Ada', 'This is Your Life', 'Special Branch', 'Dear Father'), with the pathetically restricted and local output of a company like Tyne-Tees

111

which gets hardly anything onto the national network.* The lesson here seems to be not that Tyne-Tees is 'worse' than Thames but on the contrary that by operating as an authentically local medium – for a socially specific audience which might find week-long coverage of the third Teesside Eisteddfod good entertain ment or 'Where the Jobs Are' a programme which meets its idea of public service – this company has virtually abandoned the prospect of success in terms of the values that prevail in the media generally. Yet it was this conspicuously provincial, and no doubt 'out-of-date' company which managed to produce, in 'Mr Lowry', a programme which (quite apart from being hailed by the critics as the best documentary of the year), entered the relationship of an artist to his art more subtly, more exactly and with more honest feeling for the man and his work than I have known it done before. Here television was doing superbly what it can always do well – the documentary mix of image and message through close and careful observation, so that a subject is made to speak for itself directly to an audience and on many levels. In such a programme the audience is virtually unaware of the existence of the broadcaster. The broadcaster in turn seems to feel no need to 'mediate' with art or technique between his subject and an audience; in carefully drawing meaning from his subject he himself seems to disappear. This apparent invisibility is one of the highest achievements of the broadcaster's art. What it calls for is not so much a very elaborate technology or an enormous budget but rather a simple respect for, a belief in, what one is communicating. A programme like 'Mr Lowry' surprises the regular viewer. It surprises him into seeing how dressed up, how diluted and indeed how sloppily made at a technical level most of our peak broadcasting, the broadcasting consciously designed to have universal appeal, really is.

It is, then, in relation to the core of broadcasting, the peak viewing and listening programmes, that the problem of dis-crimination arises most acutely. It arises in two forms. How, first, can one tell whether a broadcaster is doing his best in a situation governed by the fact that he wants to communicate to ten million people? How much, secondly, can you as an in-

*ITV 1971, pp. 207–9.

dividual ask of a programme which you have chosen to watch, knowing that it has been designed to appeal to ten million people apart from you? The two questions can be reduced to a third: how much trivialization ought one to accept as reasonable in a peak programme? Part of the answer, however, depends on what your range of choice is and this brings the minority programmes back into the problem. Some people are doing very much better than others when it comes to choosing programmes. The most favoured people at the present time are musical highbrows on the one hand and the audience for pop on the other. Both of these minorities, one quite small and the other very large, have in effect been given whole channels to themselves; and they also do pretty well out of the other channels. It would be ridiculous to quibble over the content of Radio 3; in providing access to music and discussion for people living too far from London to have any chance of experiencing these things at first hand it realizes perfectly the literal purposes of broadcasting; and it does so without any compromise of standards. Here the media have singled out a meaningful and coherent sub-section of the total audience and the broadcasters concentrate on maintaining a flow of communication only to that sub-section. The result is a triumph of mass communication; it is mass communication from which the concept of the mass has been eliminated. And much the same is true of Radio 1. It is broadcasting for a distinct sub-culture with very few concessions to anyone else. Actually, the case of Radio 1 is more important than that of Radio 3 because here broadcasting has not simply discovered and served an audience; it has contributed quite actively to the artistic and technical development of a sub-culture; arguably, it has been *the* medium in which the sub-culture of pop has grown – outstandingly with the emergence of progressive pop.

But excellent as it is that the BBC should have broken the grip of universality on broadcasting, this setting aside of special channels for special audience groups is a solution that raises as many problems as it solves. Lord Reith objected to the idea of a Third Programme (Radio 3) on the ground that with the intellectuals set aside the doctrine of universal acceptability would gain new strength in the main body of programmes; that when

113

concessions to intellectual standards no longer needed to be made it would be assumed that no other differences within the audience mattered. And his fears seem to have been well grounded. In the wake of the Third Programme sound radio introduced the 'magazine' programme, the scrapbook collections of fascinating bits and pieces, oddments of information, whimsical tales, tunes, and jokes, no item lasting more than a minute or two, making no demands on anyone, offering something for everyone. And the television equivalent of these radio rag-bags, the so-called 'family' programme, monopolizes the main viewing hours in the same way – programmes in which the doctrines of universal appeal or 'no offence' find their apotheosis. With the highbrows and a few other special groups set aside both media have indeed become more frankly devoted to substituting the acceptable for the authentic so far as everyone else is concerned. The new pattern of radio broadcasting introduced in April 1970 (the four distinct channels and the regional sub-channels) has given two or three stereotyped special audiences more of what they are thought to want. But it has also lent weight to the idea that the only way to escape from the problem of universality, the dilemma of accept-ability or authenticity, is to segregate particular audience groups. Given the nature and cost of broadcasting this may indeed be the case. The only alternative I can think of would involve the media in a radically different way of using their time. This brings us to the second of my four basic characteristics of the broadcasting media, their continuity.

Uniquely among the mass media, radio and television are given opportunities by time, by the fact that they have the whole day, every day, to dispose of, and that they can break up the day as they please. Not only are these media expected to provide communication for all the people, but they are expected to do so more or less all the time. How do they use this opportunity? Perhaps the advent of BBC 2 provides a relevant illustration. We were promised a 'flexible and adventurous' new dimension in broadcasting but in the event the spirit of adventure was sadly counteracted by the spirit of 'more of the same'. The most striking early innovation was the attempt to distinguish between nights of the week – 'Friday night is family night'. The Cor-

114

poration seems to have changed its mind a number of times since then about the best way to use its extra thirty-two hours. Sometimes BBC 2 looks like the 'serious' television channel. More often, it is indistinguishable from BBC 1 or ITV. The mere increase in broadcasting time has increased the range of broadcasting on all channels, however; it has allowed the media to give more time to relatively less popular types of programme, and to develop ideas which had hitherto hardly been more than occasional experiments – the dramatization as serials of classical novels, for example. If one looks at broadcasting in detail, programme by programme, I think it is clear that more time has meant more good programmes as well as more mediocre ones. But in an important sense it is not the detail but the pattern that matters if we want to see how the continuity of broadcasting contributes to trivialization. Night after night with hardly a break, the same pattern of programmes repeats itself on each channel. And the patterning of each evening builds into a pattern of weeks and months.

Men have always solved the more acute problems of everyday life by absorbing them into predictable cycles of activity, turning a hundred potential crises into unconsidered sequences of solutions which are barely thought about just because their meaning has become that of a detail in a pattern. Broadcasting has both adapted itself to existing cycles of action in daily life and worked powerfully to create new cycles: every Monday and Wednesday at 7.30 . . . for example. In particular, it has filled that small bit of life which, before broadcasting, was not structured by the cycles of work or domesticity. When everything else is strongly shaped an area of shapelessness is potentially worrying. It is available for exploitation. Broadcasting fills the last vacuum. Here it is plainly form, not content, that matters.

Regularity gives the broadcasting organizations the predictability their technology requires. It also turns programmes into habits with amazing speed. Given half a chance people will relate to a cycle rather than to its episodes. Because the cycle is meaningful, the actual programmes are relatively unconsidered. The variation of quality between one edition of a serial and the next can be enormous (especially when different writers are involved)

115

but if viewers can be caught up in the pattern of the series the
qualities of any particular programme are less closely examined.
We know that audiences do relate to broadcasting, just as people
relate to life, in this way. I suspect that broadcasters themselves
do, too. As often as not it is obvious that the only real work that
has gone into an episode of 'Coronation Street' (to take the
most familiar example), is in making the punch line or final shot
strong enough to carry the audience forward to the next episode.

To hunt up a programme that is not part of a pattern, to
organize one's time specially for it, to relate to it as an event, all
this is, by comparison to what we might call pattern-viewing or
listening, quite hard work. One brings a different and sharper
kind of attention to it. Most broadcasting is not received in this
way. And this is at least partly a result of the way broadcasters
have chosen to organize broadcasting. It would have been possible to distribute programmes through the great blocks of time
the media have at their disposal in such a way as to emphasize
the discontinuity of programmes. Suppose you turned on for
'News at Ten' one night and saw Andrew Gardner announce,
'We have found nothing worth broadcasting today. We'll be
back when we have. Goodnight'. If that sort of thing could
happen, if the decision not to broadcast for every possible minute
of broadcasting time was conceivable, it would not take long to
dispel the taken-for-granted atmosphere that lies between each
viewer and the appreciation of each programme now. Less drastic
measures might have the same effect. Time could be used aggressively – to provide successions of programmes designed *not* to
appeal easily to huge audiences, each designed, rather, for a
distinct and different minority within the mass. Such sequences
would confront audiences with constant contrasts of style and
standard without either diluting any particular idiom or making
it too easy for any particular group to withdraw into its own
viewing or listening enclave. We tend to take the existing pattern
of programming so much for granted that we do not see the gulf
between what could be done in the use of time and what actually
is done. When the media do experiment, it is almost always a
shock, and almost always a success – as when the BBC devotes
the whole of one evening to one opera.

But most broadcasting is not of this kind; it takes the flow of time for granted and is received by audiences who are not attending particularly to particular moments of communication. The media have used the opportunity of continuous communication to create patterns rather than events, to submerge most programmes in the rhythm of a broadcasting cycle – a cycle which acquires its own cogency and appeal independently of the programmes it carries. How could a series as superficially conceived and as thinly characterized as 'The Saint' have lasted any length of time unless each programme had been for many people an expected moment in a cycle, contributing to a pattern that was for the time being part of the structure of their lives? Conversely, observe how hard broadcasters have to work, how much publicity and noise is needed, to give back to any single programme the standing of an event. The very term 'a broadcasting event' has become a platitude, empty of force. Time, which could have been forcibly punctuated by broadcasting, has instead been patterned to a rhythm of acceptability. The fact of continuity, which could have been used to sharpen and expand the sensibility of audiences by the vigorous juxtaposing of firmly dissimilar and contrasting, and above all, unexpected subjects and styles, has in fact been used to develop a small number of *patterns of broadcasting* within which endless ingenious but minor variations of cast and detail will keep alive the interest of audiences switched on not to the programme but to the pattern.

The fact of continuity thus serves to compound the trivializing tendencies of the universality of these media. The whole experience of viewing or listening becomes that of the worst kind of magazine programme, a glorified 'Woman's Hour' as it were. Item follows item too smoothly and rapidly for any one item to engage the attention or grip the imagination for more than the moment of its passage. Comic items and serious items, the calamitous and the diverting parade before us in unending procession. No pause for differentiation or appraisal is allowed. The first thing the discriminating viewer has to do is to learn to switch off.

But switching off is only a start. To see a programme fully it must be detached, not only from its immediate context in one

117

evening's broadcasting, but also from the pattern of broadcasting spreading over weeks and months of which it is part. It is in terms of these longer patterns that broadcasting becomes an invisible and unconsidered dimension of people's lives. Even switching off, however, is quite difficult – as the viewing figures suggest. Once on, the set tends, in millions of cases every night, to stay on. And in this situation definition (to borrow a useful term from the back of my own set) is easily lost. It is a standard feature of the reports of people who have 'observed' groups watching television that comment or conversation about a programme wells up only to be quashed almost immediately as attention is drawn back to whatever next appears on the screen. Discussion gives way to asides and appreciative noises. The effect is of a blurring of edges, an ironing-out of differences of stature and scale between items and programmes. Like the heroes of Webster's play, individual programmes:

> Leave no more fame behind 'em than should one
> Fall in a frost, and leave his print in snow –
> As soon as the sun shines it ever melts
> Both form and matter.

In broadcasting the sun of the next programme is always shining. Within thirty seconds of an account of public executions in Nigeria, we are back with the fantasy public transport of 'On the Buses'. Which communicates as more real? Continuity in this sense reduces the world to a music-hall. Programmes are poured at us without distinction; they run together, wrapping the audience in an eiderdown of unreality; cartoon time, news, film time, a Western, domestic comedy, news, sport, cinema, news headlines, close down – seasoned or not according to taste with advertisements at every possible break; the whole blending in ways which serve, as Raymond Williams puts it, 'to deflect, postpone and cushion any relevance to actual living'. 'It's all the same, I don't enjoy it any more ...' Actually, of course, 'it' is not all the same; that is just an effect of radio and television.

And the effect is compounded again by the third characteristic of broadcasting, its domesticity. It is indeed this property that makes it virtually impossible for radio and television to escape

118

from the tendencies to trivialization which their universality and continuity encourage and permit. Radio and television are provided in the home. And because they are one does not have to make any felt act of choice in order to be exposed to them. To see a film one has to decide to go to the cinema (not necessarily to see the film one ends up seeing, though). Reading a paper or going to a football match or pub all involve a relatively deliberate effort; one chooses what to do and what should happen to one. None of this is true for watching or listening. These are activities on which one embarks, typically, unthinkingly; they are so easy to embark on. People can and do switch on in a way that is as routine as the way in which they wash and have tea when they come in. These are activities from which the problem of decision has been removed. 'Now,' as one man put it, 'you don't need to worry how you will spend your time.'

Ever present, radio and television provide alternatives, not just to other activities, but to the whole problem of thinking what to do. One BBC survey found that the more an individual watched television the less likely he was to describe himself as 'choosey' rather than 'not choosey' about the programmes he watched. And this is not very surprising. Because television is so easily available it is given functions which have nothing to do with conscious choice or cultural discrimination. For people who watch a lot it is not just what they watch but the fact of watching that is important. There seems to be a direct progression in this respect from the 'choosey' ten per cent at one end to the ten per cent of 'addicts' at the other extreme for whom watching and listening have become rewarding activities in their own right regardless of what is seen or heard. Most people are not in either of these groups of course and do discriminate to a greater or lesser degree. But the domesticity of broadcasting, combining with its universality and continuity, opens a primrose path along which the audience has an open invitation to be led towards addiction.

In one particular way the domesticity of broadcasting furthers the decline of choosiness. Because programmes are so easily and constantly available one thing that most members of the audience are likely to ask of the media sooner or later is that they provide a

119

certain minimum of wholly undemanding distraction. Radio and television are asked to do things which other, non-domestic, discontinuous, selective media cannot – to allow listeners and viewers to relax, to provide just the sort of 'cushion against reality' that Raymond Williams describes, to create an agreeable background for passing and wasting time. Because they are domestic these media are expected to be unexacting, to provide relief from routine and effort. Nor do I see how this demand, even if we call it a demand for 'escape', can be said to be unreasonable or improper. The quality and pace of modern work make it difficult to censure the use of broadcasting for light relief. Broadcasting, in short, through its special character, acquires strictly non-aesthetic, social, and psychological functions which other media do not have (or do not have to nearly the same extent). R. H. S. Crossman, indeed, goes so far as to speak of a 'right to triviality'. Certainly, a non-stop supply of programmes making rigorous demands on the judgement, attention, and imagination would deny to most viewers and listeners an important and proper use of the media.

And if the demand for background is legitimate it follows that some provision should be made in an ideal scheme for it to be met. A good deal of what is communicated by these media not only is ephemeral (as a result of the 'one transmission only' norm of broadcasting performance which is itself a by-product of universal coverage), but ought not to pretend to be more than ephemeral.

But to ask for space for the light-weight is not, of course, to endorse a flight from standards of authenticity even in light-weight programmes. The fact that the media are used for 'escape' makes it more not less important for us to have clear criteria for judging the goodness or badness of the material that is used in this way. One possibility is suggested by the sociological literature about the mass media. In this literature increasing attention is being given to the uses people make of the media and to possible side-effects of those uses. It is suggested for example that while one may use television to escape from tedious or vexatious situations of one's daily life, there may also be a 'feedback' from the material one uses for escape to the way in which one subsequently sees and handles the situations of 'real life'. What the nature of this feedback will be seems to depend not on how far the individual uses the media for escape but rather on what the escaper finds *in* the material he uses. The feedback from some media or some programmes may be narcotizing but from other media or other programmes one may gather resources of understanding and sensibility which contribute creatively to one's 'real' social relationships. Thus a serial may be narcotizing or invigorating for those who view it as 'escapist' to the extent that it disregards or respects individual personality. In this sense 'Coronation Street' perhaps qualifies as a 'better' serial and 'Here's Lucy' as a 'worse' one; although the former caricatures life, it does deal in consistent, developing personalities, people who can be enriched or diminished by one another: the latter is indifferent to personality and for all its technical ingenuity deals in stock types who relate to one another as objects.

In short, to speak of a 'right to triviality' is not to give a licence to the trivialization which seems to be the broadcasters' own favourite solution to the problem posed by the demand for background, for media that function as occasions for 'escape'.

But the problem remains. How can media with universal coverage and a limited number of channels, continuous broadcasting and domestic consumption meet the need for background, a need felt by different people at different times and in different ways, without compromising the standards of authenticity and respect for divergent tastes which in principle one wants to demand of them? Perhaps the problem is insoluble so long as British broadcasting is organized as it now is. Perhaps some limited compromises are inevitable. But it is ironic that at present the fourth and last basic characteristic of these media, their respectability, should also contribute powerfully to the tendency towards trivialization. Not only is trivial material easier to provide than authentic material (making fewer demands on the energies and imagination of already harassed broadcasters), but the official mythologies of British broadcasting themselves favour triviality.

The BBC is, and the ITA has convinced itself that it is, an 'established' not to say official institution, with appropriate commitments to respectability, impartiality between interests, and apparent self-effacement. Both like to see themselves as above controversy and party strife. Both are dedicated to the ideal of providing services in the 'national' interest, services of information, education, and entertainment. Both are sensitive to complaints about their objectivity. Both profess aspirations to help in the 'raising' of standards of public taste; at the same time both express concern to cater for every taste, to 'hold a mirror up to society', and, whatever happens, not to 'impose' on public opinion. Both seek to be fair to all points of view. Both want above all to be democratic, responsible, impartial.

Both are thus in a cleft stick of their own making. On the one hand they are anxious to lead or raise standards of taste; on the other hand they shy away from anything that can be criticized as 'imposing' on taste. In a one-way system of communication one cannot help imposing on taste. Even the variety of programmes of the type of 'Listeners Answer Back' with which the media have experimented over the years must be, in effect, shaped unilaterally by the producers. To watch, say, Robin Day dragging preselected questions about the Common Market from a preselected audience for a carefully representative and preselected panel to answer is to have the unilateral character of broadcasting made brutally clear. A mass communication system of this kind can never have the flexibility, the reciprocity of conversation. Mass communication is a gift not an exchange. The only real question is what shall be imposed; how and by whom shall the messages be pre-determined?

But one cannot lead taste if one has no sense of direction; one cannot raise standards unless one will allow that some things are better than others and some worse. And what has happened with these media is that their respectable image of their own role has made broadcasters so afraid of imposing that they do seem to have lost all sense of direction. In its place they have set up a largely spurious public service ideal of impartiality. Other mass media may have the wrong values; one's first impression of radio and television is that they have no values. The press and the cinema may glamorize the shoddy and they may have false, even vicious priorities. But at least they have priorities; they do patently select and editorialize; some things are headlined and some ignored; if a newspaper feels like flaying the government's defence policy, it will do so; it is sensible to talk about the 'character' of these media. Radio and television, by contrast, seem to have no editors, they do not admit to having conscious and consistent principles of selection – except perhaps the worst of all possible principles, the principle of 'news value'. The Pilkington Committee had a hard time getting the controllers of these media to admit that they ever chose or planned anything. What the broadcasters offered the Committee were the ideas of neutrality, balance, and the mirroring of society.

Such ideals mean different things for different types of programme; in so far as it is necessary and desirable for radio and television to function as universal public services it would seem to follow that these media ought to concentrate on those sorts of programme to which the ideal of impartiality is most appropriate (especially as, for other, technical, reasons, these are the sorts of programme which these media do best in any case). I shall return to this point shortly. First, a word is perhaps in order about the ulterior arguments on which the whole working logic of the media, as I have described it, is premised. These are the arguments about democracy, respecting public taste, and 'giving the public what it wants' which I have touched on several times already and which were made articulate by both BBC and ITA in defending their present practice and their commitment to impartiality to the Pilkington Committee.

Arguments about giving the public what it wants are the overarching claims in terms of which all the trivializing tendencies of the media are drawn together and collectively justified. Like the belief in impartiality, the appeal to what the public wants is spurious through and through. Just as something has to be selected and something rejected whether the selecting is done consciously or not, so the highly centralized structure of broadcasting means that judgements are constantly being made about the nature of audience-wants and that in practice the only test of these supposed wants is audience size. And I would suggest that to defend programmes that are more 'acceptable' than 'authentic' on the ground that such programmes have huge audiences and that these huge audiences show that such programmes are what the

123

public 'wants' is to ignore the real relationship that exists between the broadcaster and his public and to make nonsense of the idea of a want.

Gilbert Seldes, in one of his essays on the mass media, tells a story of a cinema proprietor in Nigeria who owned, and showed, only two films, *King Kong*, and *The Mark of Zorro*. Three days a week he packed the house with one of these; on the other three he did the same with the other; on Sunday as a surefire double feature he showed them both. This went on for years. The story parodies but does not really falsify the relationship between communicator and public in the mass media. This enterprising man had fastened on to a general demand for entertainment; this he had met in a somewhat specific way; and he had gone on to work up an audience for the specific form of entertainment he was able to provide; finally, since he monopolized the means of entertainment in that region, he had contrived to 'prevent an audience for any other sort of entertainment from coming into existence'.

The sorts of demands people actually make are open-ended and ill-defined. If one asks what 'want' a particular programme is meeting one very rarely finds that the want could be met *only* by the programme in question. Rather, general wants, for amusement, background, excitement, are met in the particular ways the broadcasters find most convenient. The relationship between communicator and public is a manipulative one with the initiative firmly on the side of the communicator. When television provides a glut of Westerns the public selects Westerns as its favourite type of programme; when the companies switch to providing hospital dramas the public discovers a want for these. A series of recent studies has shown with growing clarity how far, as Professor Himmelweit puts it, 'taste is the product of the producer, rather than television entertainment the response of the producer to the public's taste'. Or as Gilbert Seldes writes:

Demand is generalized and diffuse – for entertainment, for thrills, for vicarious sadness, for laughs; it can be satisfied by programmes of different types and different qualities; and only after these programmes have been offered is there any demand (specifically) for them. Supply comes first in this business and creates its own demand.

The nature and working logic of these media tend, in short, 'to create those conditions in which the wants that can be most easily satisfied by the communicator take precedence over others'. And what this means in practice is that tendencies to trivialization are built into almost everything that the media do. This is the easy and convenient way to operate; to some extent even the unavoidable way.

British radio and television are beset with this problem. And yet, as I have already suggested, the things these media do best are the things in which the difficulties of trivialization are least urgent. Broadcasters themselves tend to believe that broadcasting can do anything. Specifically the media exist to provide services of information, education, and entertainment. In effect, wherever the broadcaster tries to fill the first or second of these roles the chances are he will succeed and that radio and television will prove superior media of communication to most others; wherever he tries to fill the third role, that of entertainer, the chances are he will fail and that radio and television will prove less adequate media than many others. But it is of course entertainment that is the heart of these media, brings them their income and gives them their social importance.

In trying to decide what these media can and cannot do we must start then by setting aside the delusions of communicative grandeur created by the universality, continuity, respectability and sheer technology of broadcasting. The built-in tendencies towards trivialization which I have been discussing are of a kind to make their worst impact on programmes designed to entertain. It is in the quality of such programmes, for example, that the impact of the domestic demand for agreeable background and the effects of the spurious belief in impartiality in programme selection are likely to be felt most. The one outstanding exception is music; here radio, but not television, remains a perfect medium; not so much for the quality of reproduction or performance but for the range of music to which the listener is given access. This of course is the fruit of a deliberate policy decision. It was a decision which has given sound broadcasting an unchallengeable and distinctive function among the media. One could complain in this respect only of the fact that so much broadcast music is still

125

space-filling music, amiable noise with minimal musical character
or cultural meaning, provided I suppose to meet the need for
'background' – and on the assumption that 'background' broadcasting is necessarily vacuous. Even in this context I suspect that
proper pop, or jazz, or folk, or classical music could be played as
acceptably – that Vivaldi would do as well as Mantovani – and
after Vivaldi we might try going on to Haydn, or Poulenc. But we
are dealing with a 'supply creating demand' situation here until
someone makes the experiment. Television, on the other hand,
does not seem suited to the transmission of music; either the
camera gives a head-on view of an entire orchestra so reduced in
size as merely to strain the eyes and infuriate the intellect; or it
roams around providing an arbitrary sideshow to the music; in
either case it is an unnecessary and distracting addendum to the
music itself. There is, again, one exception. Television is an
admirable medium for solo performers. It does not add anything
to the quality of the music of course and may again distract attention from the music itself. But it does permit a scrutiny at close
quarters of a performer's technique; it gives us something over
and above the sheer sound and this is something that is valuable
to have. But what it does is essentially of a documentary nature:
it shows how music is made, it permits us to understand a craft;
this is a real aid to appreciating the music in itself. To watch
closely what, say, Julian Bream does as he plays the music at
which he is uniquely good is a privilege we could not have without
television.

Television is good, too, surprisingly, with talk, and especially
with dialogue. Sometimes the time allowed is too short, or too
many speakers are assembled for any themes or conflicts to be
properly developed – this is particularly likely to happen when it
is felt necessary to treat a complicated and controversial issue in a
'representative' way. But when the media put two interesting
people together and allow them to talk to each other at length,
or when a powerful lecturer like A. J. P. Taylor is given an hour
to unfold one of his brilliantly structured historical interpret-
ations, television seems to me to come as near as it can ever hope
to do to being a medium which directly, rather than vicariously,
enlarges our experience. In such circumstances the visual element

is typically exploited in ways that complement and enhance what is being said. As compared to radio where the normal limit for a talk is nineteen minutes, it being calculated that listeners cannot concentrate on sound alone for longer than that, in television devices of illustration have been developed which focus attention for much longer periods, and which in the hands of at least some producers do support and not distract from the talk itself. Basically, this is an educational or informative activity of course. When someone has something to say, whether it is about sixth form physics or about why we should join the Common Market, and television's visual devices for making points are mobilized in a disciplined way to help him say it, this medium emerges as a surely unparalleled means of effective communication.

The same is true for all programmes of the 'live documentary' type – interviews, news programmes, sport, discussions, straight documentaries on controversial subjects, expositions of seemingly difficult matter – for all of these television, by virtue of its special technical properties, is highly suited. Such programmes should be judged by the most rigorous standards so far as trivialization and authenticity are concerned. They are the sorts of programmes where television is capable of excellence. Similarly whenever television treats entertainment in a basically documentary way – as when it gives us not only music but a close-up of a musical technique, or not just ballet but a study in detail of what dancers do to compose 'the dance' – or when it creates entertainment out of documentary matter – as it has done in popularizing show-jumping and cooking and interior decorating – it is again potentially at its best. In all these contexts of course the standards of greatest relevance are technical not aesthetic; what matters is how effectively points are made; how relevant is the technical apparatus to what is being said; how fair and thorough is what is said in relation to its subject-matter; how honest and uncompromising is the presentation.

Problems are raised here by the doctrine of impartiality to which both the BBC and the ITA subscribe in their role as respectable public service institutions. Both are in fact required by law to be impartial but both seem to welcome the restriction. Thus the *BBC Handbook* maintains that 'For the BBC to take sides in a controversial issue would be contrary ... to its policy of impartiality', and the *Guide to ITV* seems equally to welcome that passage of the Television Act of 1964 which insists that 'due impartiality is preserved in matters of political or industrial controversy or relating to current public policy'. There is a real problem here. Impartiality in presenting news *is* desirable – and the fact that the broadcasting media have become the country's most trusted news media reflects their very considerable success in achieving impartial presentation. But what is achieved is in fact a very negative conception of impartiality, a fear of editorializing, a shunning of anything 'which offends against good taste or decency' or might be 'offensive to public feeling' or 'subversive to society as a whole'. The way these guidelines are put into practice in particular programmes should be carefully studied. Particularly as, on a day-to-day level, they are frequently counteracted by the sense in the mind of the reporter or programme editor of the relative 'news value' of different possible items of news. The notion of news value seems to me to be largely coloured by an unacknowledged idea of entertainment value – particularly in the case of television. But the good picture in this sense is not necessarily the true picture. There are one or two studies, for example the study by J. D. Halloran and his colleagues of the coverage of the Grosvenor Square demonstration in 1968, which at least suggest that criteria of news value can work very powerfully against the ideal of impartial reporting. The whole problem of the way the media handle public issues is ringed round with difficulties. They probably have no choice but to try to be impartial. But the idea of impartiality itself can easily mask lots of ways of being extremely partial – who, to take the most obvious example, is to decide what is 'subversive to society'?

It is when its attention turns to art or simple entertainment that broadcasting steps beyond what I would call its natural territory. Here the limitations of universality, domesticity, and the ideal of impartiality make themselves felt most brutally. Consequently, it is in this field that broadcasting is least likely to do well but also in this field that one has to make most allowances for broadcasting – since the reasons for its shortcomings are so largely built into its organization. Nevertheless it is here that directly aesthetic ap-

128

praisals are most relevant and it is to such evaluations that broad-casting is most vulnerable.

The basic trouble with television drama, for example, is to my mind that the psychological relationship between viewer and performance is wrong. It is a relationship that destroys the stature of what is being performed. For some reason – perhaps simply because the distancing effect of a proscenium arch is so enormously aggravated – television contrives to reduce the scale of the drama both physically and emotionally to the size of the puppet show. The alternative, of course, is to make great use of close-ups and to select plays in which the exploration of personality is paramount and collective situations and group action subsidiary. Even so television, and still more sound radio, simply because it is one-dimensional, seem to me intrinsically less satisfactory media for drama than either the theatre or the cinema. Everything about television militates against a play acquiring dramatic stature. In the first place the producers and performers know that what they are doing is ephemeral in the extreme; television plays normally have one performance only, they do not aspire to be more than momentary entertainments. I can believe that it requires at least some sense of the possible permanence of what one creates to sustain an endeavour of aesthetic merit. Secondly, the television play is not presented or viewed as a unit but as an item in a mixed programme of an evening's entertainment; here again the theatre and cinema gain in that the play or film is offered as an isolated event, a work in its own right. Even a television play of the type most suited to the nature of the medium, a play of personality in which there is some true psychological complexity, labours under these difficulties. And the sense of the need for universal appeal, domesticity, and the provision of 'background' all probably reduce the chances of such plays being put on in any case.

But what especially impairs television drama and other broadcast entertainments is the very mythology of impartiality that contributes so much to the high standards broadcasting achieves in its documentary activities. In the latter the ideal of neutrality is generally a source of strength. But in the area of entertainment it is not so much impartiality as commitment that is needed. As I have suggested, in this area the nature of the media makes any

129

Brilliant !!

attempt not to impose on taste unreal. Aspirations to cultural neutrality merely conceal from both the communicator and the audience the nature of the imposition. The 'holding a mirror to society' argument masks an act of evasion, not of responsibility, a refusal to discriminate consciously behind which there must lie unconscious discrimination, intuitive selection taking the place of purposeful and critically articulate selection. The fact that the criteria of selection are not brought to light – for fear no doubt of the charge of paternalism – does not mean that selection does not take place. However seemingly casual, random, and value-free, however plausibly explained-away as 'what the public wants', selection of material for broadcasting by the broadcasters is inescapable. And the criteria of selection become the implicit, unspoken values of the communicators. Since purposeful selection in the field of entertainment is deplored, the basis of selection is seldom scrutinized. But it does not take much study of the content of broadcast entertainment to discover behind the seeming neutrality a persistent, no doubt unconscious, diffusion of a distinct, and not at all impartial, view of life.

In the absence of other criteria the style, idiom, and values of radio and television entertainment are set, in practice, in part by the unstated values of the communicators, in part by the working logic of the media as a whole, in particular by the pursuit of universal appeal and what that is taken to mean. The nature of the ensuing 'media values', and the extent to which they mould the attitudes at least of younger viewers, have been forcibly demonstrated in many studies.

On a modest scale one can quite easily repeat for oneself the sort of experiment that has allowed media researchers to disentangle and identify the values running through different entertainment programmes. It is useful to repeat such scrutinies of the norms of broadcast entertainment, for through them one comes to appreciate just how much selection, how much pre-determining of the supposed 'mirror-image' of society is in fact involved in broadcasting. There is for example in television drama the consistent presentation as normal and desirable of what is in fact 'essentially an urban and upper-middle class society' ... 'essentially the ideology of a competitive society'. The viewer is offered

130

a world in which 'the most important qualities for success are determination and will-power; kindness and unselfishness are of lesser consequence.' Purporting to reflect the world, the entertainment portrayed by these media offers a definition of the world which is not the world known to most people and which rests on values alien to most people, and certainly alien to the professed ideals of most educators and public men. The starkest presentation of these special values, as though they were not so much values as working norms of the society as a whole, is of course to be found in television advertisements.

In evaluating television and radio entertainment one should, then, not only make certain allowances for the commitments of the media to universality, domesticity, etc. One should also have some conception of an alternative pattern of broadcast entertainment which both escapes from the unconscious commitment to 'media-values' into some more articulate and desirable commitment, and uses to the full the special facilities of these media for entertainment – facilities for the intimate as opposed to the spectacular, the detailed as opposed to the grandiose, subtlety and precision and a sense for the texture of personality as opposed to glamour and brashness and a surrender to what F. R. Leavis has called the 'illusion of technique'.

In all these respects broadcasting as a medium of entertainment lags far behind broadcasting as a medium of information and education. Yet it is still for entertainment rather than information or education that both communicators and audiences are most dependent on, and most devoted to, radio and television in Britain. We value most those aspects of broadcasting where the problem of discrimination and the dangers of trivialization are both greatest.

BOOKS AND PUBLICATIONS

Report of the Committee on Broadcasting, 1960, H.M.S.O., 1962. The report of the Pilkington Committee; still the best survey of the problems of British broadcasting, with many surprisingly frank statements by broadcasters and representatives of many pressure groups interested in broadcasting about what they feel are the aims of radio and television. It also contains a very clear account of the problem of trivialization.

131

BBC Handbook 1971, BBC Publications
Guide to Independent Television, 1971, ITA – These two guides, which
now appear annually, are together the best source of basic information
on what the broadcasting institutions are doing, their organization,
policies and (sometimes unintentionally) their values. They also contain
up-to-date bibliographies of works on broadcasting.

L. A. DEXTER and D. A. WHITE, *People, Society and Mass Communication*, Free Press, New York, 1964. Of many sociological readers on the
mass media this is possibly the best so far as radio and television are
concerned. See especially the chapter by H. Mendelsohn on 'Listening
to Radio'.

J. HALLORAN, *The Effects of Television*, Panther Books, 1970. A useful
survey of what we know about the effects of television, with particular
reference to effects on children, and of what we need to know.

H. T. HIMMELWEIT *et al.*, *Television and the Child,* Oxford University
Press, 1958. A relatively early contribution to the literature in this field
but one which is still very fruitful – particularly in using a research
design which does allow one to arrive at definite judgements about the
content as well as the effects of broadcasting.

M. MCLUHAN, *Understanding Media*, Routledge, 1964; Sphere, 1970.
Probably the most accessible of the many writings of this important,
disturbing and enigmatic critic.

6   Pop Music

DONALD J. HUGHES

1

It needs considerable imagination today to realize how difficult it was for anyone interested in music at the beginning of the century to follow up that interest. If you lived anywhere outside the very largest cities, you could have very little musical experience beyond what you made yourself. Professional concerts were even rarer than they are today; there might be a music-hall in the nearest centre of population, and in a cathedral city you could hear choral music. In the North there would be the town or factory brass band. Even if you played or sang yourself, comparatively little music was available in cheap printed editions much before the turn of the century.

This is why all children in respectable middle-class homes in Victorian England were expected to learn the piano. How else could they get musical experience? Obviously they could not join in the music-hall and public house songs. Later on they could join the local choral or operatic society and sing 'Messiah' or 'The Mikado'. But in general music, except what you sang in the bath, was a scarce commodity.

Now it is an axiom of economics that scarcity creates value. A man in the middle of the Sahara may be prepared to give a fortune for a glass of water that he would expect for nothing in a London restaurant. And a music-lover of the nineteenth century might have to make, and would probably be willing to make, considerable sacrifice of time and money to follow his hobby.

The arrival of the radio and record-player has made an almost unbelievable difference to this situation. For some people it has become a question not so much of sacrificing to experience music, as of being prepared to pay to get away from it. Music has become part of the noise system that surrounds our lives like air. It is indeed constantly on the air and in the air; it assails us in the home, in the factory, at the restaurant; and there are commercial firms that make a living recommending the right kind of background music to anyone who may ask – be he manager of a shop for selling expensive gowns, or a dentist or an undertaker.

All this means that there is a strong temptation today to under-value music, to take it for granted. Even thirty-five years ago the composer and conductor Constant Lambert wrote a book in which he complained of 'the appalling popularity of music'. Moreover, the persistent absorption of music by the ear and mind cannot be without effect. One recalls the subliminal advertising which consists of throwing messages on to the cinema or tele-vision screen for such a short space of time that the mind does not consciously identify and record their meaning, but they are received by the subconscious mind and are thereby able to in-fluence the watcher. We may not listen to the background music, we may not consciously take it in, but it is likely to affect our musical values, and maybe even our ability to appreciate other music. There is even a distinct possibility that the constant assault on our ears and nervous system by too many and too frequent decibels has a harmful physical effect; experiments carried out with teenagers in America have produced strong evidence to suggest that serious damage to hearing does often follow the kind of exposure to fully amplified music which any youth club or pop festival supplies today.

But, while the increase in sheer noise is plain for all to see and hear, the insidiousness of the quiet but permanent background of wallpaper music which creeps in our ears may be less appreciated. Surely the first requisite for discrimination (which is the theme of this book) is awareness. But the essence of the piped music which is now provided at will is that you should not be aware of it. The industrial worker engaged day by day in a monotonous repetitive task may well be thankful for a background noise of musical sounds; it may also be quite possible that his produc-tivity will be greater because of it; but he is not, and must not be, fully conscious of the music in the background. However repeti-tive his task it requires some of his attention, and so he cannot be fully aware of the music.

134

The content of such music is therefore deliberately kept simple, and indeed empty – empty not only of technical complexity but of emotional intensity; for both are equally distracting. So those who like music as a background to other activities are right to reject the music of Beethoven and Bach, because such music does not fit into the category.

It may well be, then, that the cultivation of any very general sense of discrimination where music is concerned will require as a prerequisite a concentrated campaign against the menace of background noise – both the very loud which devastates the most delicate of all man's physiological possessions, the ear, and the discreetly soft, which drugs and dulls. And those who are currently trying to attract the young to symphonic music by playing it to them in fully amplified, Woodstock-size versions may know something of the problem, but cannot be complimented on having found a solution. This is not helping discrimination.

2

But a great deal of modern popular music is worth attention, and is attended to by many. Let us trace some of its origins.

Over the years there have developed two different traditions in music. One is what we call 'art music', or (wrongly) classical music. In this the composer puts down his ideas on paper as exactly as possible, and the duty of the performer is to give as accurate an interpretation as he can of what the composer wrote, playing the 'correct' notes in the 'correct' time.

On the other hand, there is a tradition of popular music, or, as it is more commonly called, folk music, which has somewhat different characteristics. First of all, and fundamentally, the popular music tradition is an aural one. Tunes are handed down from one singer to another, and often change in the process. A singer may take liberties with a tune, may alter the notes or the rhythm, may purposely attack a note below pitch (as blues singers often do). There are some accepted common habits of performance, and an instrumentalist will harmonize a tune by ear with certain conventional and well-worn patterns of chords.

The two traditions have not always been as far apart and as

135

clearly differentiated as they are today. It is of course only since music began to be written down in accurate notation that the extended compositions of the classical writers have been possible; and even up to the time of Handel and Mozart in the eighteenth century a good deal of improvisation took place in the performance of art music. But, as time went on, the two streams diverged more sharply. As every aspect of life became more prone to specialization, the composer of art music became more and more a professional writing for an educated audience, mainly aristocratic or middle-class, and more out of touch with the peasant or factory worker. In England, the folk tradition itself lost a great deal of its hold on everyday life because the old communities were broken up and destroyed by the Industrial Revolution; and it was only about 1900 that Cecil Sharp and others began to collect and to attempt to breathe a new life into the old folksongs and dances. But while we owe them an incalculable debt for rescuing a great many lovely tunes which might otherwise have been lost, they did not always sufficiently realize that the old order in which this music had flourished had changed, and that much of it was irrelevant to a new society.

It was about the same time as this that jazz was making its first appearance in and around New Orleans. Many influences went to the making of jazz; but nearly all of them stemmed from the popular tradition – the Negro's songs of oppression, the dances of the Spaniards, and the African rhythms brought via the West Indies. Only the brass band music could be called partially an influence from the tradition of Western written music; and indeed the regular four-in-a-bar underlying pulse and the simple harmonic structures of the band marches were among the most important European elements in jazz. But it was by borrowing these and using them in the context of the popular tradition, with a great deal of improvisation, that the early jazz performers developed their characteristic music.

Jazz, in its traditional form at least, is true folk music. It has all the qualities listed above as typical of folk music and distinct from art music; and it is well known that many traditional players – not merely the amateurs – cannot read music.

It is true that in its modern style jazz is much less of a spon-

136

taneous improvised music. Both the commercial-style big band music and the intellectual conceptions of the modernists are of a very different order from trad. Yet no living means of artistic expression stands still. There is always development, and inevitably the original form of free-and-easy traditional jazz has been followed by many changes, most of which have been in the direction either of a larger grouping of instrumentalists or of more complex and sophisticated harmonies – both of which lead away from the true popular style and demand written arrangements and trained, rehearsed musicians.

Yet at the same time it is true that, whether it be mainstream or modern, or just plain commercial, you can usually trace the origin of each number to one or the other of the two basic traditional jazz forms – the blues, with its lazy, dragging rhythm, its set harmonic structure and its characteristic nostalgic note of oppression or of the frustrated search for the unattainable; or alternatively the high-spirited, noisy brashness of the four-in-a-bar quickstep rhythm, deriving from the old band marches, enlivened by the syncopating improvisations of Negro jazz musicians.

Thus the development of jazz as seen in the big bands of Duke Ellington and the commercial swing combinations of the thirties, and equally by the small 'chamber' groups, is natural and proper. Many may still prefer the spontaneity and the uninhibitedness of traditional jazz, with its simple sequences of well-used chords and its insistence on improvisation by the melody instruments; but this is not to deny to the other manifestations the name of jazz. No one can listen to the Modern Jazz Quartet or the Dave Brubeck Quartet, for example, without realizing that music has in it the essence of the jazz spirit. In both groups the drummer will create just that beat, whether it be the relaxed withheld swing of the slow blues tempo, or the exciting onward thrust of the quick movements, which is one of the hallmarks of good jazz. The curious and fascinating combinations of sound which both quartets derive from their choice of instruments may be far removed from the unsophisticated trumpet, clarinet or saxophone; and the chord progressions may contain a good deal of the chromatic harmonies of the late nineteenth-century

137

art music and be less instinctive and more worked out. But the quality and spirit are undeniably the quality and spirit of jazz.

But there is one particular feature of the original jazz which is of special interest to us. Because this music belongs to the tradition of music handed down aurally, music which is not put into permanent written form before performance, its underlying pattern must be basically simple. Thus, we have the blues form with its established formula of a twelve-bar sequence of chords. The strict blues always keeps to this same pattern of chords; it is a most restricted form, and it is amazing how much variety has been obtained within it. It is a formula which is ideal for its purposes of aurally improvised music. Every singer and performer knows the harmonic pattern and feels it instinctively through long familiarity; thus they can improvise freely within the framework. On the other hand, the rigidity of the scheme makes it unsuitable for large-scale development. It is not surprising that no one has ever written a successful 'blues' symphony. 'Rhapsody in Blue' does not use the normal blues formula, and in any case its great weakness is its scrappiness, its lack of cohesion. It is equally true that few of the art composers of the written tradition have successfully produced large-scale compositions using folk melodies. Once again we see that the essential characteristics of folk and popular music are spontaneity and immediacy, as opposed to the long span of most art music, where one of the most important things is to be able to remember what happened two or three minutes ago, and to relate it to what you are hearing now.

So an old favourite like 'Alexander's Ragtime Band' is recorded – many years ago now – by the traditional New Orleans team led by Bunk Johnson; and the number consists of seven oi eight variations improvised over the basic harmonic pattern of the tune. No development occurs, and no contrasting material is introduced; the formula is as simple as that of the blues, and as appropriate for the purpose.

3

For a long time jazz and its offspring – a bastard offspring, some would say – ballroom dance music, held sway. The commercial values of white American society and the need for an easy, not too intellectual communal recreation for the population of their great cities led to the creation of a vast entertainment industry which utilized the new Negro music for its own purpose. This industry was able to make use of men like Duke Ellington and Benny Goodman, but inevitably the music they provided altered in character from the old-style jazz.

Now both jazz and dance music, with their reliance on largely conventional instruments, still need a technical skill in performance which removes them to some degree from the purely spontaneous, and limits the number who can perform it. It was partly because of this that in the 1950s there grew up a new type of folk music. This music was skiffle.

For many years the hit tunes had been usually straightforward dance band melodies – a fox-trot or a waltz, or perhaps a Latin-American rhythm. Occasionally a sentimental ballad number might have a turn, or a song hit from a show, like 'Old Man River' or 'The Lambeth Walk'. Then came the gradual spread of interest in other types of American folk song – the hillbilly, the 'country and western', the music of Burl Ives and Josh White. Suddenly the teenage world was hit by skiffle. Boys discovered the fascination of a new easy-going form of spontaneous music-making in which the principal elements were guitars used as rhythmic and harmonic background to folky melodies ranging from spirituals and blues to cowboy songs. It was easier to play and sing skiffle than jazz; and it required none of the formal knowledge of written music. It became almost in a matter of weeks an occupation for thousands of performers and many more of their followers.

The commercial world at once saw that here was a perfect vehicle for the mass recording process. Lyrics which 'belonged', basically simple but rhythmic tunes, and a set type of instrumental accompaniment. All that was needed was to 'hot up' the style, to amplify the guitars (the electric guitar is not just a

139

different instrument from the orthodox variety, it is a much inferior one), to make full use of echo chambers and the rest of the recording gimmicks, and to find one or two recording artists of the right kind.

The social student of pop culture will probably feel that the above summary exaggerates the importance of the skiffle vogue. He will argue that the pop era really began with Bill Haley, Elvis Presley and the rock-and-roll craze which set the teenagers tapping and jiving. But these artists were using precisely the musical techniques which were also the basis of skiffle; and the latter symbolized the do-it-yourself impulse which may truly be described as popular in the sense of 'by and of the people', in contrast to the recorded and broadcast music of the stars, which was 'for and to the people'.

Skiffle was unquestionably the most universally popular music of our generation. It broke through all barriers except those of age. Between the ages of eight and eighteen there can have been few inhabitants of Britain, whatever their class, education or intelligence – down to the half-wits – who did not, for however short a period, take some active pleasure in it.*

In line with the normal order of events, the basic folk style was adapted and widely disseminated through the medium of recording, and in the process tended to lose much of its original character and integrity.

It was certainly in these last years of the fifties that pop culture in its musical aspect really established itself. Publishing firms and record companies had not done badly out of the hit music of earlier decades, but the teenage market was only now growing to that state of affluence where there was money to spend and no responsibilities on which to spend it. It was the mass media that took the new music and made it a part of the daily existence and the life pattern of their young clients. 'I Remember You' sold 102,500 copies in one day, and a quarter of a million was a fair average for a Top Ten winner.

We had seen the same process at work with jazz, though in a less frighteningly rapid way. It was only the existence of records and radio that enabled jazz to sweep the world as it did. But for

*Francis Newton, *The Jazz Scene*.

these aids it would doubtless have remained a localized folk music native to the Southern States of its origin. It would have spread to Chicago and those northern towns where Negroes had settled in considerable numbers, and might have attained some popularity among local whites. But it would no more have become a common interest of millions throughout the world than have the polkas and dumkas of Bohemia, or the scottisches and reels of the Highlands. The fortunate circumstance was that an exciting and upspringing new music grew up in a country which was the first to adapt itself to mass production and which had the opportunity of wide diffusion which came from the growth of mechanical reproduction.

Though some people deplore the fact that jazz has had such popularity thrust upon it through the workings of commercial enterprise, it is surely unreasonable to complain because so many people in so many countries have been enabled to enjoy a new experience. Yet the inevitable effects of mass reproduction of music, and particularly of folk music, are not all good. We have seen that one of the chief features of folk music is its spontaneity, its immediacy. If, on the spur of the moment, a folk musician feels like altering the tune, or improvising, he is entitled to do so. Like the comedian in pantomime, he is allowed and even expected to gag. The music is intimate, and a folk singer is in his element when performing to a small group of his associates, in intimate surroundings; there is a direct *rapport* between him and his audience, which derives from the fact that they belong to a common society and share a common inheritance.

Now these conditions are the precise opposite to those of commercial recording. What is wanted here is something which will appeal to a vast international audience; what by the nature of things has to be put on disc is something fixed and unchangeable; direct contact and mutual sparking off of enthusiasms between performers and listeners is impossible.

All this might suggest that traditional jazz and the skiffle types which derive from it are the most unsuitable kinds of music for recording purposes. And indeed this is to a large extent true. Such music is best enjoyed 'off the cuff' when you join with a crowd of enthusiasts like yourself at the jazz club or the coffee

141

bar, and the music itself lights up from the environment, and the players are possessed by the occasion.

Some of the best records, of classical music as well as of pop, have been made under conditions of normal public performance. But in general the technique of the recording studio is utterly removed from spontaneity. Takes and re-takes continue until a performance is passed as perfect; and the final issued version may be a synthetic construction from a number of performances joined together by tape and scissors as a film is cut and patched.

Inevitably this affects the style of the music recorded. If a number is to be rehearsed several times, and if the eventual result is going to be placed on permanent record, there is every reason for sticking to a written arrangement, and limiting improvisation as much as possible. And if a record needs to sell tens of thousands of copies and have an international market, it is natural to attempt to produce what is known to be acceptable and popular.

Record companies thus find themselves in the position of every operator of a mass medium of communication, which the Pilkington Committee on broadcasting so well described when they said that the programmes provided and viewed by millions are not necessarily the most popular in that they are everybody's, or indeed anybody's first choice; but they are tolerated enough to be accepted by more viewers than any alternative. Such alternatives might be more eagerly awaited and enjoyed by many, but would not be accepted by others, who in their turn would have their own positive first preferences. A middle-of-the-road mediocrity, offending no one, is the inevitable result.

The achievement of the business interests in Tin Pan Alley and the recording companies has been to manufacture a music for the new folk on the largest possible scale. They have done this, as such things must be done, by a process of standardization, by providing an article which will be accepted by most of the people most of the time.

4

There is then a conflict between the needs of the small spontaneous community and the audience which the mass media demand. The paradox with which we have to come to terms is that the very factor which makes it possible for everyone to share in whatever music most completely expresses the feeling of the time is also the agency which tends to destroy any personal and individual expression. As Colin MacInnes has said: 'As for any regional origin, if the group is successful . . . the local idiom soon vanishes. The move from the maypole (or cellar) to the international recording studio can happen almost overnight.' Yet, true though this is in general, the nature of pop music does change in ways not entirely due to the moguls of money-music. The story of the Beatles best illustrates this. They were indeed just such a local group as MacInnes had in mind. They possessed a real originality which gave to their own compositions a certain new flavour which was one of the main causes of their immense popularity. There was something of a new sound; and few pop addicts could have told you in what the newness consisted. But much was made by interested music critics of a modal flavour in the melodies and harmonies of their numbers. This may have been partly derived from experiments up and down the strings of the guitar, which is well-designed for producing harmonies of consecutive and parallel triads; and the more purely instrumental groups before the Beatles had discovered these possibilities. But to most listeners there was certainly something of a more native folk sound which contrasted with the harmonies of the blues and the trad jazz tunes and the rock numbers of American pop-folk.

Out of the ranks of the pop groups themselves had come this new sound; and before long it was widely imitated. Out of any selection of hit tunes today not many will conform to the American pattern of square Victorian-type harmonies and regular four-bar phrases; there will be modal-type progressions, ostinatos (notes or short passages constantly repeated) and other features first made prominent by the Beatles. But the Beatles' own development shows a steady trend away from their Merseyside beginnings. Their earliest hits are straightforward, spontaneous tunes with originality and vitality. Before long the arrangements were becoming much more sophisticated and the free and direct folk element correspondingly less. 'Sergeant Pepper' and 'Abbey Road' were hailed as triumphant examples of the progress of

143

pop; but they are also an indication of the difficulty which any group has in our present cosmopolitan and incoherent society in maintaining a firmly based identity. The flirtation with Indian music is only one aspect of this. The final break-up of the group can be seen as arising from a failure to sustain a real integrity of purpose in the face of the conflicting stresses of the restless outside world.

Since the Beatles there have been further considerable changes in the musical scene which emphasize the vitality present in pop. There is a significant growth within the pop world of the same kind of intellectual movement which one has seen also in jazz. Symptomatic of this is the swing in the sale of records from single 45's to the long-playing albums; the more progressive pop artists will only think today in terms of LPs; nor do they measure their music in terms of the lyric, with its set pattern, its 32-bar stanzas, and so on. Groups like the Pink Floyd and The Who are concerned mainly with instrumental sounds, with developing their music along lines sometimes as abstract as those of the classical symphonists. Like the modern jazz combinations, many of these groups perform mainly to smaller audiences like university and college clubs. Their music covers a wide range and many styles; there are echoes of Messiaen, of Ketelbey, of modern jazz. Much of the music is pretentious and naïve; the attempt to run to large-scale and quite lengthy compositions is rarely completely successful because of the ramshackle organization of ideas. (The more improvisation drops out, the more ideas derived from other forms of music creep in; and when improvisation remains, the harder it is to sustain interest in a long-term structure.) But the objective quality of the music is one of the least important things; what is significant is that out of pop there has now grown a substantial movement of both performers, who aim to express themselves with some seriousness of purpose, and listeners, who are quite ordinary young people, by no means all of them in the intellectual category, who spend selectively on LPs and listen with real discrimination to their choices. To these the commercial single is as unsatisfying as it is to most older squares.

The conclusion must be that in truth we are faced with a pop culture which contains in it a great deal that springs from the spirits and minds of those who follow it, however mingled this may be with the imposed stereotypes which the mass media still provide. Some of the new race of highbrow pop critics who write now in the daily press and weekly reviews overstate the case in claiming for this music qualities which can only come from an art which has matured over centuries; but this is not to deny the potential importance of this development.

Given this situation, the mass media cannot be seen only as hostile elements. They have encouraged much that is puerile; they have offered an assembly-line product and reduced individual creative impulse to a mechanical process; Radio One bores and ossifies with the staggering imbecility of most of its disc jockey chatter. *But* they have also, in a quite unprecedented way, made available to all the riches of the whole of music, art and popular, and therefore given them the opportunity of choice. The 'teenybopper' still goes in mainly for the singles currently in the charts; and the more discriminating (and usually slightly older) enthusiast chooses his LPs with care and listens to them with concentration.

For the educationist the essential thing is to keep the choice real and to encourage that seriousness of attention, that *valuing* of music, which will enable discrimination to play its part.

5

The folk songs of past communities came to most of the older of us through the revival work of men like Baring Gould and Cecil Sharp; and in the process they lost a great deal of their vitality and contemporary significance. Only through the work of later experts like A. L. Lloyd (cf. his *The Singing Englishman*) did people begin to realize the extent of social and political comment which is implicit or explicit in many of these songs. This awareness was well-established by the time the new American folk artists like Ives became well-known.

When the first novelty of skiffle wore off the majority of devotees turned towards the primitive forcefulness and rhythmic energy of rock. But a quite considerable minority broadened their experience in another way. Some were discovering not only the more common of American folk music songs – 'The Streets of Loredo', 'John Henry', and 'I'm Just a Poor Wayfaring Stranger '– but also the wealth of West Indian tunes – 'Linstead Market', 'Bahama Lullaby', etc. – Scottish bothy ballads and even our English heritage. The interest in American urban folk spilt over into something of a folk revival; Ewan MacColl and others popularized the industrial songs. The educationists still tore their hair because youngsters re-arranged in their own way the traditional melodies – as though this was not precisely what folk musicians have done since the beginning of time – but folk clubs began to find their way into the pubs. There were not all that many of them, but it was, and remains, a significant movement. Before long folk turned its next corner. All over the Western world there was a slow growth of the social consciousness and the revolt of the young which has been a feature of the sixties; and the songs of protest began to appear.

The lyrics of pop songs can teach us a good deal about the pop lovers. It is, after all, always easier to write and talk about words than about music. Obviously the theme of a pop song must be relevant – it must be 'about' one of the universal themes which appeal to all. Of these, the girl–boy motif is the surest winner, more especially since the growth of the teenage market has led to a special assault on that section of the community. In earlier decades other themes have had a long run for their money; the local state-love of the American led to a whole era of songs praising Wyoming, Alabama, Mississippi, Omaha; Hawaiian islands and coal-black mammies have also had their turn. But the love theme is the most universal. However, it must be love of a very romantic and sentimental nature. In the twenties they sang

> We'll have a blue room, a new room, for two room,
> Where every day's a holiday, because you're married to me.

Today it is

> Come outside, there's a lovely moon out there,
> Come outside while we've got time to spare.

There may occasionally be the lyric of the frustrated lover, but it is rarely the frustration of ordinary human circumstance; the

146

singer and the object of his or her song inhabit a dream world, seated as it were on remote clouds of insubstantial candy-floss, with nothing to think about but their romantic emotions.

In this respect there is a great difference between the real folk jazz and the pop. The blues singers did not tell of an idealized world but of a very real one where pain and trouble were common experience – where music and song might help you to overcome trouble but not by pretending it didn't exist. Jazz has been called a music of protest; and in so far as it came from a slave people, a racially oppressed people, it was just this. In this lay some of its appeal to the industrialized city dwellers, who themselves knew what oppression meant, and who felt the heartache of the blues.

> Now it's ashes to ashes, sweet papa, dust to dust,
> I said ashes to ashes, I mean dust to dust:
> Now show me the man any woman can trust.

That sort of integrity was rarely found in the lyrics of the pop which came in with Presley, Chuck Berry and others; these belonged to the world where June rhymes with moon, where there is no such thing as struggle for existence, where love does not have to be striven for through understanding.

> Dream, dream, baby;
> Dream, dream, baby;
>   How long must I dream?
> Dream, dream, baby;
>   You can make my dreams come true.

Not often did there come to them the spirit of delight which led Cliff Richard to sing:

> You are a stick of dynamite
> Sitting on a coffee bar stool.

At the time that the folk revival got its first real head of steam the commercial lyrics were at their most empty and banal. And it was a main achievement of this revival that it brought back to the songs of the people a broader basis of experience and feeling. Only a few songs since have challenged in poetry and popularity that early lyric of Pete Seeger.

147

> Where have all the flowers gone,
>   Long time passing,
> Where have all the flowers gone,
>   Long time ago?
> Where have all the flowers gone?
>   Young girls picked them every one.
>   When will they ever learn?
>
> Where have all the young girls gone, etc...
>   Gone to young men every one.
>
> Where have all the young men gone, etc...
>   Gone to soldiers every one.
>
> Where have all the soldiers gone, etc...
>   Gone to graveyards every one.
>
> Where have all the graveyards gone, etc...
>   Gone to flowers every one.
>   When will they ever learn?

But before long Bob Dylan had taken protest into the charts. Many of these new socially motivated songs were a genuine response to strongly felt emotions on issues of race and apartheid, on peace and Vietnam. Seeger had them singing about the little boxes in which they lived; Dylan gave them an answer which was 'blowin' in the wind'; and singers like Joan Baez appear at the Woodstock Festival and others alongside the biggest of the commercial names.

Any selection of hits today contains at least some numbers which treat of a different theme from the conventional boy–girl motif. Though one still hears such conventionalities as

> And for ever
>   There'll be a new world where all our dreams come true
>   To-morrow,

words are often more significant than they were. We see again a broadening of the pop scene; turn on to any session of Radio One or any commercial station in the U.S.A. or Canada and the odds are that you will hear lyrics as puerile as ever; search around in the discotheques, particularly among the albums, and you may be better satisfied.

6

I have written in some detail about progressive pop and about folk protest because these are the two aspects which over the last few years have given the greatest hope of a creative future for the new music which has grown out of the popular tradition of the century. But of course the majority of young people are still predominantly influenced by the commercial pop of television, Radio One and the record companies' singles.

At the time of the reconstitution of B B C radio programmes early in 1970 there was an interesting discussion in the 'Radio Times' between Pete Townshend, of The Who, George Melly, and Douglas Muggeridge, Controller of Radio One. Melly expressed the view that 'Radio One has at this moment a tremendous potential and it's not taking it. I think the reason it's not taking it is because it appears to refuse to admit that there is in this country an enormous body of young people aged something between 12 and 15 who are wide open to the idea that culture can be open-ended. They admire John Peel, who plays a pop record followed by a bit of Scarlatti and somebody reading a poem, and these kids will listen. But in the morning they're faced with disc jockeys who are dinosaurs left over from pirate radio, and who appear to be totally unaware that they have an enormous audience that can be moved in the direction of a broader culture.' Muggeridge's reply was 'The audience for progressive pop is very important, but tiny in comparison with the total audience for Radio One. You're suggesting that Tony Blackburn comes off and John Peel goes on in the morning from 7 to 9. If we did that we would drop an audience which can be up to 15 million over that two-hour period to an audience of something like 2 to 3 million. We would leave unsatisfied the vast majority of people who wish to listen to Radio One. How could we then justify the radio licence?'

The two opposed attitudes are clearly set out here; on the one hand the positive attempt to provide an ever-broadening range of styles to choose from – Melly was 'talking about widening taste, not lifting it'; on the other the tendency so prevalent in all the media to draw up tight categories – a process brought to its final

149

fulfilment as far as British broadcasting is concerned by the recent division of BBC sound time into its four typed programmes with no overlapping.

One can only agree with Melly's criticism of the disc jockeys. The musical fare on Radio One is generally restricted enough to make it tolerable for long only as that background music which is in the long run so destructive of attentive minds; but to have to suffer as well the moronic comments of the DJs is too much. They belong to the world of the aural strip cartoon; their introduction of every record is couched in superlatives; one would be impelled to write in protest to the BBC did one not know that pirate radio and commercial broadcasting in the U.S.A. are worse. With very few exceptions they represent one of the most stultifying influences at work in the media.

In folk music proper the performer is important because of his direct creative contribution. An enthusiast looks on the label of a jazz record not for the composer of a piece, but for the performers. In pop the performer's personality is important, but for a rather different reason. For the number to catch on, the record-buyer must be able to identify himself with it; just as the theme should be one of the universals, so the singer should be an ordinary chap – one of us. The teenage idol need bring no very great musical or technical skill to his work; but he must attract the fans, and they must be able to feel that the romantic idealized world in which he lives (in public) is one which they too, Walter Mitty-like, may inhabit.

An excellent idea of the way in which the modern publicity machine builds up the chosen artist in order to project him to the world may be gained by reading the very frank description of the launching of Tommy Steele given by his manager, John Kennedy. Gimmicks, deliberate inventions (which some people would call 'lies') and constant expenditure to keep the star in public view are all part of the tactics. With the best of them, like Steele himself, their own character and personality may carry them beyond a merely ephemeral fame; the majority do not survive their promoter's favour, and are dependent on the publicity process

150

for such success as they attain. Although the hysterical scenes associated with the early days of pop are less common today, this build-up of the performer remains and is likely to remain an important part of the pop process.

A comparatively recent growth is the large-scale pop festival – like Woodstock or the Isle of Wight. As usual the truth about these events lies in the middle ground between the extremes of comment which they have evoked. They are *not* just lawless drug-taking sexual orgies; neither are they the final apotheosis of a free peaceful community which has solved all the problems of life. Organizers of such festivals may reasonably be proud of the general spirit which prevails; but anyone with personal knowledge of other large-scale musical get-togethers of young people, such as the big youth choir festivals held in Europe, with three to five thousand involved, will know that exactly the same thing is true of these. For a few days one can live in perfect harmony with one's fellows. The glory of music is its ability to demand and receive cooperation from performers and to create a sense of common purpose and communal enjoyment. One knows also that the problems of the world cannot be solved just by vague goodwill or good intentions; they need much hard thought, hard work and sometimes hard talk. And so the claim to have found a new way of living, a new society, is no more than the excited exaggeration that is proper to young people; the Woodstock spirit is a marvellous thing, but there are still 3,500 million people in the world to be fed, and that means work, and government, and all the difficult things that the hippiest of the popsters seem to want to do without.

Besides comparable musical occasions there are other parallels to the pop festivals, some more pleasant than others. There is almost the fervour of a religious revivalist meeting; so, one feels, must the early Wesleyans have felt at a rally under their founder. Less happily, one thinks also of Nuremberg – the first place where the power of the microphone and of modern mass communications was fully realized and utilized. The crowd psychology, its fervour and hysteria can impart a sense of belonging which is

151

beyond rational conviction. The Nazis at their rallies felt they belonged. But the quality of what you belong to matters a lot.

In this respect the pop festivals must be rated something of a disappointment, though not in the Nuremberg class. Musically they emphasize the weakness of the appeal through mechanical reproduction; the music tends to a repetitiveness, a battering of sheer noise and obsessive rhythm which inhibits any subtlety or anything but the crudest emotions. The decibel content is overwhelming – and, incidentally, an invasion on the privacy of the neighbourhood, however well-behaved in other respects the participants may be. The hypnotic effect of sheer noise is in fact one of the most disturbing characteristics of modern pop, and deserves serious investigation on medical and psychological grounds.

7

The position of pop music today may now be seen as confused, contradictory and very difficult to assess accurately and with balanced judgement.

There is, firstly, the genuine spontaneous element of the folk, which burst forth in skiffle, out of which later came the Beatles' Merseyside sound. At the moment there is no very strong grassroots movement perceptible. But folk remains the music which comes most easily to the untrained music-maker, and should therefore strongly engage the attention of teachers. Unfortunately too many of these swing too easily from one extreme to another. Some continue to offer to the less devoted of their pupils the academic partsongs of the art tradition; others have learnt the lesson that improvisation and spontaneity are more important to the ordinary boy or girl than the formality of the printed copy and the studiously learnt descant. But too often they adopt gimmicky approaches, in which the sound of a car passing in the street outside, or the tearing of paper in front of a microphone are regarded as sounds of as much musical significance as the song of a human voice or the sound of a musical instrument: such educationists fail to see that music with just the qualities they seek – and attractive to teenagers – lies directly in front of their noses in folk.

Then there is the commercialized pop – the basic offering of Radio One. This is still the main fare of the younger element. It is here that we find the stereotyped product, the banal lyric and assembly-line tune, the rhythmic poverty which aims to build up excitement simply by repetition. It is with the followers of this kind of music that one needs to widen experience, to show that there are other choices and other styles.

Finally there is the so-called progressive pop. Here the media in the shape of the record companies make the material available, though its share of time on the radio channels is limited. Here lies the clearest picture of pop as a culture, in which a developing growth may take place, certainly not uninfluenced by the machine but equally not entirely led by it. Much of the output is gimmicky, shallow and pretentious; but these are inevitable growing pains.

Richard Mabey, in his interesting book *The Pop Process*, clearly makes the case that pop is, for its adherents, a whole culture, pervading all aspects of their lives; and his analysis shows that it is partly a natural response of young people to the world that they live in today, and partly manufactured by the manipulators of opinion and taste. As part of a more general culture which has grown so staggeringly in the past two decades pop music will mirror that culture and will be a vehicle for expressing the experience of its members. If the culture is limited the music will be limited. If the culture is one of narrow images, if its members are artistically inarticulate because no serious attempt has been made to develop their capabilities of artistic self-expression, the result may well be a stereotyped music lit up only occasionally, and then as often as not by the hallucinatory over-charged primitivism which is a mark of such artists as the Rolling Stones and Jimi Hendrix.

It has taken art music several centuries to reach that maturity where it can express the whole of human experience from the sublimities of the Missa Solemnis to the homespun naturalness of 'The Bartered Bride'. It has been in the main the art of a fairly small minority, but it has grown from a solid foundation of established belief and tradition in European society.

Artistic development more than almost any other human

153

activity is a product of personality, and that personality must depend fundamentally on a coherent social background which produces a strongly rooted tradition. It is a paradox that twentieth-century man seems determined to combine a narrow political nationalism with a searching for a vague and inevitably rather superficial international culture, when the necessities of the modern world cry out for a political internationalism, together with a sense of firmly-based local community in social, cultural and artistic respects. Hence the cosmopolitanism of the mass media and the cross-breeding of American, West Indian, Indian and Merseyside into one product is liable to lead to superficial results.

Throughout history, as democracy has gathered force, it has at each move led to a temporary decline of standards as new groups are brought into the circle – groups which have not previously had the privilege of developing their tastes and their potentialities. The swooning teenagers who mob Haley, the Beatles, the Rolling Stones, have their counterparts in the hysterical young ladies who fainted at the sight of Franz Liszt at the piano or Paganini with his violin. Both were a new class bowled over by the emotional impact of the new thing in their lives.

Earlier, at the time of the Renaissance, the boundaries of man's knowledge were being suddenly and widely extended, as they are today. A new music, too, was being created, establishing new patterns of musical form and new techniques of expression which paved the way for the whole flowering of European art music from that time.

Maybe we are today on the verge of a new Renaissance. But today it is not only the leisured aristocracy who have the new knowledge at their disposal; it is everyman. A new music in the twentieth century will not come from the professional composer or the intellectual music-lover alone; it will not come from jazz alone, because too much of the essential meaning of jazz belongs only to the American Negro. It will not be the product of a mass medium of communication, but these will help immeasurably to propagate it. It will grow only if new generations continue to see and use music as more than a background, more than a business,

as a personal expression of all that they themselves feel most
deeply and believe in most fully.

BOOKS

N. HENTOFF and N. SHAPIRO (eds), *Hear Me Talkin' to Ya*, Penguin
  Books, 1962. Jazz men talking informally about their music and
  background.

DONALD HUGHES, *Let's Have Some Music*, Museum Press, 1965.
  Attempts to bring all kinds of music under one cover; written for
  teenagers.

JOHN KENNEDY, *Tommy Steele*, Souvenir Press. Kennedy was Steele's
  manager. A frank and entertaining book.

A. L. LLOYD, *The Singing Englishman*, Workers' Music Association.
  The English folk-song story from an unusual but challenging
  angle.

RICHARD MABEY, *The Pop Process*, Hutchinson, 1969. An interesting
  account of the whole growth of the pop movement.

GEORGE MELLY, *Revolt into Style*, Penguin Books, 1972. A recent
  book by one of the soundest commentators on the pop scene.

REGINALD NETTEL, *The Englishman Makes Music*, Phoenix. Some
  account of the social background of English musical life.

FRANCIS NEWTON, *The Jazz Scene*, Penguin Books, 1961. The best
  short introduction to jazz.

7   Magazines

with special reference to the
exploitation of pseudo-sexuality

DAVID HOLBROOK

Every day in the local paper shop the assistants dispatch a large
pile of periodicals. Among them are technical and professional
papers, such as the *Police Review, Buses Illustrated,* the *Off-
licence Journal,* the *British Bandsman,* the *Funeral Service Journal*
and the *Farmer's Weekly.* There are papers for members of small
sects or groups: *Dziennik Polska,* the *Baptist Times,* and the
Short Wave Magazine. There are children's papers: *Tiger and
Jag, Playhour, Mad,* and *Look and Learn.* There are women's
papers – many are women's papers – *Woman, Woman's Realm,
Nursery World, The Lady, Mother and Baby, Woman and Baby,
Woman and Home, Woman's Story.* There are some newer
'sharp' journals for women like *Nova* and *Vanity Fair.* There are
men's papers: *Farmer's Weekly, Motor Sport, Hot Cars, Guns
and Ammo.* There are papers for adolescent girls: *Christian
Novels, Red Letter, Mirabelle, Valentine.* Others such as *Weekend,
Reveille* and *Titbits* are taken for 'the family' (and are probably
read by children, too). There are papers for special interests and
hobbies: *Prediction,* the *Bee Journal,* and *Melody Maker.*

Among these are journals which represent serious intellectual
interests, some of which (like the more specialist journals) are
usually available only on order – the *Listener,* the *New Statesman,*
the *Spectator* and so on. To these we must add the 'underground'
press – *Black Dwarf, IT,* or *International Times,* and *Oz,* and a
new range of bold 'sex' magazines, such as *Penthouse, Curious,
Forum* and *Man and Woman.*

The *Writers' and Artists' Yearbook* lists about seven hundred
journals, and this omits both local provincial papers and some
of the more technical and trade journals such as the *Fish Trades
Gazette* and the *Meat Trades Journal.*

Some of these magazines are remarkable technical achieve-

156

ments – as is *Vogue*, for instance. Printers, typographers, photographers, block-makers, art directors, and editors, all are highly skilled, and produce with accuracy and regularity millions of copies of beautifully printed magazines. Many, like *Valentine*, are, by comparison, inferior products – some twenty-eight pages of unevenly printed matter, with indistinct half-tone blocks, poor typography, crude drawings on yellowish-grey newsprint, much of the copy put together from handouts from the publicity offices of 'pop' star promoters. In between these extremes come all sorts: respectable papers, mediocre in appearance if efficiently produced, like most of the women's papers; elegant glossies like *Country Life*; and crudely produced papers, with poor impressions of saucy 'cheese-cake', and yellowish-grey copy, such as *Reveille*.

A good deal of the matter in popular commercial papers is obviously put together according to the time-honoured and rather crude principles that one finds laid down in courses on 'writing for profit'. But a good many popular articles have taken some serious effort to prepare, even articles which begin 'You're going to be a new woman – fitter, slimmer, healthier – because you've discovered that FITNESS IS FUN. Now continue your exercise programme under Dr Warren Child's expert guidance ...' or 'Under Canvas ... holiday in a tent. By parents of a two-year-old boy'.

Serious effort is still more evident in the technical papers and papers for specialists. Obviously, to write an article for *Farmer's Weekly*, or the *Illustrated Carpenter and Builder*, a contributor must not only be able to write, but must know his subject at first hand, or near enough first hand. Of this most useful, informative and instructive kind of periodical press, England probably has the most varied, numerous, and most widely circulating in the world. Such publications are a most valuable element in an educated democracy, and some represent important sectional groups who study and protect their own interests keenly and vigilantly. It was a small group of local anglers who some years ago won their case against Derby Corporation over river pollution, and forced the installation of purifying plant costing a million pounds. Such incidents, a mark of health in the community, are often the

157

result of a sense of cohesion, and an understanding of issues, rights and courses of action, among those interested in a particular field – footpaths, canals, historic buildings, noise, the protection of archaeological sites. Many important interests are expressed and championed by such specialist journals. So, apart from an occasional objection to their tendency towards typographical conservatism and mediocrity, one has nothing but respect for such periodicals as *Accountant*, *Aeromodeller*, *Aeronautics*, the *Amateur Ciné World*, *Amateur Gardening*, the *Amateur Historian*, the *Amateur Stage*, *Angling*, *Animal Ways*, the *Antique Collector*, *Apollo*, the *Aquarist and Pond-keeper*, and so on throughout the alphabet, right down to the *Yachtsman*. To these we may add the successful development of papers which, representing intelligent critical attitudes to our kind of society, have become wide-selling *because* they do not underestimate their public, such as *Which?* and *Where?* Besides these there are also many sound journals produced for professional groups or small minorities, such as the *Architectural Review*, the *Musical Times*, *Geological Magazine*, and the *Lancet*. Many of these are valuable in that they represent a disinterested preoccupation with 'the best that is thought and known' about their subject.

These valuable professional and minority publications, many having a specialist readership, do not represent the major cultural influence in the sphere of periodical publication in England today. They do not form the main arena for exchange of opinion nor on the other hand do they belong to the mass-sale magazines. Yet they are probably the most important section of all periodical journalism nowadays, because they represent at best what Mr Fred Inglis has called 'a community talking to itself'.

Indeed, they seem now to be of more positive value in this essential process of democracy than those papers which are supposed to serve the function of the irrigation of public opinion among the minority who should be informed and influential. We assume so often that, as education improves, our culture will move towards higher and higher standards. But is this true of our 'minority' periodical press? If we compare today's *New Statesman*, say, with the *Nation*, the *Adelphi*, or other papers of the twenties and thirties – has there been a steady improvement? If we examine the magazines on display in any university senior combination room, do our weekly journals really provide the serious critical arena we need – need especially since higher education has been expanded? If we compare them with their equivalents of a hundred years ago do we find they are equal in substance, influence, or width of effective public? If we compare the leading critical journals of the nineteenth century such as the *Westminster Review* or the *Quarterly Review* – available in some central and most university libraries – with our weeklies, we find that they are more serious, and more responsible, than ours – and less concerned to entertain. Perhaps only the *Listener, The Times Literary Supplement,* and the *Economist* come up to the weight and intellectual seriousness of (say) the *Edinburgh Review* or the *Quarterly Review*: nothing as influential today can equal the *Westminster* on which George Eliot worked for a time. Moreover, the readership of the more serious journals was not negligible numerically. The total readership of the nineteenth-century 'minority' publications has been estimated as 220,000 in 1812 in a population of about 10,000,000, of whom 1,000,000 lived in London.* The equivalent today would be over 1,000,000 really serious readers, and many more interested in 'instruction' as well as amusement. The discussion of public questions and aspects of morality, the concern with the quality of life, and the criticism of cultural matters, were responsible and related to learning and the values of civilization, at the level of higher education and learning.†

*Figures from R. G. Cox, in a Ph.D. Thesis at Manchester University. In 1804 the *Edinburgh Review* was read by 200,000 people; the *Quarterly Review* printed 12,000 in 1818; *Blackwoods* printed 5,000 in 1831; the *Westminster Review* 3,000; the *Examiner* sold 6,000 a week in 1895; the *Saturday Magazine,* 60,000 (1833); the *Cornhill* about 80,000; other figures are the *Penny Magazine,* 200,000; the *Mirror of Literature, Amusement and Instruction,* 80,000; *Chambers,* 50–80,000; *London Journal,* 170,000; the *Spectator,* 3,500. Journals were much more widely circulated from hand to hand, of course, in those days. See R. G. Cox, 'The Reviews and Magazines', *Pelican Guide to English Literature,* ed. Boris Ford, vol. 6.

†These assertions would take too long to substantiate in detail. The reader can turn to discussion of *The Report of the Select Committee on Public Libraries* (1849) quoted by the Hammonds in Chapter XVII of *The Age of the Chartists*; E. E. Kellett on *The Press in Early Victorian England.* See also L. Marchand, on *The Athenaeum*; M. M. Berrington on *The*

By contrast, our periodicals seem much more concerned, even at minority level, with entertainment rather than the 'irrigation of public opinion'. The need to entertain demands that the writers and reviewers, as George Eliot once complained, 'must always be saying bright things', and this has led to many journalistic vices so that university staff in the humanities, dissatisfied with the existing outlets, often attempt to produce serious papers of their own and reject 'the muddled and distracting powers of journalism' (Peter Abbs, *Tract One*, *The Politics of Imagination*, Gryphon Press, Llanon, Cardiganshire, 1971).

Although our 'minority' journals pride themselves on their 'enlightenment', they tend today to display a somewhat dogmatic coherence of attitude, a good deal of political expediency or horse-trading, and not a little narrow-mindedness (compared, say, with *Le Monde*). The *New Statesman* spoke of itself recently in these terms: 'There has never been so strong a need for a journal like the NS which is wholly independent and entirely dedicated to the improvement and enlightenment of society' (Paul Johnson on handing over to Richard Crossman in June 1970). But how 'independent' is it? In a recent article based on a study of this paper, Ian Robinson, editor of the *Human World*, saw the paper as representing a fairly clearly defined clique, with its own staunchly loyal public. A certain complacency and smugness pervade the *Statesman* on many issues (e.g. 'the inalienable right of a woman to decide on social grounds whether to bear an unwanted child') while one might also detect in its voice a 'hatred and distrust of the British people':

'Better the liberal élitism of the statute book than the reactionary populisms of the market-place. Referenda or plebiscites . . . notoriously confirm right-wing acts: they do not voice left-wing opinions' (the *New Statesman*). The will of the people is therefore whatever will get left-wing opinions past the opposition and onto the statute book; only one of the sets of civilised men represents the people.*

As Robinson says, such a passage depends heavily on the stock

---

Saturday Review; E. Everitt on *The Party of Humanity* and on *The Fortnightly*: and J. W. Robertson Scott, *The Story of the Pall Mall Gazette*.

*Ian Robinson in the *Human World*, February 1971.

responses of the already prejudiced reader, and the recognition of an assumption that there is only *one* true élite. The paper is also narrowly selective, even among left-wing opinion: Raymond Williams complains (in a private communication) that 'I haven't been allowed to write for the *New Statesman* for about eight years.'

By degrees, the established 'minority' journals have gradually been overcome by the effects of the increasing costs of producing them, and by their own nemesis in becoming institutions. The *New Statesman*, for instance, for a time employed a girl who, according to *The Times* Diary (7 June 1971), went round the editors of other papers, trying to urge them to give the magazine publicity. This kind of 'promotion' must surely lead to a decline of integrity? The present writer once tried to intervene in a series in the *Guardian* on 'permissiveness', but his article was returned with an indication that this series had not been planned by the editorial staff at all, but by the department concerned with increasing circulation, in connection with a series of television advertisements.

Are these not indications that, today, as Raymond Williams says, 'opinions are now subordinate to selling, and it is no longer even felt appropriate for content to be anything other than sales appeal, (*Communications*, p. 33). This represents a 'narrowing of the cultural conditions of democracy' (*op., cit.*, p. 34) not least because this is associated with the narrowing of ownership. In magazines this tendency goes not only with an increasing decline of serious debate, but an increasing exploitation of the symbolism of hate, by which greater 'impact' can be made.*

While undoubtedly there are areas in the 'serious' weeklies which are still deserving of attention, such as Raymond Williams's own reviews of television in the *Listener*, it would seem from a

*See *The Masks of Hate* by the present author. Symbols of hate are those which arouse primitive anxiety, hunger, rage or dread in the reader – and they include bare breasts, frightened faces, tarred and feathered figures, dead bodies, wounded men, and scenes of disaster. Where such images are justified by relevance to the news they would seem to be acceptable: too often, however, they are used to draw a shocked attention to advertisements. Dead Indians or sad-looking 'problem families' are often evidently displayed to draw attention to the glamorous drink ads in the colour supplements, for instance.

161

study of nineteenth-century journals that we have less by way of 'irrigation of public opinion' than the nineteenth-century reader. One's experience as an author is that there is less and less space for reviewing, while reviews seem to become less and less adequate. Newspapers and journals continually complain of shortage of space, while articles become shorter and shorter. There are few magazines with a wide general circulation which can take a substantial piece of writing of 2,000 words or more, at the level of a university audience. The direction of our minority magazines, and their columns, becomes increasingly taken up with journalists of a new and 'sharp' kind who belong to the new world of lively television commentary, with its parry and thrust, and the demand for a 'good show', rather than for considered judgement. Even magazines devoted to a 'sociological' or 'scientific' approach are edited by those with fiercely partisan views over such questions as pornography, who seem often to be resisting serious challenges to the 'permissive' orthodoxy. This is partly an ideological matter: strictly rational and 'objective' criteria are believed to be the exclusive road to truth (see Roger Poole, *Towards Deep Subjectivity*, Allen Lane The Penguin Press, 1972). But it is also a tendency in a journalism that serves a materialistic and pragmatic society and fails to question its aims and values. It certainly hardens into dogma.

One may often be shocked today by the inadequacy of the account of an event such as (say) the *Oz* trial by David Dimbleby in the *New Statesman*, or the treatment of (say) psychological theories derived from experiments with rats, applied recklessly to sexual politics. To the serious student of human problems it is often clear that what looks like 'enlightenment' is rather a calculated posture, of playing to a public for 'success'. There is a new journalism, competing today with television to make an immediate 'impact'. This kind of journalism is at its most characteristic in the colour supplements: but it has influenced the minority press too. As the reader will know, there is a kind of article, at all levels, and a kind of television programme, which appears to raise 'grave' and 'deep' issues. But when one examines such 'shock issues' one finds that the reason for exploring the theme (lesbianism, ageing, madness) arose from no sense of the necessity of exploring reality, of gaining insight into human nature, of finding the truth, or seeking to persuade us to help put things right. These subjects are too often 'exposed', to arouse feelings of anger, disgust, or disquiet – but not to direct these in socially effective or even compassionate directions. Feelings are really aroused *to sell the journals*, or 'hold' an audience, for good entertainment value.

As an instance of this kind of tendency as one meets it, the present writer once hastily withdrew from a 'prestige' television programme when it became obvious that the producers wanted to use the text and drawings of the work of a disturbed child for sensational purposes, but were unwilling to allow proper time for this example to be qualified by comment. This is a typical and recurrent situation for anyone who has to do with the mass media. Just as working people will often refuse to be interviewed on television because they are afraid of being 'slanted' against their own class and trade unions, so more and more intellectuals feel like Peter Abbs that journalism is a mere distraction, and that it is impossible to enter into journalistic debate without compromising one's standards. This is destructive of good journalism itself.

Meanwhile by compromise and a certain suspension of conscience and integrity, by 'brightness', by *fâcherie* – a kind of deliberate rudeness – and by the display of a carefully calculated 'persona', some journalists who are less troubled by doubt and values gain rapid influence, while 'serious' papers tend to merge into the world of popular newspaper journalism, and superficial television debate. (The *Human World* even alleges that *Private Eye* has become more serious than the *New Statesman*; see No. 2, February 1971.)

Inevitably, in such a situation, it becomes gradually impossible for any writer to stand outside the 'trends'. A leading Sunday paper, I was once told by one of its more serious women writers, actually held a conference at which the editorial staff decided to be 'brighter' – which meant 'harder', or more sharp and brittle. If people are to keep their jobs, and certainly if they are ambitious in such a situation, they have to compromise. So, there are fewer and fewer really free spirits, and it is increasingly difficult for any

163

effective body of opinion to exist, outside the special kind of optimistic and falsely lively 'brightness' that pervades the journalistic scene.

Moreover, economic necessity demands a certain kind of cohesion among journalists, in terms of a generally accepted philosophy of life. Today this is aligned very much towards an 'amoral stance', which pretends to be based on a radical reconsideration of the whole traditional pattern of morality. Arrogant advertisements have appeared, in which those who write for money are acclaimed as being equal to genuine creative writers (see the 'Cossack Vodka' advertisement analysed in *The Masks of Hate*) while in some articles, especially in the colour supplements, depersonalized sex and even the use of drugs are spoken of as acceptable ('even the pot-and-sex parties have a strange air of innocence about them ... English girls are fresh and eagerly alive ... they take to sex like candy ...').*

This development has taken its lead from the most extreme advocates of 'permissiveness'. Their attitude that 'everything goes' perhaps originates in the advocacy of Lars Ullerstam, the author of *The Sexual Minorities*. His kind of argument is one that has deceived many liberals – if nothing is taboo, the old repressions will lose their force, people will get bored, the interest will exhaust itself. As David Boadella, the author of a study of Wilhelm Reich and the 'sexual revolution' says, 'It takes a deeper insight to realize that such a programme ... is something other than a helpful therapy service to encourage disturbed people to work off their repressions and improve their health, and so lead to greater happiness.'†

Such an abolition of qualitative distinctions, says Boadella, carries with it the implication that we are all healthy already, and that we have been conditioned by 'society' to see ourselves as sick. All that is needed is reverse conditioning, on a mass scale – this is the basis of the widespread new 'amoral' permissiveness adopted by Fleet Street. As Boadella says, what we are taught by

*'London – The Most Exciting City', the *Telegraph* colour supplement, 16 April 1966, see my analysis, *op. cit.*

† *Wilhelm Reich, The Evolution of His Work*, Vision Press, 1972.

this pseudo-revolution is that 'split-off, depersonalized, compulsively intrusive sexuality is perfectly normal, natural, and healthy, and that we need look for nothing better.'

This is the basis of vindications of the exploitation of sex in the *Sun* newspaper, *Mayfair, Vanity Fair,* and *Nova,* and the passion with which all this is defended. At the time of the *Oz* (*Schoolkids' Issue*) trial, *The Times* had a revolt on its hands, as forty-four members of staff signed a letter to the Editor protesting against his editorial. A columnist in the magazine *Where?* spoke of the *Little Red Schoolbook* as 'lovely' although it gave dangerously false information about the harmlessness of venereal disease, and might well have led a disturbed child into a perverted seduction. Yet this magazine refused to publish a counterstatement, pointing out the doubts of psychotherapists, while several distinguished educationists went into the witness stand to defend journals which could well be accused of child seduction.

The public has been widely misled, by a pseudo-revolution that ignores even the distinctions made by the sexual revolutionaries (Wilhelm Reich warned against a new 'brothel religion' arising from those who sought to exploit the new permissiveness to live out their sick and sadistic fantasies). As David Boadella says, 'Such a mass-conditioning amounts to a progressive prostitution of culture, and involves a hidden and subtle control over people's feelings that is more insidious than the old repressive system, because that was fought as an enemy, while the new threat is welcomed as a friend.' This mass-conditioning has been largely brought about by magazines and newspapers in England – not least among young people. Moral debate on these sensitive issues is nowadays almost impossible, because young people are often simply not aware of the problems, or are totally misled by pseudo-sexuality.

Much of the propaganda in favour of the pseudo-revolution may be associated with the commercial promotion of 'pop'. 'Pop' promoters offer an ersatz life-style, disguised as an 'alternative' way of living. Quality papers which want to keep their young readers bring in bright writers to make this spurious development seem intellectually respectable – and so Schubert, Bach, Baudelaire and Wittgenstein are all solemnly mentioned in

165

connection with 'pop'. The consequent blurring of values and levels is combined with a forceful propaganda for 'the new amoral society we have created' (the *Guardian*). Thus, this is more than confusion – it is propaganda for a new demoralization, aggressively and arrogantly urged on us as a herd trend:

living openly with someone without marrying him, having a child out of wedlock and so on, lead to no general public outcry ... Films and theatres are able to show scenes which previously would have been confined to blue films or erotic 'exhibitions'. On television the first male frontal nude has just put in a rather tentative appearance, but naked breasts and bottoms are a commonplace ... teenagers put the case for and against pot and promiscuity with an unselfconscious ease ... Permissiveness, while not total, is nearly complete, in the sexual field at any rate...*

George Melly's tone throughout his book is one of enthusiastic acclaim for developments which others might regard with dismay. There are many psychotherapists, philosophers and educationists who might perhaps feel that such a cheerfully hypomanic attitude to the new 'freedom' is not only trivial, but, in its happy enthusiasm, likely to prove harmful when it is absorbed by young people. But Mr Melly goes on to proclaim confidently that 'it (pop) has affected our sensibilities and to the good. We are more open, less stuffy. Less intellectually snobbish, more loving ...' – and he is widely believed. The influence of such a journalist today is enormous, and such individuals have created a new orthodoxy of enlightenment in England. The views of those who scribble their weekly thousand words would not matter if they were not taken so seriously in England today, or if alternative, more serious views were equally widespread. There seems to be a gulf between serious opinion in the sphere of medicine and psychotherapy, and attitudes in fashionable culture, as there is not, I believe, in Australia or America. Mr Melly's view seems hardly reconcilable with that of Dr R. S. Morton, who says in *Social Freedom and Venereal Disease*,

The accumulation of cases of long-term individual misery and venereal disease as a direct result [of the use of the pill] is more calamitous than anything precipitated by thalidomide ... Pill prescribing ... as a

*George Melly, *Revolt into Style*, Penguin Books, 1972.

means of reducing illegitimacy has been a conspicuous failure ... gonorrhoea was thrice as common and growing faster among women on the pill than among those who did not use it.*

This attitude to sex would be rejected in the 'Arts' pages, and the split marks a trivialization of our intellectual life in the sphere of the humanities. Alas, so convinced has the British public become that the Sunday-newspaper journalists represent the 'intellectual life' where the humanities are concerned, that when a woman is needed to join a scrutinizing committee to study violence on television, it is a Sunday-newspaper journalist, and when the National Theatre needs an Artistic Adviser it is a newspaper drama critic (and pornographic impresario). At the moment the journalist individual of this kind is gaining almost unchallenged power over our culture and intellectual life, in the absence of an effective consensus of substantial opinion, available in serious journals.

At the same time, people at large seem to assume that we are to congratulate ourselves on the amount of satire and lampoon today directed at the Establishment and institutions. Yet in fact the 'satire' we have is all too safe: written by more or less the same kind of people as preserve the orthodoxies of enlightenment, it seldom tackles abuses in a penetrating way which yet invokes passionate concern for human good (Compare *Le Canard Enchaîné* or *Der Spiegel*). Rather, it relies upon playful obscenity and abuse on the one hand and the reinforcement of 'progressive' prejudices on the other. The pyrotechnic derisiveness of such a paper as *Private Eye* marks a new stage in the abrogation of a 'point of view' altogether, and of the need for serious and committed opinion behind social satire or lampoon (cf. Cobbett, Hogarth, or Dickens).

To conclude this survey of those periodicals which are generally taken to keep us in touch with serious ideas, and with developments in culture and science, there is a great deal of room for improvement. Yet improvement seems unlikely to come – because of rising costs, increasing competition for advertising, declining editorial responsibility, greater (and more ruthless) ambitiousness, and increasing trivialization.

*The Times, 13 January 1972.

167

Way out beyond these areas of established fashionable journalism is the 'underground' press. While no doubt some of the material published in these papers deserves our toleration in the name of freedom of expression, a survey of them reveals a degree of subversion and rage that deserves little respect – and barely deserves the right of free speech. The present writer does not subscribe to the prevalent fashion to uphold free speech at all costs; though some revolutionaries undoubtedly have important criticisms of society to make, this cannot be taken to justify their attempts (say) to thrust perversion on children, or to encourage sabotage or violence at large. Here we encounter the difficult problem of how to deal with the 'schizoid minority' who need to thrust hate into the world, and to invert values. If their dynamics are 'fascistic', then we have hideous lessons to learn from history, about the consequences of mere toleration (lessons we should have learnt over racist propaganda).

Richard Neville has admitted that 'There is a lot of fascist stuff about', and the present writer is deeply disturbed by the anti-human elements in much of the 'underground' press – despite the evident passionate convictions of its promoters and writers. The ugliness of the papers, their inverted morality, their drug-dream lay-out, their coarse ugliness of image, their destructiveness of tone, their abysmal obscenity, their essential conformity of extremist non-conformity, all seem, rather, manifestations of nihilism, decadence and the collapse of discourse, rather than healthy protest. They often seem to be pursuing with fanatical immoralism the destruction of those very institutions and modes of thought and action in which any hope for the future may be found. How can we feel that liberty is outraged when such papers are prosecuted for publishing a 'Schoolkids' Issue' which both describes perversions and offers them in small advertisements – with no concern that some unhappy child might be emotionally harmed? The images and modes of these papers seem often disturbingly like those in *Der Stuermer*, except that the rage and hate are manifested in pornographic directions, or in cruel humiliation of woman's image, rather than against racial scapegoats: the hate, however, is the same.

This, of course, raises a wider question of the whole avant

garde movement. Some underground papers belong to a sinister political trend which seems to be seeking to invert all moral standards. They can be seen as a manifestation of that fanatical bohemianism which Michael Polanyi analyses so well in his *Knowing and Being* and compares with the origins of Nazism. As Masud Khan and others have pointed out, there is a whole vast movement in our culture which has developed a cult of the mentalization of instinct, which leads, however, in an opposite direction from human 'meeting', insight, or creative sympathy. It is full of hostility, sadism and rage – and its predominant symbol is that of woman being humiliated and degraded. This also involves the humiliation of man and it is the other side of the penny of much contemporary nihilism. Yet such rage and subversion are imprisoned in their own dehumanization, and can never find any essential freedom, as we shall see. If, as Marjorie Grene says, our freedom is bound up with discovering the human values in knowledge, the anti-intellectualism of much of the underground press (and student 'protest') is an even greater threat to our freedom than the 'Establishment' press which serves commerce and advertising.

Besides the periodicals discussed above there are political papers which vary according to the colour of the editor or group in charge for the time being, such as *New Left Review*. There are very small literary magazines such as *Outposts* and *Poetry Review*. The standard of production and writing in these is uncertain and often amateur, while their editorial standards vary a great deal. Some small journals, however, like *New Blackfriars*, the *Critical Quarterly* and the *Human World* contain genuinely thoughtful and independent material.

There are also university journals and minority journals with circulations of about 2,000 to 5,000, their contributors unpaid. Their long-term influence – sometimes world-wide – should not be forgotten in the general picture. This has been true of the best literary magazines of this kind in our century, the only equivalents in our time of the great nineteenth-century papers, such as the *Calendar of Modern Letters* (1926–8: reissued by Cass and Co., 1969), the *Criterion* (which yet contains little one would want now to turn back to), the *Adelphi*, and particularly *Scrutiny* (1932–53,

169

reissued complete by Cambridge University Press). Various attempts have been made to establish successors – the *Cambridge Quarterly*, the *Human World*, and the Aberystwyth series of *Tracts*: but we do not at the moment have anything to be compared happily with the most distinguished journals of the past in the arts. There are of course scientific journals, such as *Nature*, which have an immense prestige and value: science has been able to maintain its standards of intellectual irrigation as the arts have not.

This is as much as can be said about 'quality' periodical publication in England at present. We may turn now to the largest field of all periodical publication, which has close links with advertising. Here there are some distinctions to be made, between smart, 'homely', and 'pop', but all belong to the same species. Their function is that of making a commercial return to the proprietors as a branch of the entertainment industry, and their income is often largely dependent on advertising. The 'smart' papers, such as *Vogue*, *House and Garden*, *Harper's Bazaar*, *Queen*, *Vanity Fair* and *Honey* have obvious links with the high-class furnishing, travel, fashion, clothes, cosmetics and entertainment businesses, and serve these in their content and promotion modes. The 'respectable' or 'homely' journals consist of the many women's papers – *Woman*, *Woman and Beauty*, *Woman and Home*, *Woman and Shopping*, *Woman's Companion*, *Woman's Day*, *Woman's Illustrated*, *Woman's Journal*, *Woman's Outlook*, *Woman's Own*, *Woman's Realm*, *Woman's Story Magazine*, *Woman's Weekly*, *Housewife*, *Homes and Gardens*, *House Beautiful*, and so on. These follow fashion and cosmetic promotion too, but also help to sell a wide range of household goods, furniture, articles of hygiene, confectionery, and foodstuffs. The 'pop' papers range from *Reveille* to *Weekend*; these papers carry 'mart' advertising of the kind one used to find in such papers as the *Radio Times*, which have mammoth circulations, but which we now find even in *The Times*. These advertisements are a grotesque chequerwork of skin balms, body builders, slimming aids, books on etiquette, home-shopping catalogue agencies, 'The Exam Secret', shampoos, secretarial courses, schools of salesmanship, baldness cures, clothes, holidays, cosmetics, jewellery, guitars, wigs, bust developers ('Kurvon tablets') and extraordinary forms of bizarre underwear (Frou-Frou set, The Famous Bare-a-Frontery, the Bikini Jama, Daring Golden Bra and G-string, 'sizzling' Flamenco Bra and Briefs). It is a mark of present economic difficulties that even newspapers for the 'top people' depend upon such advertisements today for their very existence (and dare not even refuse advertisements for doubtful sauna-massage centres, abortion agencies, pornographic stage shows or chastity belt vendors).

But these small advertisements do not represent the major *raison d' être* of the periodical press. This whole press could not survive unless it provided the media for the general advertising of household consumer goods. And, while there is a modicum of independence in journalism, it is essentially the advertisers of fashion goods, whisky, cigarettes, cars and household goods who call the tune for English popular journalism. The general link between these mass-sale papers, advertising and commerce is made plain by advertisements in the national 'quality' press, such as the following (with a drawing of a woman relaxing with a magazine):

SHOPPING STARTS HERE FOR $7\frac{1}{4}$ MILLION WOMEN
Week after week, in the colourful pages of WOMAN'S OWN, this woman, and 7,239,000 like her find a combination of editorial and advertisement content which adds up to one of the world's most successful and trusted women's weeklies. At this moment, while relaxing with her favourite magazine, she's choosing her new clothes for Spring. In the women's mass market, WOMAN'S OWN sells everything a woman needs – and carries more advertisement pages, year after year, than any other women's magazine.
If you would like more detailed information about WOMAN'S OWN *to assist you in the planning of your next campaign in the women's mass market, please contact The Advertising Director,*
WOMAN'S OWN
– WHERE SHOPPING STARTS

The reader who has read Frank Whitehead's contribution will be aware of the way in which the overall dominance of advertising has caused certain deep changes in our society, through the educational effects of the media. All culture depends upon 'trust': yet

171

the advertiser can never be trusted in his use of symbolism. He demands (indirectly) a certain 'combination of editorial and advertisement content'.

The clue to the nature of this combination is indicated here by the words 'successful', and (especially) 'trusted'. The other term on which to fix one's attention is the word 'relaxing' – whose implications are that what is most important for commercial purposes is that the *reader's defences should be down*, so that advantage can be taken of him or her. In no previous society has culture been so widely used in this deceptive way, by a small and powerful minority, for a purpose quite other than a cultural one.

'Relaxation' and 'trust' are often achieved by a clever play on the deepest existential fears. A characteristic example of the trivialization of deep feelings is such a piece of 'true life' drama as an account of the death of Von Trips, the motor-racing driver, in a picture paper. The news item was about a year old at the time, but the skilful magazine writer drags the old story out for the sensational juice it can still yield, 'handled properly', and warmed up. The writer seeks to play upon the reader's fear of death – his natural preoccupation with the fact that 'in the midst of life we are in death'. This is the province of the poet. A creative writer would be able to share a genuine anguish with the readers, so that the reader could share his search for meaning in the face of death, and our existential 'nothingness'. This would be true mourning in the face of mortality. Art is inevitably compassionate, because the creative writer is seeking by words to share his agony with others.* As we know, all children – not least 'backward' children – can be artist-writers in this sense: but they are using symbolism in a situation of trust for quite different purposes – to explore their world, not to gain a hypnotized attention.

*A small proportion of art makes an assault on the reader, viewer, or member of the audience, and so some would question this assertion. However, the present writer believes that such art has often regressed to 'acting out' and is deficient in creative content. (cf. Genet, and the discussion of him by Masud Khan in his papers on perversion, and in *An Existentialist Aesthetic* by Eugene Kaelin). I would certainly use as a value judgement the degree of insight and empathy given by a cultural work: the degree to which it answers the question, 'What is it to be human?' As E. K. Ledermann has said, 'radical solutions' should not become 'radical dissolutions' (*Existential Neurosis*, Butterworth, 1972).

The popular magazine writer pretends to be using words for the same kind of end. He assumes a serious moral position – he pretends he is 'condemning' the thing he writes about. Here motor racing is called THIS CRUEL GAME, but the excitement is derived from the excitements of motor racing itself, particularly its liability to lead to maiming and death. Though the writer *appears* to be telling his story in compassion for the protagonist and his family, and for those hurt and killed by the crash, he is in fact doing all he can to revive the compulsive sensationalism of the gladiatorial event. Under the guise of moral righteousness he is exploiting the most poignant and horrific moments of the suffering of others. He is not doing this for any serious moral purpose – to try to get motor racing banned, or made safer, or even to defend it as a necessary blood-sport. He is certainly not concerned to help us to come to terms with the presence of death which is inevitable in our lives. He is simply playing on the reader's nerves, to hold him in distraction a little while, to fray his feelings, and then, having roused him, leaves him hypnotized – and attentive in a certain way. This kind of attention suits both advertiser and the need of the paper to establish a habit.* The writer is arousing sadistic, morbid, and anxious feelings but offers little to help the reader to come to terms with these. Public execution and the horror comic were prohibited because it came to be recognized that the stirring of savage feelings in crowds in public could have a degrading effect, to an extent which threatened personal and public order and well-being. Such sights evoke feelings of anxiety, cruelty, horror and rage which, evidently, distract energy from creative living. Such spectacles not only brutalize people, but tend to deprive them of their potentialities. Yet today great play is made of fantasy 'spectacles' of a parallel kind, many of which are brutal, too.† The huge periodical industry nowadays depends upon arousing such

*Vance Packard, I believe, makes the point that television programmes which were 'too good' were found to alienate viewers to advertisements: advertising demands 'relaxation' in a context of mediocre entertainment.

†The appeal of stage sex is its unconscious sadism; in film this is nowadays more apparent. In Saturday afternoon all-in wrestling on T.V. sadism is also a way of compelling rapt passive attention, when there is little else to do. The girlie magazine is a parallel appeal to sadistic feelings: see below.

feelings, which are often, as here, full of deep anxiety – while little is offered that is creative, to help overcome anxiety.

Here are some representative paragraphs designed to give a juicy shock to the emotions. The page shows colour pictures, accidentally taken at the track, of Von Trips in his crashing car. The unfortunate driver can be seen in his seat, and one is invited to identify oneself with the man at the point of death ('As the crimson Ferrari rocketed on, Von Trips had a hundredth of a second to realize that this was the end'). Short of describing the actual maimings and terrible bodily wounds the writer squeezes the maximum horror from the incident. He builds up the lack of expectation in the spectators, with 'human interest':

Poppa Piero Carpani, grocer, and father of four, squinted anxiously at the sky before he made his big decision.

Neither Piero, his wife, nor the children, had ever seen a motor race before.

In the Ferrari pits at Monza, mechanics swarmed over the five blood-red cars, bearing the name of the famous Italian manufacturer.

And so was beautiful American millionairess Sally Ringling, twenty-seven-year-old daughter of one of the seven Ringling Circus brothers. Her friends called her 'race-crazy' – but this was one race Sally had not wanted to see.

Only a week before, she had flown back to America, filled with a ghastly presentiment of disaster. Then the cable arrived. It said: *Come to Monza. I am going to win the World Championship. I want you to be there.* It was signed 'Wolfgang'.

Debonair Count Wolfgang Von Trips ('Taffy' to his fellow drivers – 'Count Crash' to the crowds) had loved her from the moment they first met at the Le Mans twenty-four-hour race two years before.

On the morning of the big race, the pale, slim German nobleman proposed. And Sally accepted. But she was the unhappiest person of all the 50,000 who thronged the death-circuit on September 10, 1961.

Note that the race track is now the 'death circuit': both the writer and the reader know, in a cynical way, that all they are doing is treading the same old weary circuit of sensation-mongering with the subtle play on feelings about sex and death. The cars are 'locked in a crazy embrace', 'the Ferrari rocketed on'. Schoolboys can write pastiche of this kind of thing with great efficiency, alas: one remembers the maxim attributed to

174

Lord Northcliffe, 'our readers have a mental age of fourteen and a half'.

Then comes the meat. Of course, it 'holds one':

Von Trips had a hundredth of a second to realize that this was the end. He tried to free himself as the car spun through the air before spinning end over end on to the track.

The chances are that he never even *saw* the blur of horrified faces as his car slashed into the crowd. He was killed instantly when . . .

The 'Death Circuit' had claimed one of the greatest motor-racing drivers of all time. And fifteen men and women who went to see the fun.

There was no victor's laurel for Von Trips. But every three days for a month afterwards, a fresh red rose was found on the spot where he died – laid there by a young Milan student, Francesca Guadenzio.

'I was just a friend,' she said.

Such is the general level of diet in the popular commercial journals of an 'educated' democracy.

To anyone concerned with the health of the language, in relation to people's capacities to deal with life, what is distressing here is the banality, the commonplace quality of the cliché, and the crudity with which English words are handled, from 'end', 'blood', and 'fun' to 'miracle', 'loved', and 'death'. This example is typical of thousands poured out by Fleet Street every week. While this industry continues to be in hands indifferent to its inevitable moral influences it will continue to damage and weaken both language and attitudes to life at the popular level. What such matter damages is the 'life-world' in which each individual lives, and by which he or she perceives reality, and creates a world to live in.

The interests of commercial companies demand that this kind of exploitation of language and feeling be developed by mass journalism. The staple themes remain the same as those set out by Northcliffe at the end of the last century – death, money and sex ('Everything starts with sex' a woman's journal editor said recently). These requirements impose very considerable restrictions on the freedom of the popular periodical Press. So they are barred by their limitations from functions which could really help develop public opinion, extend insight or understanding, or contribute to the well-being of society, except insofar as they promote

175

the sale of useful products. At best they are a harmless form of distraction: at worst they corrupt feeling and attitudes. It is of course little justification to say that bloodthirsty and violent stories have always been popular. After a hundred years of popular education one might hope for something better, while the world today is in no state for reckless brutalization to be added to in intensity.

If we accept the view of philosophers such as Susanne Langer and Ernst Cassirer, that man is the *animal symbolicum* – that is, a creature whose primary need is meaning, and who is distinguished from the beasts by his consciousness of his world and his vision – then this widespread exploitation of the banal is disturbing.

From our culture and entertainment we can at best derive a sense of human sympathy, insight into human nature, understanding of ideas and other kinds of experience, values and standards, and a sense of meaning. These, for instance, people once had, at a popular level, at best, from folksong to Dickens. By comparison with primitive societies (as observed by anthropologists) or with (say) medieval or Elizabethan society (as we can judge from a study of both minority and popular culture) our society nowadays seems seriously deficient in opportunities at large for people to find sound nourishment for the imagination, and to exercise symbolism in creative ways of all kinds. Yet as Susanne Langer has said, 'Symbolizing is a primary need of man'. A periodical press could help to nourish such needs more. But at the moment, while from most other sources of supply for their everyday needs (such as shops which sell material goods), people get a reasonable deal, if they turn to those centres which have to do with *communication* and *meaning* – the bookshop or periodical stall (together with the cinema or record shop) – what they get too often is the mis-use of symbolism that offers them false solutions. They are frequently offered, indeed, something essentially anti-human. For not only are certain elements in this irrational, like horoscopes, but actually likely to promote harm: a horoscope in *Vanity Fair* gives such advice as 'Tuesday will be a good day for sex – so just give yourself away!'. Many periodicals, like much other commercial culture, tend to falsify symbolism, and so they

176

inevitably affect people's feelings about the meaning of life at a time when their need for a sense of meaning is desperate.

The need of the periodical trade is to create 'trust' in a 'successful' magazine for the purpose of selling. Their dependence on advertising and commercial optimism promote a certain kind of spurious attitude to life even at best. In the fashion papers for women and the 'home' journals it is usually falsely optimistic, and exaggeratedly idealized – the seas were never so blue as they are in *Vogue*, the women so elegant, the foreign places so halcyon: if a dirty old tramp or a camel are there, it is only to provide 'atmosphere' and contrast with the image of an ideal – a bejewelled princess posing elegantly and impossibly by the moonlit wall (with a caption telling you where to purchase the clothes she is wearing). The same bright dream-like optimism is promoted in various degrees in all those magazines, where every face bears a smile and titled people appear in our midst, while the same manic light imbues the glamorous boys and tousle-headed love-lorn girls in the strip stories of *Mirabelle*.

There is a new brashness which is not the same kind of thing at all in the newest and sharpest women's papers such as *Nova*, *Vanity Fair* and *Honey*. The main appeal of these is a new 'frankness' about sex. It is no exaggeration to say that their treatment of this subject is often perverted, as we shall see. In much of all this, the human person is implicitly reduced to the status of an object, a commodity. Humanness is sacrificed to the needs of a commercial society to exploit human beings in that way. The consequent schizoid dehumanization is a focus for the arousing of anxiety about the point of life, and about one's identity, for commercial purposes.

How can we substantiate such value judgements, in discriminating between the genuine use of symbolism, and its mis-use in journalism? It is becoming obvious from the work of many students of human nature, from an 'inward' point of view, that our capacity to perceive the world, and to deal with it effectively, is the product of love, relationship, and culture. Psychoanalysts like D. W. Winnicott have traced the way in which the child's ability to see the world, from a secure and integrated self, emerges from the long years of 'play' between infant and mother,

177

from play at the breast, to an adult personal culture (see *Playing and Reality*). Similar observations have been made by 'existentialist' psychoanalysts such as Rollo May in America, while philosophical biologists in Europe, such as F. J. J. Buytendijk, have studied what they call 'encounter' between human mother and child (see *Approaches to a Philosophical Biology*, Marjorie Grene). From the first smile of the baby, there develops a complex system of sign and symbol, the growth of which is bound up with the child's identity, and his grasp of reality. All these observations confirm the view of those who see culture as primary in human life. Moreover, they show that the emotional life is closely bound up with our capacities to deal with other people and the world.

Any mis-use of symbolism, therefore, is likely to cause considerable harm to man's relationship with his whole world. And here we need to look especially at the increasing use of the symbol of woman – her face and body – in such contemporary forms of culture as the magazine. Images of woman, and woman's breasts, are the predominant images exploited by contemporary commercial entertainment. They are able to exploit these images because they are the most powerful ones, in drawing the attention of the camera and, so, the attention of our eyes. This is so because, of course, the first object on which we fixed our eyes was a woman's face, and then her breast. In the beginning, as Winnicott indicates, her breast was the world, and we were at one with it.*

In consequence, the image of woman may be called a symbol of the *anima*, to use Jung's word. This is the 'female element' in human beings. The woman's face, and her breast, are objects over which we can throw our most intense idealizing vision, because they stand for our deepest aspirations. They draw out of us feelings of wanting to be alive, to create, to worship. They thus stand for the intentional and emotive aspects of human nature – our 'female element', that creates more human beings, artistic works, and, indeed, makes the world we live in. The image of a woman nursing her baby is, of course, one of the most powerful

---

*As Winnicott explains 'breast' here means all the care she offered us, in tending us as well as feeding us. It is the creative response which enables us to become ourselves.

of all religious symbols, and the naked figure of woman can be the most inspiring of cultural symbols.

In creative works the image of woman enables us to discover, and to pursue, the richest human potentialities – as we recognize in Botticelli's Venus, Shakespeare's Cordelia, Dickens's Little Dorrit, or D. H. Lawrence's Ursula. But such creative uses of symbols also involve us in pursuing answers to that question, 'What is it to be human?' and this brings us closer to the reality of human beings as they are. It involves, for instance, recognizing that we have emotional needs, that we are sensitive, that we depend on others, that we need to love, and that once we were totally dependent on a woman, as Christ was on his mother (which is what the ikon reminds us of). Thus, the images of true femininity, as in Sir Kenneth Clark's book *The Nude*, or in the works to which I have referred, remind us of our human weakness and existential doubts: often, as we know, the greatest discoveries of vision, round the subject of love, devotion and meaning, are bound up with the contemplation of death, as in *King Lear*, *Romeo and Juliet*, and *Women in Love*.

This kind of true creative use of symbols, evidently, would not do for commercial exploitation. If we are urged to be merely acquisitive, it will not do for us to be mindful of our end, or to be troubled by existential doubts. Commerce therefore demands that we are in a 'manic' mood so that it can promote optimism and trust.* The useful word *manic* from psychoanalysis describes a mood in which we tend to deny the existence of death, fear, guilt and hate – as we do when we 'live it up' at a party, which is a deliberate cultivation of the manic mood. (The opposite to manic is depressive, and manic is a denial of the existence of the guilt that causes depression.) So, in commercial culture, the image of woman is very cleverly detached from humanness. The breast is displayed apart from the body: the girl's face often has a somewhat blank schizoid expression, with all the human qualities drained from it. Or it tends to be glossy, bright, smiling, and hopeful, in ways technology makes possible.

The psychological term for this manifestation is 'part-object'. The image of woman is an image of the object of relationship,

*It is well known that trade falls off during an international crisis.

179

as when we first looked at the breast. But there can also be a 'partial object' (as a child's toy may be 'a part of mummy'). The schizophrenic who has never learned to relate will dream of his need for love as a 'part-object' – a stream of milk, or a separated 'breast' which he feels he has 'stolen'. Much of the imagery in magazines (and films and television) today is of this 'part-object' kind. The advantage of this kind of 'split-off' breast is that it is not bound up with a whole human being so it does not remind us of our emotional problems, or burden us with responsibility. We can just 'take' it with our eyes and, as we shall see, there is a good deal of 'rape' in this, and an essential cruelty. (It reduces women to the humiliated level of the Bunny Girl play-thing.)

At worst, in pornography, the image of woman is a 'split-off' which is subjected to humiliation and contempt. For, because we are afraid of our emotional vulnerability, we can easily be persuaded to project our hate over the *anima*, and ill-treat it, much as the racist ill-treats the Jew or negro, over whom he has projected his hatred of his own humanness.

But in the general commercial exploitation of *anima* symbolism, what we have is an image of a depersonalized sexuality of the kind which technological society can exploit. Commerce deals with us largely in terms of mechanical organisms, which need products, as if we were machines which needed fuelling and servicing. The images in magazines and other media thus tend to symbolize these concepts which our society develops. Human beings are reduced to mere bearers of sensations, and mere functioning organisms. So, too, the emotions aroused belong to this essentially technicist concept: magazines supply us with amounts of sensation, unconscious sadistic feelings of 'feeding' on the seductive image, as at a breast, or, indeed, on a breast. The magazine *Nova* some time ago had a big colour double-page spread of bare breasts. (Such an image may seem strange in a woman's paper. But we may suspect that *Nova* is read by women (and by their men!) who are somewhat uncertain of their own femininity, and perhaps despise it. Just as the insecure man enjoys pornography, because he sees in it his 'female element' being humiliated, and can feel he is 'better than any woman', so the 'sophisticated' woman enjoys seeing her female element humiliated, so that she can triumph over it in a rather male way.)

In these ways, such human proclivities as sexuality are exploited in commercial media, in quite different ways from their exploitation in creative art. Discussing the work of Reimut Reiche (*Sexuality and Class Struggle*) David Boadella says, 'The façade of pleasure and fun disguises a latent need to attack and destroy the real love-needs'; and we cannot ignore any longer the negative effects of this exploitation of symbols. He quotes Reiche, who says, 'Sexuality becomes radically similar to capitalist forms of consumption, in which goods have no intrinsic worth outside the value attributed to them by advertising, and the rising scale on which they are consumed. Translated into sexual terms, the principle is: I get no satisfaction from any individual thing I buy because I only wear it out, not really use it. Therefore I might as well wear it out thoroughly, give it the highest possible market value, and persuade other people of its merits, photograph it, treat it sadistically, etc'.* The pseudo-sexuality inculcated by such media as magazines, therefore, may be associated with a radical failure of people at large to find a meaning in their life, in an acquisitive society. It is also bound up with 'commodity' thinking, transferred to concepts of man, and leads to a tendency to treat others as if they had no value.

The culture and symbolism of creative culture (and, it should be added, of popular culture of the past) helped people to find 'goals beyond themselves' to which they could devote their energies, in the pursuit of meaning. The symbolism of mass media culture tends merely to alleviate the need for meaning, by placing an intolerable burden on pseudo-symbols, from the intense hysteria of the football match, to the pseudo-sexual pursuit of quantities of mere sensation. Most people today live in an environment which is shapeless, sprawling, and anti-human. It contains far too few opportunities for creative symbolism, and active participation in sports or other adventures. It contains few architectural expressions of any larger-than-personal

*From an article, 'The Return of the Repressed', by David Boadella, on the work of Reimut Reiche, published in *Energy and Character Journal*, Abbotsbury, Dorset, 1972.

meaning. People travel vast distances to work (and on the journey they read manic journals and magazines, which supply them with sensations). They move from one meaningless sprawl to another, for the inner city environments become increasingly impersonal and ugly. There, they are largely engaged in meaningless tasks, which offer them no sense of personal value. They are offered relief from the meaninglessness of their work and environment by office flirtations, pin-up and pop-singer cults, film and television talk, cosmetic and fashion preoccupations.

As Denise Levertov writes:

> In tiled and fireproof corridors
> the typists shelter in their sex;
> perking beside the half-cock clerks
> they set a curl on freckled necks.
> The formal bird above the doors
>
> is set in metal whorls of flame.
> The train goes aching on its rails.
> Its rising cry of steel and wheels
> intolerably comes, and fails
> on walls immaculate and dumb.
>
> Comptometers and calculators
> compute the frequency of fires,
> adduce the risk, add up the years.
> Drawn by late-afternoon desires
> the poles of mind meet lust's equators...

(Typists in the Phoenix Building)

On such pursuits the modern office or factory worker often spends a disproportionate amount of income, in a desperate search for a sense of identity and meaning. Yet, as we know, people also yearn for much more exacting, or romantic, or challenging opportunities – as youth does especially. At home, the mother, alone in her comfortable, efficient, and hygienic living-box, often suffers from isolation, frustration, and boredom. She has few opportunities to find something meaningful to which to devote her life, beyond herself. As the suburban dweller ranges farther out

182

from the city centre the tedium and strain of commuter travel and the lack of meaning in his work and leisure – all threaten him with dehumanization. So, he bravely tries to find meaning in his family life, or in what social life he can find, amid the deficiency of provision for creative leisure, or service or 'giving out'. But his life tends all the time to make it more and more difficult to find individuality, humanness and meaning, and this schizoid dehumanization is felt increasingly in all great populations of suburban sprawls from Tokyo to Greater London.*

In such cultural deserts the periodical press can only superficially and temporarily relieve the cultural starvation of the population at large. The first *Daily Mail* speaks in an editorial of being designed for commuter travel, in 1890. Since then, increasingly, the mass media have educated us to believe that the solution to the problem of life is through the *acquisition* of personal possessions and sensations and, implicitly, that an acquisitive attitude to all experience is a valid one. That we find the point of life through acquiring things or even experiences is a lie, and it is this deceit implicit in popular commercial entertainment which makes it nihilistic in effect, by contrast with the true arts and live entertainment.

The Bible, folksong (*The Raggle Taggle Gipsies!*), Bunyan and Dickens often told their popular audiences that the greatest happiness comes from giving up preoccupation with material things altogether, and 'dropping out'. Learning to find ourselves human in 'encounter' is learning to *give*: our deepest satisfactions are in 'meeting', which is finding value in others, by contrast with the 'taking' attitude which depreciates their value. Folksong, folklore, and ritual often express a genuine sense of man's tragic 'nothingness', and a sense of the meanings by which he can transcend it. Many young people, especially the hippies, are trying to drop out of the acquisitive society: they too glimpse that meaning is to be found in 'love' or 'being' – however much their love is too random, and their approach to being is too solipsistic (as in the drug cult). But in emphasizing 'doing' and 'taking',

*See the chapter on 'The Meaning of Work' in *The Doctor and the Soul* by Viktor Frankl; also Rollo May's analysis of the schizoid nature of our society in *Love and Will*. See also Lewis Mumford, *passim*.

183

and by linking the sense of identity to acquisitiveness, much popular culture today is inimical to that quest for meaning which the existentialist philosopher and psychoanalyst see as man's primary need.

In a situation in which so many people's circumstances are lacking in meaning and satisfaction, insecure because of unemployment, and menaced with insignificance because of unsatisfactory community life, the magazine image of smart and trendy 'success' surely deepens unhappiness and discontent at large? If people are influenced at all they are surely likely to become worse at developing and cherishing those real personal relationships and modes of living in which genuine satisfaction may be found? If they have any effect on living, such periodicals are surely likely to exacerbate those hankerings by which we tend to become dissatisfied with our partners, with our real life and our actual home, and with the exigencies of love, marriage, and parenthood, in favour of some hallucination – which exists nowhere except in the prostituted imagination of the ad-man or in our more primitive hungry dreams which he is skilled at exploiting?

The 'wants' inculcated by the 'feature' periodical, as we know from personal observation of ourselves and others, tend to condition our behaviour in the direction of acquisitiveness, even in attempts to conquer the personal difficulties and conflicts between the ideal and the real. We take a great deal of this in, at the less conscious levels, and all of us swallow something of the persuasion. If only the home is made gay, the wife given new clothes and make-up, and we take a holiday in Italy . . . Alas, the other half of the equation – 'then we shall be happy' – simply doesn't follow, for reasons which might seem obvious (say) to a psychotherapist, or philosopher, or to anyone who has responded to a number of works of art (from *Women in Love* to *Das Lied Von Der Erde*, or from folksong to *Another Country*), but these reasons are seldom pointed out in popular magazines.

Of course, at the 'homely' level the advice and moral implications of the contents of popular magazines are respectable, and largely sound. The traditional women's papers convey a belief in the home and family, love and marriage, and conventional moral values, many of which are unobjectionable. They encourage self-respect and such virtues as mutual kindness, and can even suggest resistance to the false daydream. Here is a typical 'reconciliation' at the end of a romantic story in *Woman's Mirror*, 'Keep a Dream Safe', by Val Weedon:

He sat down beside her and put his arm around her shoulders.

'A dream,' he said, 'everybody needs a dream. When you get ratty – no, don't deny it – I think of Louise. When I'm depressed, I think of Louise. When I'm bored, I think of Louise. Twenty,' he said. 'Young, beautiful. Let her stay that way.'

Nancy was silent. She wasn't sure that she liked the idea.

'That fellow,' Bill said at last. 'Mr Whatsit.'

'Who?'

'Old pieface. That chap you were nearly engaged to.'

'Frank,' Nancy said. 'Oh, him. What about him?'

'How do you think he feels about you?'

She didn't know. It had never occurred to her that Frank would pay her a second thought.

'You know how you look?' he said. 'Young. No lines here,' he touched her forehead. 'Happy. Smiling. That's the way you look to him. For ever.'

'Oh,' Nancy said. It was an oddly comforting thought, almost as if a sort of immortality had been bestowed on her.

'And you,' he continued, 'you have someone too. Everyone has.'

And she knew that she did, and that it had all happened a long time ago, and that the young man's face was very dim now, but all the same he was a good escape hatch in time of need. The might-have-been that one never wanted.

'Yes,' she admitted. 'It's true.'

'So – no Louise.' Bill tapped his forehead. 'I'll keep her up here.' Then he leaned forward, touched the old green dress and said breezily: 'But don't we look beautiful tonight! You and me both,' and he ran his hand over his head. 'All scented and shorn and beautiful. It seems a pity to waste us, we should be showing ourselves off.'

He took her arm.

'Let's go out,' he said, 'and paint the town red.'

Even so, the implications about personal relationships are shallow, and the typical story is one that ends happily – as incidents in real life often do not – by wish-fulfilment.

The staple fare of the 'homely' popular journal is reassuring

185

platitudes – at their most typical in Godfrey Winn (from the same issue):

> What I mustn't forget to tell you before I sign off for another week, is about the carved wooden slogans hanging from the ceiling of The Pig and Whistle at Minehead, where everyone congregates in the evening, between dances.
> I picked out three. One for husbands, one for wives, one for everyone. Here we go.
> *Try praising your wife ... even if it does frighten her at first.*
> *A clever wife is the one who convinces her husband he is cleverer than she is.*
> *If your face wants to smile, let it, if it doesn't, make it.*
> But you don't have to make it at Butlin's. At least I never have.

The essence of such cultural fare is that it must keep to platitudes and conventional moral attitudes because the reader's 'relaxation' must not be disturbed, in case she becomes less accessible to the blandishments of the advertiser. This necessarily limits the scope of such periodicals. Thus, for example, the 'Problem Pages' touch only slightly on common peccadilloes, rather more for their 'human interest' than for the advice itself. Their real intention is to hold the audience and sell the paper by supplying a spurious 'human interest'. A sub-editor who becomes too involved in the reality of some of the heart-rending problems sent in may be told (as a journalist once told me he was instructed) to 'forget it and make some up'. The main object of the more conventional periodical is to establish an ersatz trust, and simply hold a reader for a while, so that the advertisements may work on her. Journalism of this kind seldom acts as a real clearing-house for human troubles as a Penguin paperback may do, or offers positive help in living, such as a creative novelist can provide in his art. *Woman* receives 30,000 letters a month: but, however well prepared the replies to these are, such activity surely indicates a failure in our society of culture and community life which no magazine is capable of tackling – not even by helping to relieve the terrible loneliness revealed.

Yet, of course, the apparent offer of 'help' and 'advice' is a main plank in most periodicals' appeal, and when papers misuse this trust they are being most vicious. When the values are respectable, as in the mass 'homely' women's papers, traditional values are often reduced to a lowest common denominator of platitudes. These may seem more 'enlightened' than the old codes, but are less helpful than what the family and community themselves used to provide at best: the mass media may even have fostered the decline in community care evident in our society. On the other hand some changes, such as the decrease in social guilt about illegitimacy, may have been helped into being by sound advice given in the best popular women's papers.

Yet some of the attitudes promoted are ridiculous or could even prove disastrous.

Flirting's fun! And it's high time the art came back. Men – and women – cannot live by bread alone! Let us practise the brief but charming art of lowering long lashes at an unexpected compliment . . . the fleeting touch of the hand . . . the quick turn of the head and flick of the lashes that leads a man to believe you and he share the same brilliant sense of humour. Yes, it's high time.*

In the last few years a new kind of woman's paper has developed, which is very different from the traditional 'homely' kind. In this new kind of paper the old formula about flirting and such romanticism have been extended into the ethos of 'permissiveness'. A new 'bold' approach is taken to problems such as adultery, frigidity, sexual perversion and so forth. There may be some advantages in this new frankness. It may be that some women fear (for instance) that they have a 'deformed' vagina, having examined themselves for the first time, and it may be valuable for *Woman and Home* to be able to reassure them on such intimate matters. However, it seems difficult to believe there is still so much anxiety about problems like impotence, and ignorance about other sexual matters, to justify such continual discussion of them. Are there such vast benefits to be had from discussing the more intimate sexual problems outside the personal context, as (say) between doctor and patient? We should perhaps rather see this manifestation as a commercial exploitation of anxieties. Certainly no new journal, it seems, can be launched

* 'From 101 ways to make yourself more exciting to look at, listen to, with live. . .', *Woman's Own*.

today without its ingredient of 'frank' sex-talk, often accompanied by voyeuristic pictures. At extremes (as in *Forum*) the 'advice' columns are merely titillation.

Besides 'medical' advice however, there are developments which are still more doubtful. There is a certain increasing cold-bloodedness about sex even in the more traditional journals. Over such problems as adultery (*Need adultery wreck your marriage?*) there is an increasing tendency to treat sex in a brutally functional way, separated from values and human truth, as (say) they are recognized in serious works on psychotherapy. Such advice often fails to emphasize the realities recognized in any work with patients or children in school. The belief that today (because of the pill or some new 'liberation' of attitudes) we have escaped in some way from all the deeper problems of our relational needs and our need to love, is absurd. In some sophisticated papers an even brasher emphasis on sexuality is offered with an increasing indecency of tone ('We only went to the West Indies for the screwing'). The most astonishing aspect of this is the undisturbed complacency with which women sit reading the flagrant obscenities in these new journals under the hair-driers, or in their genteel drawing-rooms. Magazines such as *Vanity Fair* print extracts from the latest 'sex' books, such as *The Sensuous Woman* (described by an American psychoanalyst as the 'ultimate reduction of the human being to the status of object'). Presumably the intention is to engage 'trust' in a new way – by enlisting the reader in fashionable attitudes, believed to belong to a 'new dimension' of 'liberation'.

In *Nova*, for instance, a group of 'swinging' couples recently reported on their private experience in bed after trying various supposed aphrodisiacs – with no sense of the degrading implications of making such suggestive public revelations from their intimate married life. As Erwin Straus indicates, in his essay on shame in *Phenomenological Psychology*, such exposure of the realms of one's privacy to 'the public in all its forms' is likely to menace the essential creativity of the erotic life. Moreover, such essential voyeurism has the effect of objectifying human beings in this sphere – the effects of which have also been explored by philosophers and psychologists such as Viktor

188

Frankl, Maurice Merleau-Ponty, Masud Khan and Rollo May.*
There is a great deal in our popular culture today that has this
effect of threatening inward meaning and uniqueness by reducing
human beings to mere *machines à plaisir*. As Masud Khan has
said, it makes the human body 'an ideal machine that can be
manipulated to yield maximum products of sensation'. The
effect of such 'trends' has been to demoralize English people at
large, in middle-class fashionable, or would-be fashionable
circles, in a deeply nihilistic way and the dynamics of this developing cult of the acquisitive pursuit of sensations in pseudo-
sexuality has become a new and destructive flight from life.†
Unless they are taking part in sexual activity of a certain kind
some people, who are anxious to be recognized as 'with it', may
feel 'out of things'. Yet the kind of activity they feel they should
be engaged in may seem to a psychotherapist perverted or psy-
chopathological.

While most people, no doubt, behave in normal and decent
ways, as reasonable people always did, there does seem to be
more anxiety among those who are uncertain of their values and
their emotional security (see Rollo May, *Love and Will*, which
suggests an increasing anxiety at a deep level, and a new psychic
impotence). This is hardly surprising when people are subjected
to so much falsification of sex and other personal realities by
television and journalism. A magazine recently quoted a leading
actress ('a pace-setter') who said that when one was in love 'it
was difficult to be unfaithful': trendy fashion obviously seemed
to her to demand that one should sleep around a little, while
love was something of a hindrance, because it meant one had to
show a certain amount of integrity. There is no doubt that such
'swinging' absurdities put about by fashionable journals in
England today have undermined people's confidence in their own
good sense – and in their own chastity, which Professor John
MacMurray defines, in *Reason and Emotion*, as the capacity to

*See my *Sex and Dehumanization* and *The Case Against Pornography*.
†See Masud Khan, 'Pornography – or the Politics of Rage and Subversion': *The Times Literary Supplement*, 3 February 1972. Khan finds the
more extreme forms of the aggressive mentalization of sexual sensation
'inherently fascistic'.

189

be true to one's deepest emotional needs. If indeed people do find support in trendy journalism for their aberrant activities, such as wife-swapping, they may be able to overcome guilt* in giving way to the acting out of pornographic and perverted fantasies. Yet such activities menace psychic health. As David Boadella says, 'The façade of pleasure and fun disguises a latent need to attack and destroy the real love-needs which are repressed by this kind of narcissistic behaviour' (*op. cit.*). The elements of hatred and revenge in such activities have been pointed out by writers such as Reimut Reiche.

From the point of view of Marcuse, we can see such manifestations as the pseudo-sexuality of today's journalism as 'repressive desublimation'. Those who need to live out their sick and sadistic fantasies exploit the new permissive ethos, to 'imprison others in distorted concepts', and urge them towards pseudo-gratifications that can do nothing for their real relational needs. This is all disguised by the liberal-progressive tendency to believe that what we need is a reverse conditioning, in the way I have discussed above. As David Boadella makes clear, the genuine sexual revolutionary sees this as a parallel to the deadening effect of capitalist society itself, and as the 'institutionalization of sexual pseudo-gratification' – which gratifies nothing, because it is mental, split-off from bodily life and 'meeting'. The voyeur's sick need is to seek to maintain permanent sexual tensions – and this is now the stock-in-trade of the magazine industry. Today we cannot even open a copy of *Vogue* without seeing an image of a couple having sexual intercourse in bed, in the film news pages (November 1971, No. 15, Vol. 128, p. 152). The copy of *Nova* we pick up on the table of the doctor's waiting-room will present us with a sequence of film frames showing a woman undressing, ending with her suggestively undoing the opening of her panties.† In the same issue there is an advertisement showing a girl dressed only in a towel looking out of the window at a

---

*The attempt to dispel guilt is also assisted by drugs. *Nova* recently repeated the myth that L S D increased potency. In fact, as Dr Masters has pointed out, it causes impotence.

†From *How to Undress in Front of Your Husband.*

young man who is gazing in, and crouched in a rampant pose. The implications of such new advertisements is that immodesty and voyeurism are socially acceptable. In our colour supplement, there is a man in period costume undoing a girl's dress in bed, selling us not only brandy, but the implication that it improves promiscuous potency. Next to this perhaps there will be an article describing how an underground film director filmed himself copulating on a heap of offal, with an image of Andy Warhol's superstar, sitting naked in a discussion about his latest voyeuristic film.

All these images are, in their context, perverted images. They are serving no other purpose than to draw the eye, by evoking a kind of sexual excitement which is split-off from the kind of excitement that arises between lovers. When the present writer complained about the use of naked girls to draw attention to cars at the Motor Show in 1971, the directors of the Motor Show retorted that there was 'one time-proved method of drawing the attention of the camera'. We may interpret this as meaning that to serve commerce in a machine-society people must be treated as things, and parts of their bodies which arouse sensations must be used to attract those who prepare images by various forms of technology, so that we, in turn, may be mechanically manipulated by the sensationalism of techniques. In the course of this, woman is symbolically humiliated, as are the meanings of the body. The same phenomena are being exploited in the contemporary theatre and cinema, on television, and in journalism by the cynical exploiters of powerful technological media, and by a technicism that reduces man.*

As the *New York Times* has said, of sex on the stage, the use of explicitly sexual imagery now marks the 'final step in the erosion of taste and subtlety'. In the theatre, 'it reduces actors to mere exhibitionists, turns audiences into voyeurs, and debases a sexual relationship almost to the level of prostitution.' 'Far

---

*See Masud Khan, *op. cit.* Khan believes that since the Industrial Revolution man has come to have an image of himself increasingly based on his own machines. See also Robert Daly, *The Spectres of Technicism*, discussed in my book *The Pseudo-Revolution*. See also Boadella, *op. cit.*

191

from providing a measure of cultural emancipation, such descents into degeneracy represent caricatures of art', it said, and 'the utter degradation of taste in pursuit of the dollar'. (Characteristically, our liberal English newspapers and journals today hardly ever dare speak in such clear terms of discrimination.) The same process is happening in the world of journal and paperback publication. Recently in Exeter I went into a fashionable paperback shop and found myself confronted with covers showing a naked male torso with a sadistic-homosexual flavour (a book by Genet); a naked man with prominent genitals, beside a naked woman (*The Body*); a cover showing a black man in a sexual position with a white woman*; a naked woman with her hand grasping her breast (novel by Edna O'Brien, Penguin Books). I should stress that these images were not in themselves works of art, however much the books may have been. They were photographs, and so it would be possible to object to them on the grounds indicted by Robert Stoller, when he points out that nude photographs depend for their appeal on inviting us to feel we are taking something from the *victim* of the camera, that they would not voluntarily give. There is thus a kind of rape involved, as well as sadistic feelings. The trouble is that we have been brought to accept such images by 'enlightened' good taste, believing this to be 'liberation', like stage morality and *Playboy* – and yet many such images evoke sadism and hostility for sales purposes, rather than the kind of admiration and humanity evoked (say) by the painted or sculptured nude in a work of art. What is released into society is growing indifference to nudity

---

*The bigotry of 'enlightenment' being so blind today, I suppose I must add that I have no objection to sexual relations between people of different colours. What I do object to is the use of coloured persons to spice the titillations of pornography. This is a common trick in Scandinavian pornography, in which a blonde woman will be shown being humiliated by a black man; in *Oh! Calcutta!* the same use is made of a black girl. This symbolism complements the well-known play in racist jokes on the negro's mythical sexual potency, and the hate to which this is exposed in racism and its vindications. 'Liberated' pornography today is thus based on the same essential mechanisms as the Nazi rejection of the 'degeneracy' of other races. Others (see Mary Stott in the *Guardian*, February 1972), have noted the similarity between the use of ugly images, as of negro women in *Oz*, and the images in *Der Stuermer*.

192

(which is a pity) and an unconscious hostility, even contempt, for others. Van Den Haag has spoken of the possible dangers of a reduction of empathy, as has Masud Khan.*

The motive behind this gradual development, by which we have come to find grossness socially acceptable when it should not be, is primarily an economic one. The money to be made out of arousing voyeuristic expectations in the public is enormous. As E. J. Mishan says, 'Although drawing support from writers and liberals, the steam behind the movement for the abolition of all forms of censorship, and more specifically in favour of complete freedom of erotic subjects, is predominantly commercial.'† The arguments in favour of increasing tolerance are based on the assertion that in 'freeing' the urge to look at sex, these developments are 'liberating' us. It is assumed that we are now 'free' and secure enough in our permissiveness, to be able to tolerate such things. Khan is scornful of such protestations, while E. J. Mishan suggests that this view is a delusion.

He says that the rapid economic growth of the West over the last half century 'has not been accomplished without traumatic effects on . . . populations'.

Tension is everywhere more evident than harmony, disproportion more evident than proportion. The gross overdevelopment of the acquisitive instinct has its genesis in the industrial free enterprise system of the Classical economists. The increasing obsession with sex, and with sexual display masquerading as fashion, the technique of distilling the carnality of sex, as though it were an essence to be poured lavishly into all forms of modern entertainment, these too owe much to private enterprise and advertising. The effect . . . is a gross displacement of public libido . . . ‡

As the expectations are created, and excitement is aroused, as in the London audiences or the customers in newsagents, so commerce reacts eagerly to it – and 'there are no countervailing forces at work today to coax it back into a proper scheme of

---

*See 'Stealers of Dreams', an interview with Masud Khan and Mary Miles in *The Times*, 8 December 1971; and 'Is Pornography a Cause of Crime?', *Encounter*, July 1967. Both are reprinted in the anthology, *The Case Against Pornography*.

†*The Costs of Economic Growth.*

‡*Op. cit.*, p. 158.

things.' In small towns, as a local newspaper found in a recent investigation, newsagents are being blackmailed into taking a certain proportion of 'sex' magazines.* They were told that if they did not, other shops would be set up to put them out of business. The controllers of all the media have a power over people which people now feel they can no longer resist. This is probably the effect of receiving so much through the television screen, from remote centres, through a technical device (many programmes not even being live, and those who put them out being faceless and concealed). How can one, in any case, protest? In the face of public passivity, every possible step is exploited by the moguls of the media, to push the limits of exhibitionism further and further back. In this they are quite irresponsible about possible public harm – and every naïve declaration of the 'harmlessness' of pornography naturally encourages them to go ahead with increasing arrogance. Obscenity trials are carefully studied and sometimes tape-recorded, for foreign firms who are waiting to exploit any gaps that may appear in the defences of morality. Such legal confusion has meant a new and startling grossness on the bookstalls, as in film.

As Mishan says,

with the 'experts' divided and the public perplexed, it is not to be expected that the law will hold out much longer against the mounting commercial pressure, backed by naïve writers and liberals, to abolish all forms of censorship, leaving a morally fragile and edgy society to cope with the flood as best it can . . . †

The spectacle is one of publishers waiting for the opportunity to be as irresponsible as their economic needs force them to be. When pressed, the advertiser or journal publisher protests his responsible capacity to control himself. Yet as soon as he is given a chance, he seizes the opportunity to push the limits yet further ('this year the models took everything off') – whatever the effects may be. So in Denmark, through the influence of a small pressure group of people working in journalism and photography, total tolerance has been obtained for pornography.

*The *Mid-Devon Advertiser*, reporting on pornography in shops in Newton Abbot, October 1971.

†*Op. cit.*, p. 159.

194

There was no popular demand for this, as the Chief Constable of Copenhagen told Lord Longford's research team. But there is now no going back: for that would be 'reactionary' and no-one would want to be that – certainly no political party. Yet the law there cannot even enforce the protection of children: although there are laws supposed to prevent the exhibition of obscene posters and magazines to children, these laws are not properly enforced and children can, in fact, buy pornography from slot machines there at any time.

What may be being unleashed is psychic damage of a profoundly anti-social kind. There are several studies which cast doubts on our cheerful assumptions that pornography is harmless. For instance, Khan makes it plain that there are malignant elements in perversion – such as the unconscious desire to annihilate the other person, a manifestation in perversion that is sometimes acted out (as in the lives of de Sade, Brady and Joe Orton). Perversions such as pornography are bound up with primitive impulses to spoil, devour and destroy – which are the kind of unconscious impulses often acted out by delinquents and criminals, for reasons we do not yet know. Other writers have emphasized that the 'primary dynamic is hostility.' Van Den Haag believes that by reducing the human being to an 'impersonal bearer of sensations' pornography diminishes those capacities in us which prevent us from being violent to others.*

Erwin Straus, the phenomenologist, criticizes the generally held view, based on Freud, that to 'release' voyeurism is a good thing, in the name of 'freedom', because it represents a 'heightened urge to look' – and so has suffered painful restriction in previous ages. Straus argues, with Khan, that voyeurism represents a break-down of an individual's relationship with reality, and with 'the significant other'. The voyeur concentrates on the 'parts, the words, and the functions'. He always keeps at a

*See 'Acting Out in Perversions' by Masud Khan, in *Sexual Behaviour and the Law*. See also *The Psychology of the Criminal Act and Punishment* by Gregory Zilboorg, on the acting out of primitive destructive fantasies; 'Does Pornography Cause Crime?' by Ernest Van Den Haag in *Encounter*, December 1967; 'Pornography and Perversion', by Robert J. Stoller, UCCA. The two latter essays are in *The Case Against Pornography*. See also *The Case of Rudolph* in *Existence – a New Dimension in Psychiatry*.

distance. The lover, by contrast, uses his eyes to move towards making love – towards half-light, concealment, secrecy. The voyeur cannot bear this because he fears the creative commitment to time, and to the new development of life which love represents. When we are overlooked we feel irritated, and that is because the intrusive looking of a voyeur threatens our creative capacities for the erotic. Straus's conclusion is that the natural shame *makes the erotic possible.* Continual intrusion into the sphere of sexual experience, by the voyeuristic camera, could thus threaten our capacities to 'go with' erotic experience, and menace it with 'the public in all its forms'. This is, in fact, the effect of the ordinary bookshop or newspaper stall of today whose main source of appeal is voyeurism. This threatens our response to the creative sexual moment in life, by making the depersonalized sexual image banal, commonplace – so that all the essential uniqueness of love is implicitly assaulted.*

Straus's approach has in the background the work of Merleau-Ponty, the French philosopher. Merleau-Ponty argued that the use of nudity in a trivial way can lead to a profound loss of freedom, because the individual who is submitted to a contemptuous glance is reduced to the status of a thing.† The person who is casually exposed to others suffers a kind of enslavement. Such a denial of the freedom of others has political dangers – so that an American sociologist has spoken of the 'sexual fascism' of *Playboy*.‡

We have been persuaded, by strange and sinister developments in pseudo-sexuality, to be blind to certain widespread offences to human nature and now something that may be called a disease is an integral and substantial part of our magazine culture. It is now necessary to insist that, from the point of view of 'philosophical anthropology', such manifestations as the *Sun* newspaper and *Vanity Fair*, the 'girlie' magazine, and certainly papers like *Penthouse* and *Curious* are commercial exploitations of perversions. This intrusion of perversion into the periodical

*See Straus on shame in *Phenomenological Psychology*.

†See 'The Body in its Sexual Being' in *Phenomenology of Perception*, by Maurice Merleau-Ponty.

‡See Calvin Herton quoted in *Love and Will*, Rollo May. Leo Abse M.P. has also spoken of sexual fascism (*Observer*, 2 May 1971).

trade is the reason for giving it so much attention here; as local newsagents intuitively recognize, this is a threat to psychic health at large. (Some newsagents, recognizing this, are delivering magazines themselves by hand, to prevent them falling into the hands of newsboys and other children.) Dr Robert Stoller, of the Gender Identity Research and Treatment Centre, Department of Psychiatry, Los Angeles University, says that 'there is no non-perverse pornography.' He says that when we look at a nude in a 'girlie' magazine, we are in fact taking from her in a cruel way:

where it is implied that the girl is calmly unaware that she is being secretly stared at and used. In fact (in fantasy) there is, however, force, something that smacks of rape, of taking from the posed girl what it is imagined she would not give the observer freely...

This sadistic element is, of course, often emphasized by the wearing of chains, or by certain tricks of clothing (jeans with open flies, etc.) that emphasize the girl's victimization. Dr Stoller emphasizes that 'there is always a victim: no victim, no por-nography'. And the essential dynamic of pornography is hostility. 'I do not mean here simply activity, benign aggression, but intent (even if unconscious) to harm.' Pornography contains an inter-mixture of sadism, masochism and voyeurism. The sadism is inherent in the implicit attack on woman. One's own femininity and one's 'bad' experiences of femininity are projected over the woman victims in pornography, and attacked in fantasy. The masochism is more difficult to see: the female element in oneself may also be projected over these victims in pornography, and humiliated in them: there is an unconscious identification on our part with the depicted victim.

The reasons for this are complex, but one unconscious impulse according to Stoller is that men have always had a problem over female identification in their lives, and a man wants to put him-self, in fantasy, to the worst test he can imagine. He 'becomes' a woman in fantasy, and suffers the deepest humiliation by seeing the woman – as in the little image of a woman showing her bare posterior that advertises *Oh! Calcutta!* in the satirical magazine *Private Eye*. If the man can become sexually excited by the humiliation he survives triumphantly. He is 'better than any woman' – an attitude of racial (or gender) superiority evident in

197

the *Playboy* ethos. But, of course, promoted at large, such indulgence of sadism must foster a deep hostility to woman, and a desire to make women into lesser beings. When the bored Sultan made the women of the Harem run round naked, like mares, we may feel this was a shameful exploitation of women as lesser beings. But when we see the same process happening for our appeal on the covers of magazines and paperback books, we feel this is a 'liberation'.

Of course, sexual depiction can be a way of exploring the realities of what was once forbidden sensuality. But the reaction which is growing against pornography is also a protest against the possibility that hostility may be released into the community. What commerce is exploiting at the moment, by its glossy images of nakedness and sexuality, are sadism, hostility, the impulse to humiliate, primitive anxieties, masochism, anti-feminine impulses, and hate. The effect of titillation is to bring out our capacities for unconscious hostility and the anxiety associated with it. This is now the basis of the workings of most commercial journals and many publishers, and its roots are in a deep anti-human cruelty. As costs rise, and the demand for returns on investment becomes more assertive, editorial control and responsibility gradually give way to this new ruthlessness of exploitation, of which sexploitation is the most anti-human manifestation. It is likely that, as in films, unless these trends are resisted by public opinion there will follow an increasing exploitation of violence.*

Children read the worst papers, they get into 'X' films, and it is thus appropriate that the community at large has begun to question the effects of such forms of education, which are without doubt deeply affecting the attitudes of impressionable youth. It seems worse when papers intended for youth are themselves improper. *Honey*, in a recent issue, offered its readers a 'Seduction Game for Lovers', a kind of combination of Snakes and Ladders and Postman's Knock, in which the forfeits were sexual ones –

*A magazine *Seen*, on sale in Danish Sex Fairs, juxtaposes images of dismembered bodies with pornographic images. A film editor of Hammer Films has recently resigned because of the exploitation of scenes of rape and perverted sex. See the stills from *Straw Dogs* and *The Clockwork Orange* in *Films and Filming*, which children read.

from 'tell a dirty story' to taking part in depersonalized sexual activity. Another magazine, discussed at a Conference of the National Council of Women in November 1970, advised its girl readers on 'how to get a man into bed as quickly as possible – and if not a man, then a woman companion.' *Valentine*, early in 1971, instructed its girl readers of fourteen where they could go to get picked up in London – and was criticized for this on television by Bernard Braden. It is not only that the curiosity and anxiety of young people are thus being aroused by all the powers at the disposal of modern persuasion techniques: they are also being sold, often glamorously, quite damaging answers.

One disturbing aspect of this trend is the increasingly flagrant attempt to demoralize young people, and to tell them there is 'nothing wrong' with sexual manifestations which in any medical context would be approached with concern:

Lesbians can only be considered 'abnormal' in that a minority of women indulge in it. It's certainly not 'unnatural' – homosexuality can be observed in animals from mice to elephants ... Just as it's a mistake to despise homosexual people for being 'perverted' it's wrong to pity them as 'sick'.*

Such writing is really a form of titillation, arousing a kind of 'bad thinking' about sex which has the appeal of giving a flip to one's sense of being 'alive' in the manic way. But, accompanied by romantic photographs of women lovers, such an article not only conveys the impression that sexual relations between members of the same sex are to be simply enjoyed: it implies by its tone that they are possibly superior to heterosexual ones and even conveys a hatred of men ('men are just so conceited ...') while tending to reduce natural protective shame and discrimination. There is, the article implies, such a thing as a 'true' lesbian:

'We don't want anyone to think we're corrupting anyone,' Cynthia said. 'Also until a girl's twenty-one I don't think she can really know for *certain* if she's a true lesbian or not. After all, nearly all normal girls go through a period of homosexuality at one stage, having crushes on the gym-mistress or whatever.'

In the light of studies like those of Masud Khan, on the basis

*19 magazine.

of the treatment of perverts, such articles can be seen as conveying the pervert's need to break down discrimination and self-respect in those who could be made use of, if the occasion should arise. In the light of psychoanalytical studies the effect might be to help 'fix' a young person in a homosexual tendency – and to deepen anxiety in someone who knew, deep down, they wanted to escape from some homosexual involvement, to fulfil themselves in a normal way. In general these papers are a form of social conditioning that 're-inforces and imprints a sick and distorted concept of sexuality (which) must block and impede the development of mature feelings and genuine sexual expression' (David Boadella, *op. cit.*).

The question to ask here is – to what extent have the writers and editors of such articles forgotten their responsibility to the young under pressure of the need to sustain circulation? The editor of *Petticoat* recently told his writers, 'No parents!' Ten years ago the parents appeared in such papers, albeit as hostile, indifferent or misunderstanding 'squares'. Today they have disappeared altogether. Jules Henry, speaking of the American situation, sees the attempt to appeal to a whole generation over the heads of its parents as reminiscent of Nazi methods of breaking down traditional values for other purposes (Jules Henry, *Culture Against Man*, pp. 262–74).

The inculcation of trends in behaviour and the deliberate breaching of traditional and personal sanctions in behaviour begins even with reading matter designed for children. Children are being urged towards sexual precocity at a very early age. Here is an example from a girls' picture paper:

A KISS TO REMEMBER

* It takes two to make a memorable kiss. You and him! So don't leave it all up to him. You need a little technique, too.
* Don't stare at him. You'll only put him right off. Close your eyes and part your lips oh-so-slightly.
* Kiss as though you really mean it ...
* Use the indelible kind. (Of lipstick)
* Soft ... that's how your lips should feel under his ...
* ... well, make it a kiss he'll remember. He'll come back for more.

There is no need to labour a verbal analysis. It is enough to say that nothing is sacred to Fleet Street – not even the most spontaneous, tender, and naïve of life's experiences, the first discovery of kissing. Here is the source of the precocious 'knowingness' of the adolescent that, as teachers and doctors know, can lead to personal disaster. While we may have gained much through permissiveness, we should perhaps question the degree to which children and adolescents are being continually subjected to propaganda for less responsible sexual behaviour – as they are, by 'pop', drugs, 'pop' promotion papers, television plays, films – and magazines. The climate is such that a fifteen-year-old girl will report in court that girls in her school carry contraceptives, brag about the men they have slept with and pull her leg because she admits she is a virgin (*The Times*, 8 March 1971). Between 1959 and 1969 the number of illegitimate children born to girls under sixteen increased by two hundred per cent: such figures may be an index of the effects of cultural persuasions of an irresponsible kind. We must always be concerned, surely, about putting stumbling blocks in the way of the weak? Teachers and doctors know how much children are suffering from the inculcation of pseudo-sexuality in our culture.

There are resistances in normal children, but the pressures are now more prodigious than cultural pressures have ever been in history, and where there is any disturbance in a child's natural safeguards they are easily broken down in the ethos being created by our culture for commercial purposes. Perhaps the most disturbing aspect of it all is the indifference of the public to this seduction of the innocent, as cynical journalism urges each new generation into sexual experiences for which they are not ready, with consequent damage to their later emotional development. The teacher knows at school how much, inwardly, the readers of such papers as *Marty*, *Mirabelle* and *Roxy* are still children, while children who read trendy papers like *Vanity Fair* and *She* are often deeply shocked, as some have confessed to my own children when no adults were present. But sexual precocity is today even promoted among children of eight to twelve: *Princess*, a paper for these ages, has inset features on 'pop' stars and their private lives though, of course, its other copy is appropriately and properly childish.

From their early teens children are conditioned in pseudo-sexuality, at first in a light-headed romantic way, as in *Mirabelle*. Apart from a number of romantic strip cartoons and a few articles such papers contain a good deal of straight publicity material put out by the promoters of 'pop' singers. 'Trust' is established by Fan Club items, a horoscope ('love lucky dates are tomorrow (Tuesday) and Saturday'), and by features ostensibly offering advice from the 'pop' idols themselves – 'Ask Adam ... A Boy's View of A Girl's World' ('*When a boy whistles at me, can I whistle back*? No, he's supposed to be the wolf, remember. Try a slight smile to show you don't mind him whistling'). On the centre pages Sylvia Ferguson asks Mark Wynter (star of *Just for Fun*) 'Are Engagements Square?':

'I think teenagers are more sensible today than they were say fifty years ago. They are given more responsibility and they were kept under the thumb. You know, "children should be seen and not heard",' he grinned.

'Nowadays things are very different. Teenagers run the music industry today, that's for a dead cert!'

What seems like a new recognition of children's rights and freedom is in fact a commercial ploy: but this 'movement' towards 'child power' has even become an aspect of the fashionable 'left' scene in education. (*Children's Rights* employs 'Dennis the Menace' from *Beano* as a symbol of desirable subversion.)

Later, papers for older adolescents are bolder, and offer endless advice about life, in order to establish an ersatz trust. They tell young people how to attract others as though there was nothing else in life but to be 'bright', to attract the opposite sex, and to pursue continual sensation. One cannot be a 'success' (they imply) until one *has* certain experiences – and certain clothes and other possessions: and relational experiences are approached in the same way. Here are quotations from one issue of *Honey*: 'Are you ready for marriage?', 'How to be a hit at a dance', 'The art of small talk gets you more dates', 'Don't put on the big act or you'll fail', 'You too can sparkle by starlight', 'Do relax, you're here to enjoy yourself', 'It's fun to try a private moment', 'As every girl would agree, it's better to have boy-trouble than no-boy trouble'.

The ad. copy cunningly directs these implications into the realm of materialistic acquisition. 'Only a seam can give the most elegant legs in the world', and so on. The purpose of the paper behind the helpful front is to gain the 'trust' of a generation, to hold before them a pretend-world in which they will feel they cannot live successfully – and *love* successfully – without certain know-how *and the equipment to go with it.*

But the emotional conflict this kind of commercial journal must create is evident when we look at any serious advice given in the same paper. The advertisements and general fun-seeking air of the paper are calculated to 'turn the reader on', sexually. But then the paper offers serious advice from an 'expert' such as Dr Eustace Chesser. This advice is utterly at odds with the general suggestion of the rest of the paper. The text and the ads imply 'Sweep him off his feet' – you are not with it unless you have wildly romantic experiences! But then a psychiatrist is roped in, for prestige and trust, to say 'wait!' But, of course, what he 'reveals', as of promiscuity, stimulates the mental consciousness yet further!

Occasionally there is a piece of good advice. In the first issue of *Honey*, by Dr Keith Cameron:

> I wouldn't for a moment suggest promiscuity or even the full expression of sex in any individual case, as part of the essential process of 'getting to know men'. Indeed, promiscuity will do just the opposite, because you can never have a total relationship that way at all. You simply isolate sex at the expense of everything else.
>
> I'd go so far as to say that the promiscuous people are not on the whole over-sexed, but *under*-sexed; they have to keep trying to prove to themselves that they're 'normal'.

This is loose language for a psychological writer, but it seemed to me closer to truth than the rest. But, above all, Dr Cameron's remarks on immaturity *are true of this kind of paper itself.* It encourages 'promiscuous' appetite, evoking all the time the presence and force of sex, to sell goods. It is surely cruel, so to stimulate sex-consciousness, and then to produce a medical man to give a cold-blooded piece of advice on 'how to behave'. Too late! No medical man can have enough prestige, despite his 'frankness', to overcome the impression made by the rest of the

203

magazine – with its whirl of bare thighs, straining bosoms, kissing mouths and romantic stories* – that the reader is a failure unless he or she is engaged in sexual adventure all the time: a message which has been definitely conveyed to young people, to their widespread distress.

While those who pour out this material are loud and arrogant in their assertion of the need for 'freedom of expression', the truth is that their view of culture is extremely dictatorial, and from this authoritarian position they brush aside any objections raised by the public. As Raymond Williams points out, their view of culture is that of a few educating the many – with every right to do so, according to certain formulae of 'the market's needs' such as one finds in the *Writers' and Artists' Yearbook:*

... young, gay, lively ... we welcome fresh, original ideas from freelance writers for Profiles, humour ... the art of living – *and loving*. If it's new, we are interested. Fiction: first-rate writing well-plotted, with situations *and* problems *with which the reader* can identify herself. Particularly the short short story ...
[my italics]

'Happy endings' are essential, to preserve 'relaxation'. Identification is necessary for the promotion of a dream world, in which acquisitiveness and a desire to be 'with it' may be stimulated.

... Required scripts for picture serials and complete picture stories with *emotional plots* and with the love interest maintained from first to last: happy endings essential ...

Imagine Tolstoy, D. H. Lawrence, Guy de Maupassant, Mark

*And an increasing sophisticated suggestiveness that seems to verge on obscenity: *e.g.* cartoon of two girls going upstairs, caption 'I said to him I've got nothing to hide ...' Today magazines for young people discuss such topics as male nudity (*19*, for instance, recently discussed the proportion of men who have been circumcized in the cast of *Oh! Calcutta!*, and the effects of male nudity: 'Yuk!', said the girl writing the piece). Some features such as the Ward Report in *Petticoat* have surprised lecturers and students by their lewdness: Mr George Watson and his student teachers at Saffron Walden College of Education found this feature 'sick and disgusting'. See also Margaret Duggan, 'Lost Innocence' in the *Church Times*, 28 January 1972. Of material in *Romance* and other I.P.C. papers for young people she says, 'This is *real* pornography, for it is attempting to turn a generation of girls ... into ... anxiety-ridden courtesans.'

Twain, or Charles Dickens responding to the injunctions I have put in italics above, from Fleet Street!

In this sphere the exploitation of sex has become increasingly cynical – under the cover of 'enlightenment'. The intellectual does not shudder when a 'pop' song writer reveals, in an article in the *Guardian*, that 'the secret of success is to get the boy and girl into bed together without really saying so.' With great rapidity the bookstall and bookshop have become dominated by pseudo-sexuality. But now it is obvious that those persuasions are resulting in herd trends, not least among the young. As F. R. Leavis has said, 'The suggestion that enlightened reductivism, the vacuity of life, and the irresponsibilities induced by "pop" are intimately related won't now be dismissed with the easy jeer of a short time back' (*The Times Literary Supplement*, 29 May 1969). The creation of trends has become a cultural feature, at all levels, and from our point of view these are likely to inhibit personal growth by encouraging people to submerge individuality in mass group stereotypes. They are encouraged to feel afraid of breaking the herd patterns, and thus becoming ostracized or isolated: but some herd trends are today led by fanatical immoralists. Many become less confident in their own good sense, and so open to moral inversion. 'Everybody does it' has become a powerful threat to traditional sanctions and values, and psychiatrists are now reporting that children feel it is 'chicken' not to try premarital sexual intercourse – long before they are emotionally ready. At extremes, young people are persuaded that public sex at 'pop' festivals is a 'liberation', while many today no longer seem to be able to see what is wrong with (say) sadistic films, or suggestive magazines.

In psychoanalysis it was long ago recognized that the theory that therapy 'released instincts' would not serve to explain what happened in work with children. From this realization, the work of people like Winnicott has drawn attention to the ways in which children build up a human identity and reality sense, through their culture. It will not do, therefore, to apply to children the pseudo-beliefs that all expression of sex and violence should be 'liberated', even if we accept them for adults. If we apply more recent theories from psychoanalysis, we must see the young

205

person's needs as being primarily for good relationships, love, and creativity. Society is the expression of man's best potentialities, rather than an enemy, while the quest of each individual is for his own 'potentia' – what he may become, from his own 'formative principle'. Perhaps the greatest enemy to this kind of constructive personal development today is what Viktor Frankl has called a 'thoroughly decadent sensuality', imposed on young people by their culture.

As Masud Khan has emphasized, pornography is a masturbatory stimulation of mental excitement, divorced from the body, and from relationship. Nothing could be worse for the young sensibility than to be caught up in a false 'liberation' that drew the cultural life and expectations into such a nihilistic *huis clos*. Yet this is what much in the world of 'pop', film and magazines does today, for the young. Of magazine journalism we may say, I believe, as Raymond Williams says of our popular culture as a whole:

In the worst cultural products of our time, we find little that is genuinely popular, developed from the life of actual communities. We find instead a synthetic culture, or anti-culture, which is alien to almost everybody, persistently hostile to art and intellectual activity ... given over to exploiting indifference, lack of feeling, frustration, and hatred. It finds such common human interests as sex, and turns them into crude caricatures or glossy facsimiles. It plays repeatedly around hatred and aggression, which it never discharges but continually feeds. This is not the culture of 'the ordinary man': it is the culture of the disinherited...*

The need to reform journalism and to free it from the debasing influence of commercial pressures is urgent. But it seems unlikely that there is any hope of expecting such an improvement towards the level an educated public would deserve. Occasionally a Press Commission or a UNESCO Report hopes for an improvement: but none ever comes. The commercial press has been content to follow the Northcliffe formulae (Sex, Money, Crime) profitably, for nearly a century. The arrogant assumption of the commercial interests that they have the right to teach the public in their ways, for profit, hardens as costs rise. The hard core of commercial attitudes can be studied in the *Investor's Chronicle*.

Communications, p. 109.

Grave social consequences must inevitably follow from the effect of leaving widespread and powerful cultural influences in the hands of those whose sole motives and responsibilities are commercial ones, and who are prepared to promote dehumanization. Yet, as Susanne Langer has said, even sociologists fail to make the proper connections between destructive and disruptive trends in our society and the influence of corrupt art. To tackle this state of affairs would involve widespread changes, and would require subtle legislation; yet only by greater discrimination, backed by legal sanctions, could the popular periodical press become truly 'free' enough to improve and really serve public needs in a positive way. Meanwhile it is left to the teacher in school to cooperate with young readers, to examine the fare journalism offers us, to demonstrate to them that they can write all the varieties of 'features' much better themselves, and that there are other possibilities in life than those so dismally and limitingly exhibited on the railway bookstall.

BOOKS

This essay is written from the point of view of what the author has called 'philosophical anthropology'. This means the study of man by taking into account problems of meaning, and the phenomena of consciousness. The term was perhaps first used by Ernst Cassirer in his book *An Essay on Man*, Yale University Press, 1944, in which he tried to find the way to a unifying concept of man. Susanne Langer is a disciple of Cassirer, and her approach may be studied in *Philosophy in a New Key*, Oxford University Press, 1957, and *Philosophical Sketches*, Johns Hopkins, 1962. She and Cassirer emphasize that man' sprimary need is symbolism.

Other writers who place an emphasis on man's 'inward' life from this point of view, include certain philosophers of science such as Marjorie Grene, in *The Knower and the Known*, Faber, 1966 and *Approaches to a Philosophical Biology*, Basic, 1968. Again, in these, man's inner needs and the primacy of culture are emphasized. We may also include the existentialists who follow Martin Buber in philosophical anthropology – see *The Philosophy of Martin Buber*, ed. P. A. Schilpp and M. Friedman, Cambridge University Press, 1969. In psychoanalytical psychology there are the 'object-relations' therapists, such as Harry Guntrip (*Personality Structure and Human Interaction*, Hogarth Press, 1961), D. W. Winnicott (*Playing and Reality*, Tavistock,

207

1971) and others, on the one hand, and the 'existentialist' psycho-therapists on the other – these include Rollo May (*Love and Will*, Souvenir, 1971, *Existence – a New Dimension in Psychiatry and Psychology*, Basic, 1958) and R. D. Laing (*The Divided Self*, Penguin Books, 1965).

There are also the phenomenologists in psychology such as Erwin Straus (*Phenomenological Psychology*, Tavistock, 1966) and Maurice Merleau-Ponty (*The Phenomenology of Perception*, Routledge, 1962). The author has tried to show, in *Human Hope and the Death Instinct*, Pergamon, 1971, that, in the light of this whole body of thought, many of our assumptions about man and society are absurd. Many of the things about human life and reality taken as 'truths' by the world of journalism are not truths at all, but delusions.

This falsity is especially serious in the realms of sex and violence. See also the author's *Sex and Dehumanization*, Pitman, 1972, *The Pseudo-Revolution*, Pergamon, 1971 and *The Masks of Hate*, Pergamon, 1972. Masud Khan's essay on 'Pornography – or the Politics of Rage and Subversion' is included in *The Case Against Pornography*, ed. David Holbrook, Tom Stacey, London, 1972, as are articles by Erwin Straus, and the essays mentioned by Robert Stoller, Ernest Van Den Haag, and Professor John MacMurray (from his *Reason and Emotion*, Faber). See also Viktor Frankl, *The Doctor and the Soul*, Souvenir Press, 1969, and David Boadella, *Wilhelm Reich: the Evolution of his Work*, Vision Press, 1972.

Other relevant general books are:

E. J. MISHAN, *The Costs of Economic Growth*, Penguin Books, 1969
RAYMOND WILLIAMS, *Communications*, Penguin Books, 1968
DANIEL BOORSTIN, *The Image*, Atheneum, 1962
EUGENE KAELIN, *An Existentialist Aesthetic*, University of Wisconsin Press, 1962
GREGORY ZILBOORG, *The Psychology of the Criminal Act and Punishment*, Hogarth Press, 1955
PETER ABBS, *English for Diversity*, Heinemann, 1969
ROGER POOLE, *Towards Deep Subjectivity*, Allen Lane The Penguin Press, 1972.

8 The Film

RICHARD COLLINS

The nature and status of popular culture have long vexed and provoked debate and inquiry; the deployment of terms like 'natural', 'organic', 'civilized' in cultural or social criticism, implicitly or explicitly, acknowledge the pertinence of popular culture. The debate takes on an enhanced significance with the development of mass communications in the twentieth century, when the process of disintegration of independent communities, whether of the order of village or nation, initiated by the industrial revolution accelerated towards the consolidation of human societies in 'the global village'. Clearly the nature of information mediated by mass communication systems, its content, has its importance and influence augmented in proportion to the pervasiveness of its propagation.

Although the precise status of cultural evidence remains indeterminate, a consensus seems to exist that generalizations about the nature and value of a human society may be made from the evidence offered by the nature and qualities of its artifacts. Professor Hoggart's formulation is appropriate:

The literary imagination can give insights into the nature of society itself, insights which cannot be contained within a self-enclosed aesthetic world.

The work of the Centre for Contemporary Cultural Studies has developed through an exploration of the relationship between culture and society and the status of cultural evidence; that a relationship exists is generally acknowledged and one may assert that the vitality and health of a society is related to the vigour and quality of its artistic and intellectual life, a life that is present in vernacular artifacts and behaviour as much as in the 'high culture' of a society.

209

The mass media are perhaps the most powerful and pervasive cultural influences which contemporary British society experiences and it is characteristically their content that is examined in the process of generalization about the quality and nature of modern life. Whether these generalizations follow the line of examination of the effects of mass communications or of comparison with a folk culture and quality of life that has substantially atrophied or vanished, mass communication seems to me to be preponderantly given – mistakenly – a determining significance. It is assumed more or less *a priori* that the quality of experience mediated in a popular culture compares unfavourably with that of the traditional culture, and that the advent of mass communications has provoked a decline from the real, if in some ways very limited, achievements of folk culture; a decline that is all the more lamentable and dangerous for being broadcast ubiquitously.

I said earlier that the nature and status of pop culture is a vexed question; it is perhaps characterized by a pervasiveness, a quality of being embedded in daily life, that is not shared by high culture. Behaviour must be general before it may be regarded as popular, and so an activity like watching television rather than concert-going would characterize pop culture. If popular culture does, or did, exist as a distinct entity, it must differ in kind from the phenomenon we usually imply by 'culture' or 'art'. As it is generally understood, an interest in Bach or Debussy, Wordsworth or Melville, Delacroix or Vermeer, in Resnais or Bergman, is not an interest in popular culture; yet it is extremely difficult to make categorical distinctions between the works of 'culture', the enjoyment and production of which are associated with an élite (whether defined socially or educationally) and which profoundly engage and animate the intelligence and sensibility of its audience, and those of popular culture, springing from and utilized by a large undifferentiated public. The distinction between folk culture and contemporary popular culture is perhaps easier to make: we may describe folk culture as the generation of artifacts and patterns of behaviour in a society in which work and leisure remain undifferentiated and in which moreover specialization or professionalism in work activities has not been generalized.

210

Thus it is a quality of folk culture that the activity of production is collaborative, necessitating the creation of human relationships, and that it is one in which decorative and creative impulses may be satisfied. The life of peasant Europe, structured by largely self-sufficient communities – the so-called 'organic community' – may be taken as a type; the difference between this kind of experience (which lingers on in some parts of the British Isles – in Shetland for example with its marvellous knitting) and that of an overwhelmingly urban and mechanized Britain needs no labouring.

It seems to me profitless to lament the eclipse of the traditional society and thus to divert attention from the task of recognizing the identity of contemporary experience and locating the ways in which it may be more creatively re-structured. Given that mass communications constitute an important area of our experience, we would do well to reflect on their achievements and possibilities – this will not be done if educationists construe their role as one of fighting a rear-guard action against the depredations of the media.

The assumptions voiced in the Resolution of the N U T Conference of 1960 (quoted in *The Popular Arts*: 'This Conference believes that a determined effort must be made to counteract the debasement of standards which result from the misuse of Press, radio, cinema and television') live on, reflected perhaps most grotesquely in the cult of liberal studies in further education, where too often mass media studies are conducted more in a spirit of homoeopathy than of elucidation. It is common currency that popular art offers forms which may be annexed by great artists and in which works of definitive excellence may be created; the debt of Shakespeare, Jonson and Webster to the popular Tudor and Jacobean theatre, of Mozart to café entertainments, of the young novel to eighteenth-century journalism, and of Dickens to nineteenth-century melodrama, has been clearly established. Yet the relationship between artist and form is more complex than that of genius transcending the restrictions of a common form. It is dishonest to maintain a categorical differentiation of 'culture' and 'popular culture' by annexing all considerable artists for 'culture' and explaining away a possible

211

association with common forms and concerns as contingent and transcendental.

The concept of authorship is a key one here, I think; the inheritance of an ethic of individualism, in which the twentieth-century West shares, leads to an expectation that a single unique consciousness creates a literary or cultural experience and that the qualities of that consciousness are articulated by that experience. So we speak of Shakespeare's themes, Dickensian characterization, and propagate scholarly squabbles over the authorship of 'The Changeling', the nature of the collaboration between Wren and Hawksmoor, Pugin and Barry. The importance of authorship in a twentieth-century scheme of assumption receives its definitive and grotesque articulation in the market for fine art. A genuine Vermeer is of astronomical value, a Van Meegeren forgery of trifling importance, although the qualities of the picture, its communicative value, may have been sufficient to engineer a comprehensive deception of eye and taste. A painting wholly by, say, Rembrandt is taken to be of greater value than one from his studio created in collaboration with his pupils.

Squabbles of this nature seem to me to be profitless and to divert attention from the intrinsic qualities of the art object in question. The assumption of value inherent in qualities of uniqueness or individual authorship appears to constitute an inheritance that is particularly inappropriate and misleading in the context of twentieth-century mass communications, for much of twentieth-century art is the progeny of a collaborative genesis, indeed of industrialized procreation. The source of the confusing distinctions between 'culture' and 'popular culture' may lie in attitudes formed when 'culture' was distinguished by ownership and 'popular culture' was unequivocally of the folk.

It is only in the recent past that 'culture' has become generally available although in some circumstances wealth still determines the accessibility of works of art. It is now uniquely to fine art, pictures, sculptures etc. that high intrinsic value attaches; this was not always so – before the development of printing, books were extremely expensive, and even in the eighteenth century costs remained high. Music, before the piano, was the property of great magnates who could afford to hire or maintain orchestras, and although in the nineteenth century it became available to the bourgeoisie with the piano and an increase in the number of public concert halls, it was not until the introduction of the BBC's public service broadcasting in the 1920s that orchestral music became generally available. Familiarity and inwardness with fine art remains a prerogative of the wealthy; the situation is mitigated to some extent for those living in great conurbations where public collections exist, but very important works are still privately owned and inaccessible. Thus fine art remains in the hands of the collector and connoisseur and the definition of an élite in cultural terms is now a matter of familiarity with 'art', particularly with fine art to which access is restricted. The definition of contemporary cultural élites by what are effectively social criteria follows a pattern articulated in the era prior to the development of printing when literacy functioned as a social distinction; in the eighteenth century the appropriate qualification was a familiarity with the classics (the patrician sneer magnificently deployed by Fielding and Swift in projecting their animus frequently takes this as a locus). The identity of social and cultural distinctions are defined representatively in Lord Eccles' book *On Collecting* in which he describes the pleasures and qualities yielded by works of art as essentially those of acquisition and ownership:

The argument in favour of the private ownership of works of art begins with the need to satisfy in some way or another the acquisitive instinct which is implanted in us at birth. What does the exercise of this instinct feel like to a man engaged in collecting? I have compared my experience with that of friends and we agree that when we buy something the purchase makes us feel better, more secure, and in some way enlarges our personality. If we are asked why we bought this porcelain figure or that modern painting, we reply that we simply had to have it. We were hungry and had to eat. We gave way to the acquisitive instinct which is in every man.

Communicative value or the excitement generated by the formal properties of the work assume an insignificant place eclipsed by the rewards of collecting:

All vast possessions (just the same the case
Whether you call them Villa, Park or Chase).

So too the act of attendance at a performance, theatrical, musical or operatic, carries normatively an implication of social self-definition rather than that of an implicit engagement in a communicative process. This is not to affirm the reverse; to switch on a television or attend the cinema does not *ipso facto* imply a readiness to attend to the subject of the film or television programme. However, much of the animus and suspicion that have focused on the mass media comes from this patrician nexus of values:

The cinema is unlikely ever to reach the level of the best literature and will never satisfy the most exacting demands of the minority. It must always remain to some extent popular and democratic and on a lower level than its contemporary art forms.*

The status of a mass medium as an agent in a social process has too often defined, *a priori*, a response to the achievement of the medium; whether a disdain for the productions of Hollywood, because American, industrial, and marketed for mass consumption and *ipso facto* trash, or enthusiasm for the Soviet cinema, sustained not by the felicity of Soviet films but by an enthusiasm for all art uncontaminated by the dead hand of the bourgeoisie. The cinema, as the first of the mass media of entertainment, experienced and continues to experience reductive attacks derived from basic assumptions about the nature and value of a mass medium and from the postures of cultural élitism I have adumbrated above. The report of the National Council of Public Morals 1917 on 'The Cinema: its present position and future possibilities' concerned itself with investigating the effects of the cinema, its emphasis falling on the cinema as a social rather than a cultural fact; much evidence was adduced concerning the physiological effects of film-going and the behaviour of film-goers within and without the cinema. The report, within its own set of assumptions and terms of reference, is generous and humane, concluding that the cinema performs a generally felicitous social function, but its findings have little to

*W. Hunter, *Scrutiny*, Vol. 1.

do with the nature of experiences mediated by the cinema, or with the content of the medium.

FINDINGS

10. The cinema can bring within the range of the child's experience a fund of valuable information which it would not be possible to obtain by other means.
11. Evidence has been given to us of the vividness and permanence of the visual impressions given by the cinema to the older school children.
20. We regard the adequate filming of stories of acknowledged literary merit to be a matter of primary importance in the interests of both children and adults.
22. The moving picture is intensely exciting, intensely realistic, and can cover an amazingly wide field of information. But these very characteristics, which may make it such a powerful instrument for evil, guarantee its future possibilities as a potent instrument of culture.

Findings 20 and 22 imply a wholly instrumental role for the cinema in mediating the traditional values of 'culture'; there is no recognition of the possibility of the cinema functioning as an autonomous art. It is easy to understand this position: by 1917 – in spite of the work of Griffith, Ince, Abel Gance etc. – the potential of the cinema remained unachieved. More deplorable is the contemporary pervasiveness of attitudes appropriate fifty years ago; school outings are characteristically confined to films of literature, drama, opera or public events; serious film study in British higher education is of negligible proportions; films are regarded, like T.V. programmes, as undifferentiated cultural noise:

To sit on the padded seat in the warm smoke-scented darkness, letting the flickering drivel on the screen gradually overwhelm you – feeling the waves of its silliness lap around you till you seem to drown, intoxicated in a viscous sea – after all it's the kind of drug we need.*

In the educational orthodoxy of inoculation of pupils against

*George Orwell, *Keep the Aspidistra Flying*, Penguin Books, 1962.

215

the invariably noxious and trivial products of the mass media, we risk impoverishing our understanding in a wilful disregard of the perceptions the cinema may offer, as I hope to show in later discussion of specific films. Our collective danger is perhaps that of perpetrating a like mistake to that of the nineteenth-century literary establishment, of Sir Leslie Stephen and Matthew Arnold, who deplored the impoverishment of the popular English novel in comparison with poetry, 'the crown of literature', and with the works of foreign novelists safely distanced by geography and language, whilst ignoring home-grown popular authors of the stature of Dickens.

Although the cinema has not yet gained admission to an orthodox pantheon of the arts it is an acknowledged social fact. The experience of film-going is shared on an international and virtually global scale; in spite of the decline in attendance of British cinema-goers more people go to the cinema each week than attend football matches or buy books. Not surprisingly perhaps, the preponderance of attention focused on the cinema has attended to its effects. By now the scrutineers have switched their gaze to the television but the suspicion that animated the 1917 inquiry continues to inform inquiries into mass communications – a disquiet arising out of individuals, often children's, social behaviour, comes to bear on the content of the mass media, and an inquiry into the effects of mass communications, particularly the forces generated by the portrayal of violent or sexual behaviour, is prosecuted.

The report of a television research committee, the Halloran Report of 1964, may profitably be examined as representative of the mode of inquiry that follows the mobilization of sociology in the quest for a scientific, value-free analysis. Mr Halloran states:

The weight of evidence is ... that the heavy dosage of violence in the mass media, though not a major determinant of crime or delinquency, heightens the probability that someone in the audience will behave aggressively in a later situation...

and a propos of the relationship between cultural studies, impressionistic and value judgements, and the work of social scientists:

Social science research is not concerned with making value statements, it is concerned with social facts and with drawing a distinction between social fact and social value.

Mr Halloran clearly shows an insensitivity to language in permitting himself to regard 'heavy dosage' as a neutral value-free statement, but that is of secondary importance when compared to the crucial lack of recognition that a critical judgement has been made, and needs to be argued and sustained. In describing mass media content as partly a 'heavy dosage of violence' there is no indication that depiction of violence can be anything but harmful or that definition of an act or event as violent might be a judgement that needs reflection and argument. One wonders whether Mr Halloran encountered a production of 'King Lear' on the television in the course of his investigation. Is the blinding of Gloucester to be enumerated as one more act of violence contributing to the 'heavy dosage' provoking aggressive behaviour? If so, is not the whole process of undifferentiated enumeration thrown into disrepute? And if not, it can only be excluded through the use of critical criteria that are the reverse of value-free, leaving aside the interesting question of the propriety of including disturbing material on television or cinema programmes (surely there is a way in which it is entirely proper for an audience to be disturbed, its scheme of values and behaviour thrown into question?); it is only through a scrupulous interpretative attention to context that meanings may be defined and elicited. I have assumed a positively ridiculous naïvety in the researchers, for no doubt the accretion of cultural respectability around Shakespeare enforces a recognition that the experience of 'King Lear' is radically different from much T.V. soap opera (though this is not to say that children and adults may not be disturbed by specific scenes and by the play as a whole). My purpose in raising this here is to indicate that a consistent, informed and rigorous assessment of the content and meaning of mass communications is a *sine qua non* of mass-communication research. And this assessment can only be the reverse of value-free; subjective, impressionistic; though that is not to say that it need be irresponsible or that there are not criteria for enforcing discriminations between different

217

and mutually exclusive descriptions and evaluations of individual artistic phenomena.

In fact I think that the report of the television research committee forfeits much of its potential force and value by its unreadiness to differentiate between programmes, other than on the grounds of a very narrow definition of content. Statements of the importance of 'comparisons with the earlier study showed that taste had become more standardized and uniform: the stereotyped and predictable were preferred to the challenging' lose much of their force when sustained by evidence of this order: 'four out of five of the Secondary Modern school and over half in the Grammar school chose Westerns as their favourite fare'. It cannot be glibly assumed that Westerns are by definition meretricious and the antithesis of 'challenging'. I hope to show that there are ways in which an interest in Westerns is a perfectly proper taste and may be an index of a lively and mature interest in art. None the less there are very good reasons for the prevalent suspicion of mass media and of the cinema in particular. Much of the output of the mass communications industry is of derisory interest.

But the nature of the production processes of the mass communications industries is complicated, particularly in the case of the cinema, and we cannot, I think, fully understand the output of the commercial cinema without some consideration of the modes of its genesis. I would further argue that in some ways the market orientation of the popular cinema, the definition of conventions and the reliance on stereotyped accounts of experience that this orientation implies, have in some ways proved positively enabling rather than universally debilitating.

THE INDUSTRY

British and European film manufacture has been dominated by American production since the First World War. The sustained dominance of the American film has its roots in the very large home market enjoyed by American producers, a home market that has enabled Americans to establish production on a large continuous scale. Monroe Stahr's estimate in *The Last Tycoon* was pretty accurate: 'I think we can count on a million and a quarter from the road show. Perhaps a million and a half altogether. And a quarter of a million abroad.'

Since the thirties the foreign and particularly European markets have become more important, but still the large American home market established and maintained the American film industry in a position from which it has not been dislodged. During the early days of the cinema the American studios set up vertically integrated chains of production, distribution and exhibition which, though broken up later by anti-trust legislation, foreign tariff barriers and commercial pressures leading to a growth in independent production, established a hegemony which still exists. During the time of American domination patterns of audience expectation were formed, comprehending a stable repertoire of stars, situations, and relationships distinctly those of the American cinema, and although protectionist legislation by European film-producing countries and a decline in cinema attendances together with the slow growth of a more adventurous film-going public have qualified American domination, it is still American products and American systems of production that constitute the bulk of the film experience available in Britain.

Any feature film is the product of a collaborative process of creation; scriptwriter, cameraman, director and actors all exercise a greater or lesser degree of control over the performance and collectively make a preferred version, but the preferred version may be, and often is, re-edited or otherwise re-structured by producer, distributor, exhibitor, or censor. The possibly debilitating effects of censorship need no elaboration: it is only in the last decade that the British Board of Film Censors has discarded criteria implicit here: 'the general public is embarrassed by the subject, so until it becomes a subject that can be mentioned without offence it will be banned'. The attitudes of the censor, whether the Hayes office in the U.S.A. or the B.B.F.C. in the U.K., have done much to make films as bland and trivial as they are: but censorship is only one among a number of pressures. The changes demanded by studio or producer may prove equally destructive to the unity of a film and it seems that, as often as not, changes provoked by 'front office' considerations

219

make for incoherence and dissonance in the final version. But of course the pressures imposed by attention to market requirements can prove salutary; much European cinema is unconstrained by these requirements and displays itself as recondite, self-referential, and merely personal – it is rare indeed that films from British or American studios display these characteristics; if often banal they are rarely less than lucid.

A feature film may cost over one million pounds to manufacture, of which an infinitesimal proportion is devoted to the cost of final prints; thus once a final print has been made further prints for multiple exhibition cost almost nothing. Given this property of film production and the disposition of manufacturers to recoup production expenses and maximize profits as early as possible, the preferred pattern of distribution and exhibition will be to a mass audience. A mass audience made up of different nationalities, ages and social classes may only be secured if the experience made available, the film, is one to which all may respond. An appeal to the lowest common denominator of audience interest has distinguished much of the work of the film industry (though declining audiences have to some extent provoked a readiness to pitch films for minority interests); this together with a tendency for any process of production to aspire to repeatability, mass-production, has engendered formula pictures constructed out of a fixed repertoire of recurring elements, often following in an ever diminishing and sterile circle the characteristics of the last success.

The pattern cannot but be a stultifying one; experiment and development are put at a heavy discount, the industry becomes more and more concerned with short-term quick returns, films inclining either to the merely fashionable or tilling already well-turned ground. The continued youth of Cary Grant, the ludicrous spinning out of the British 'Carry On' formula and the parasitic exploitation of series pioneered on television – 'Till Death Us Do Part' and 'Dad's Army' – are the fruit of the film industry's inability to adjust to new market conditions, or to supplant distribution and exhibition policies developed in the days of regular cinema-going with models more appropriate to contemporary conditions. The squeeze on company profits has led,

220

particularly in the U.S.A., to a change in production patterns, with independent production supplanting the work of studios. This potentially liberating development has not been generally welcomed by film directors nor has it produced a range of distinctive individual films. Directors reared in the bad old days of the Hollywood studios, when they might be assigned to a series of uncongenial projects, voice a nostalgia for the technical excellence of the studio team and the possibility of developing novel treatments which, if successful, might profitably initiate a new series for the studio, if unsuccessful could be borne, thanks to the profits from other products. The pluralism and discontinuous nature of the predominantly independent production that has supplanted the reign of the studios has provoked both an increased reliance on an often very tired formula and an almost manic search for a new and profitable gimmick. Fine films none the less continue to be produced and distributed but it is difficult to imagine the return of a situation in which directors like Anthony Mann and Vincent Minelli could, through a process of consistent development of popular forms, move towards the articulation of a rich and very individual version of experience. Both Minelli's musicals and Mann's Westerns constitute bodies of consistently impressive work and enact a development made possible by the secure system of production offered by Hollywood and the range of conventions available in popular genres. (Jim Kitses' book *Horizons West* discusses Mann in some detail; English writings on Minelli are to be found predominantly in *Movie*.)

The aspiration towards mass production in commercial cinema, especially in Hollywood, led to the establishment of genres which proved the source of a fundamentally enabling fund of situations, characters and conventions within which film makers were able to work fruitfully; in short the establishment of genres in the American cinema offered directors a language. A comparable development has never occurred in the British cinema, though there are promising signs that horror films may provide a rich perspective in which film makers may define themselves and engage the vital interests, conscious or unconscious, of general audiences.

221

Post-romantic theories of art, which constitute much of our intellectual and critical inheritance, do not dispose us to think well of the notion that the subject of art is formed in a wider context than that of an individual creative consciousness. We do well though, particularly in a consideration of popular or mass art, to consider the function of the cinema as myth, as expressing the concerns and characteristics of a mass consciousness. Although the status of myth (indeed its definition) is a notoriously vexed question, its function may be described as the mediation of an understanding of a human existential condition: thus the importance of an action in a myth resides not in its status in a causal physical world, but in its representativeness. So we may say that the sacrifice of Isaac by Abraham is of trivial historical importance but informed with great mythical significance. It follows that testing the historical authenticity of realistic films may not be the most appropriate way of responding to them: instead we should perhaps consider their efficacy in mediating an understanding of existential crises.

I intend to focus my attention on the American cinema in discussing characteristics of the cinema as an element in popular culture. This is a strategy that is imposed both by the nature of the subject, since much of the British and world film experience is constituted of American films, and also because it is in the American cinema that the potential qualities of a popular cinema are most fully realized. I realize that this may be a somewhat unfamiliar and even controversial judgement; none the less I think it is true, though it remains equally true that much American production is fit only for consumption as 'chewing gum for the eyes'. It is perhaps in the American cinema that one's discriminatory faculties are most fully and consistently exercised.

One of the perennial themes of Western art and thought has been the conflict between individualism and collectivism: this issue I suggest animates much of the American cinema and in particular lies at the roots of the Western. Thus we may fruitfully plot a changing view of the American past, and by extension a changing view of American society in the nature of the experience communicated as the Western genre develops through time. The confident positivism of the values of 'manifest destiny' and

222

in the colonization of the American frontier that informs John Ford's 'My Darling Clementine' made in 1946 is modulated in the films of the 1950s. Bud Boetticher's 'The Tall T' shows the west as a landscape of destruction and nihilism. The final series of combats that secures the hero's survival virtually eliminates everything else – his gesture of trust and neutrality is turned against him and a realization of man's condition of Hobbesian isolation enforced through Boetticher's insistence in the film's final shots of the continuity between hero and a landscape of aridity, isolation and death. Sam Peckinpah's 'Guns in the Afternoon' gives us a Western, later in historical time than Ford's 'My Darling Clementine', in which the settlement of the west, far from establishing a community distinguished by a capacity for individual autonomy and generous association with others, unfettered by the corruption of the city, exhibits qualities of rapacious exploitation of natural resources, and the disfigurement of the landscape with a squalid mining camp centred, not as in Ford's film around a church, but around a brothel.

The kind of process that the different views of experience enunciated in these three films enacts is, I suggest, one that has its correlative in the development of American society and in its collective consciousness. To tease out these relationships would require a considerable essay and I offer the example not only as a provocation to further study but as an example of the way in which the cinema may constitute cultural evidence of the kind alluded to early in this essay and as a statement about the nature of the American cinema. To imply that the difference between the three films is more than that between three individual authorial consciousnesses is to say that the difference is one which locates shifts in the orientation and development of the genre. For example Peckinpah's model has proved an exemplary one, and cinemas in recent years have been full of Westerns affirming waste, corruption and a sense that traditional moral values are threatened by, and out of joint with, a materialist, exploitative social ethic. The content of the films, though seemingly not dealing with contemporary life and problems in the way that realistic films about, say, racial integration or the dissonance between the

223

values of Madison Avenue and the Bible belt do, none the less explores and records issues of contemporary disquiet.

The existence of a genre with tight conventions exploring modes of behaviour in a closely defined temporal and geographical context, characteristics often regarded as the properties of a stereotype, acts in certain cases as a positively enabling force. Through the limited range of possibilities offered by the Western and its finite referential scheme some film makers have been able to achieve films which are as dense and as fine as the best works of the European cinema and which invite comparison with the major works of the nineteenth-century novel or theatre. In his book *Art and Illusion* E. H. Gombrich talks of the development of languages of expression in fine art and the establishment of traditions as a necessary condition for the achievement of resonant expressive art. He says: 'All human communication is through symbols, through the medium of a language, and the more articulate the language the greater the chance for the message to get through'. It is just this development of a tradition that we find in the genres of the American cinema, particularly the Western, the customary butt of mass media critics, a tradition that has, like that of the novel or landscape painting, been attended by its masterpieces.

Within the constraints of an essay of this length I cannot justify my propositions with anything approaching exhaustiveness and must lean heavily on other works, some of which are indicated in the bibliography. Any theories of art or criteria of excellence are finally only useful if they assist in developing and enlarging an understanding of individual works, and it is only in the individual works that the perceptions and ordering of experience which constitute the claims of an artist on our attention can be bodied forth in a context of realized intensity. Accordingly I propose to discuss a film which is definitely of the popular cinema, which I do not unreservedly admire but which has its own excellence and in which both the strengths and inadequacies of the Hollywood system of production are apparent. I hope to show that the Western has a genuine claim on our attention and is a form through which the nature of both historical processes and states of feeling may be elucidated, ordered and realized. In short that the general claims made for the richness of the cinema as a medium of communication may be grounded as well in the popular cinema – the product of a collective, collaborative, industrial enterprise – as in the works of individual masters.

NICHOLAS RAY'S 'THE JAMES BROTHERS'

Hollywood is archtypically the temple of distortion and the high altar is where sacrifices of truth and historicity are made to the aggrandized reputations of criminals. A review on the occasion of the British release of 'The James Brothers' contrasts the Hollywood version with that of the dictionary of American biography:

Jesse Woodson James (1847–1882), American outlaw. He belongs to that doubtful order of champions who began with guerrilla warfare and a grudge and end as bandits; robbed banks and held up trains; murdered quite a number of people before being murdered himself; his brother Frank stood trial and was remarkably lucky to be acquitted; his mother had her hand blown off by besieging Pinkerton men; most of his life was spent under aliases in hiding; he had dyed hair and bow legs. It is as well to know what stuff a popular hero is made of. In 'The James Brothers' the whole family reappears purged of its squalors; Jesse is upright in stature and almost in intentions; Frank breaks away and is willing to face the music, Ma with hand restored can be proud of her terrible boys. They make a handsome hunted pair in this new version of the legend directed by Nicholas Ray which sets out to take the eye and engage the sympathy.*

But of course the characteristically favourable account of the James gang is that of tradition. Jesse James was and is a popular culture hero and folk heroes do not take on a wide popular appeal in defiance of authority's version for no reason.

The James Brothers stand as a type of the outlaw hero in Western films: they pre-eminently embody the disorientation and flux of American society after the Civil War, and their position is in some way exemplary. During the long history of the Western (dating from 'The Great Train Robbery' of 1903) directors have selected a repertoire of situations, antinomies and motifs from the mass of material available in the history of the American

*William Whitebait, *New Statesman.*

225

frontier. Drawing on the history of the frontier (the 'subject' of Westerns) they have enunciated a series of focal situations in which historical, mythological and personal crises are encapsulated. The gun fight, drifters from a defeated south, confrontations of cavalry and Indians, ambushes, gambling, cattle drives and railway building are all familiar to film-goers and in these representative situations crucial meanings may be embodied by directors.

The conflict between individualist and collectivist ethics is one that has excited the American consciousness and informed American art from the time of Madison and Alexander Hamilton and before. This opposition lies behind the struggle between north and south in the Civil War, animates much American literature (e.g. the characteristic theme in Hawthorne and Melville of the artist struggling for a *modus vivendi*, a way of relating himself and his work to general shared social activity) and constitutes the central problem explored in both Western and gangster films. It's a continuing preoccupation and finds lodgment in contemporary youth culture, where a cult of individualism is linked to a specific nostalgia for the south: Bob Dylan in 'John Wesley Harding' and 'Nashville Skyline', The Band, particularly in 'The Night They Drove Old Dixie Down' and in the work of the felicitously named James Gang – a group whose music has no connection with the south but who have annexed the title of outlaws as an index of their own relationship with contemporary straight America.

In this struggle the south was firmly identified with local autonomy, pluralism and individualism. In John Taylor of Caroline (a Virginian senator of the early nineteenth century) political and social theories are representatively Southern:

I believe that a loss of independent internal power by our Confederate states and an acquisition of supreme power by the federal department, or by any branch of it, will substantially establish a consolidated republic over all the territories of the United States though a federal phraseology might remain; that this consolidation would produce a monarchy, and that the monarchy however limited, checked or balanced would finally become a complete tyranny.*

*Tyranny Unmasked, 1805.

Outlaws and bandits clearly have an affinity with the individualist ethic; their mode of behaviour is one of exploiting and attacking the agencies of collective action through which wealth has been concentrated. Some outlaws, including the James Brothers, are explicitly associated with the south and their depredations were predominantly at the expense of the institutions of the colonialist collectivist north – their victims, banks and railroads. Indeed most Westerns are set in a post-Civil War temporal context in which these conflicts were particularly acute.

During Reconstruction the treatment of the south as a conquered-territory policed by Unionist soldiers and Pinkerton mercenaries and administered by carpet-baggers and scallawags provoked an intense need for culture heroes; and men like Jesse and Frank James who continued their war time guerrilla battle for the Cause in attacks on Yankee banks and railways, enjoyed very considerable popular sympathy and support.

Around the spectacular career of the James Brothers an accretion of legends and myths has gathered and precise differentiation of myth and history is no longer possible. History and myth are customarily regarded as antithetical. Myth is emphatically a question of belief, true for those with pre-existent convictions, and false for those without: rather, mythology pervades and informs responses to experience and offers models for its comprehension and ordering. The mythology that has accumulated around the career of the Jameses, much of which has come from the entertainment industry – the dime novels and Wild West shows of the nineteenth century and the range of films about the James Gang, ranging from 'Jesse James' in 1911 to the 34-episode serial recently screened in Britain on I.T.V. – dramatizes their part in the American struggle between individualism and collectivism. Professor Thistlethwaite, in his book *The Great Experiment*, characterizes the Civil War as a water-shed in this struggle; and in terms of a struggle between collectivist forces, sustained by a capitalist economy into which individuals sink their identity in corporate endeavour among political equals, and individualists, sustained in their turn by a hierarchical social order (the old south) in which a stable and secure place in that order is substituted for the political equality espoused by the north, a defeated

227

individualist is likely to regard continued resistance, a heroic posture of individual mastering experience and determining his own role, as preferable to subsumption into the new collective order, the Union as proper. The activity of the James Gang during Reconstruction won them considerable support from contemporary southerners and it is out of the perspective of a struggle for national self-definition that their heroic stature came: the continued popularity of films and novels about western outlaws, and specifically the Jameses, indicates that the conflicts their legends enact and explore are still alive.

The theme of the man who won't be reconstructed recurs again and again in the Western, whether as Rod Steiger leaving the defeated south to join the Apache nation in Sam Fuller's 'Run of the Arrow', John Wayne in John Ford's magisterial 'The Searchers' drifting between the Mexican wars, Indian fighting and casual work, or Clark Gable in Raoul Walsh's 'The Tall Men', flirting with Yankee collectivism but finally eschewing it and returning to farming in Texas. If then we can analyse historical events in terms of cultural, ethical and moral conflicts then the depiction of those events in fictional terms will assume those dimensions and manifest a meaning in those terms. When conflicts are played out in exemplary situations between heroes, men whose actions are representative and transcendental, the dimensions of the fiction become mythological.

The cycle of films about the James Gang may, I think, fruitfully be considered in terms of myth. David Bidney in his essay reproduced in *Myth: A Symposium*, edited by Sebeok, sets up a triadic model of man's understanding of the world: mythic, epic and historical. He suggests that the transition from mythic to epic occurs when man bases his conduct on some notion of the model man or the cult of the hero. The historical stage emerges when man ceases to look to the exemplary past and sets up for himself rational objectives and means for their attainment. The films about the James Gang inhabit and inform all three areas.

A film like the Republic serial 'The Adventures of Frank and Jesse James', 1948, is of a primary mythological order: Jesse and Frank engage exclusively in virtuous action, they signify repentance and goodness, their good fortune in finding a gold mine

228

enables them to become capitalists and repay their debts! The epic is represented by Henry King's 'Jesse James', 1939. Frank and Jesse respond to reconstruction and scallawag politicians by fighting Yankee capitalism. They offer themselves in the film as models to other dispossessed and deracinated southerners and to the audience of 1939 as a model through which a response to twentieth-century slump economics may be defined. The film is very like the contemporary 'Grapes of Wrath', the role of the James family like that of the Joads, each evicted from their small farm by bullying landowners, each farm crushed by the symbols of the onward movement of nineteenth- and twentieth-century technocratic capitalism – the railway locomotive and the bulldozer. Indeed the films share two actors, Henry Fonda and Jane Darwell, whose fictional personae in each film mutually consolidate each other through their similar roles in the films; indeed in a more general sense each actor brings his or her iconographical meaning, established elsewhere, to the part.

The American cinema is notorious for its star system – a system that is both an index of its general reductiveness, reducing actors to the status of a commodity of constant and predictable specifications, and of its market orientation, the aspiration to a consistent and identifiable product image. But the star system does have real strengths. An actor may play a series of similar parts extending in each the definition of his persona, creating a normative pattern of behaviour in which deviance assumes a commensurately great significance. Thus a language of expectation, of conventions, of symbols, is established in which meaning may be communicated with precision and economy.

Nicholas Ray's film may inhabit Bidney's third area: the historical; indeed the original title of the film, the one used in its U.S. release, 'The True Story of Jesse James', invites consideration of the authenticity of the experience and historical moment it presents. The film constitutes both a statement about the lives of Jesse and Frank James and an account of myth-making in action and enjoys, I think, an exemplary status. It seems a really intelligent attempt to come to grips with the problem of defining the kind of truths about Jesse James that are available.

'The James Brothers' too is an interesting Hollywood case

229

study: Nicholas Ray said in his lecture at the National Film Theatre in 1969 that he did not like the film and had not seen it since it was made; not surprising perhaps in view of its production history. He had planned a film about his favourite concern – young people:

My preliminary production scheme was to do the whole film on stage as a kind of legend with people coming in and out of areas of light – making it a period study of war and the effects of war on the behaviour of young people, but doing it as though it were a ballad ... the result was, I think, a very ordinary kind of film.

The film is predominantly realistic, mostly shot on location and distinguished by Ray's customary excellence in placing characters in a landscape that is revealing and informative. As Jean-Luc Godard stated in his review of the film for *Cahiers du Cinéma*, the film exhibits 'Ray's ability to render tangible and clear concepts as abstract as those of liberty and destiny'.

Producer, studio and, in Britain, distributor, have all functioned as major determinants of the form the film takes. Their influence seems to have been instrumental in the choice of narrative procedure adopted in the film – a dialectic of past and present flashbacks juxtaposed with a fictional present – and to have infused a greater concentration of 'genre' elements than the director wished. It's clearly much more of a Western than Ray desired; his aspiration was towards a 'Rebel Without a Cause' out west. In fact the centre of the film's moral scheme is the conflict of individualism and collectivism that I described as a general property of much American art and specifically of the Western. It is not a theme that is central to Ray's other films. We may, I think, be grateful to the producer and studio for diluting Ray's very personal scheme; less happy though is the interference which recut the film, interposed dissolves through flame and deleted several key scenes.

The film as it stands is a construct of episodic intensity governed by the dramatic irony created in the first magnificent sequences of the Northfield raid seen from the townspeople's point of view. The film begins in violence and confusion – a motif that recurs throughout the film but which is ordered through the audience's developing understanding of events and their connection: the audience knows the final fate of the gang and is able to assess the significance of the forces bearing on the lives of the protagonists in a way they themselves are unable to do.

I do not propose to go through the whole fim and discuss the force and function of each scene but will comment on particularly striking and significant episodes.

The baptism scene that follows Jesse's return home after fighting the Civil War as a Confederate guerrilla is representative of Ray's originality and audacity – unprecedented in earlier films on the same subject. The scene is invested with considerable grace and harmony; Jesse and Zee (who becomes his wife) are baptized by a minister; the two young people, one dressed in black and the other in white, are immersed in a large pool, watched by a community who participate in the ceremony of initiation administered by a benevolent and distinguished representative of temporal and spiritual authority, the minister. The baptism is a key scene in the film signifying reconciliation – black and white, male and female, individual and community and the establishment of Jesse James in a harmonious relationship with others, his rebellion and dissent laid aside in submission to the minister.

The central sequence of the film is a spectacular train robbery and it is in this scene that the theme of individual locked in a struggle against collectivism receives its most resonant symbolic articulation. A lighted train travelling at night containing collectivized man, neatly separated and organized in compartments, is followed by an individual from the outside, who affirms his mastery of the collective and its creation, the machine, by leaping on to the roof of the train, dancing, as it seems, along the carriages, halting the train and robbing the passengers. The following scene has a similarly important function in enforcing a realization that the lives of the heroes proceed on unique existential terms. They have solved the problem of action in a chaotic and changing world. In command of their experience, and able to order life on their own terms, the outlaws do not live as the prey of contingent or superhuman forces but are able to order and structure their experience as they wish.

The James gang are fed by a distressed widow who explains

that her rapacious landlord is about to foreclose her mortgage and evict her. Jesse James gives her sufficient money to pay the mortgage and instructs her to secure a receipt, the gang leave the house, watch the landlord enter and leave, and then steal the money paid him by the widow. Stealing therefore enables Jesse James to redress wrongs and punish transgressors at no cost to himself. The gift of money to the widow relieves her want, the theft from the landlord returns the gift to the donor and punishes an avaricious rentier.

The second view of the Northfield raid offered in the film, that through outlaw eyes, is a very representative embodiment of Ray's directorial talent and displays his consummate ability to realize events with extraordinary vividness and immediacy. Communication of the chaos and violence of the event is a matter of the sudden intrusion of a gun barrel into the image threatening the outlaws from a totally unexpected direction, from behind the camera. Similarly farm machinery (the motif of Yankee technocracy – collectivism again) takes on an unexpected and sinister role as an obstacle; the brothers escape the trap by riding through a shop window. The director's investment in them of a capacity for rapid assessment and response to new situations is also an index of his own creative originality.

After their escape from the abortive raid the brothers hide in a cave, and the film returns to the question implicitly raised in the title and explicitly in the early sequence, where a gang member suggests that Jesse engaged in his criminal life out of a desire for fame. The continuous process of speculation about the true story of Jesse James that the film enacts shifts to a metaphysical perspective in the brothers' conversation in the cave. They discuss their lives, Jesse maintaining that they were 'driven to it' (his behaviour is inconsistent with his own view, as he behaves as if man created his own destiny but believes himself driven by the furies). Frank offers a more pragmatic analysis and believes that the brothers have created their own fate and that Jesse has chosen to seek death and invite self-destruction. The behaviour of the Jameses explores three existential possibilities – man as hero, man as victim, and man engaged in an irresolute struggle with opposing forces for his own destiny. Jesse's neurotic inconsistency

232

derives from his own individualism, from his own *raison d'être* – when triumphant an individualist is a hero, when defeated an anachronism, the prey of organized collectivism and the victim of forces beyond his control and therefore beyond his comprehension. Frank retains possession of himself and is able to encompass the rival demands of individualism and collectivism; his upbringing and allegiance to the Confederacy, and the changed circumstances of later life – Reconstruction and the colonization of south by north.

The death of Jesse, very like that of the Jacobean revenge hero, killed from behind with his own weapon, augments rather than diminishes his stature as hero of the myth. He has the distinction of course of having died before making an inevitable compromise with the Yankees and embracing Reconstruction. His commitment to the Cause, to the fight for the defeated Confederacy, ends with his integrity uncompromised.

Fritz Lang, the eminent German film director who left Germany after the Nazis took power and worked in Hollywood until the late fifties, has spoken of the importance of the Western as a repository of myths and therefore as an agency for mediating existential truths: 'The Western is not only the history, of this country (i.e. America), it is what the saga of the Nibelungen is for the European'. If the Western corresponds to the Nibelungenlied then Jesse James, killed from behind by a friend, is surely its Siegfried. He embodies in his struggle the model of authentic conduct in the fight against collectivism.

Simply to establish the Western as an agency for the mediation of existential truths does not of course imply that discriminations between individual works are not appropriate; the experience of seeing 'The James Brothers' is very different from that of seeing the recent television serial about Jesse James. Whilst both film and series are susceptible to content analysis and thematic definition in much the same terms, in one the experience is much more resonant than in the other. In the Ray film it is 'proved upon the pulses'.

The scrupulous differentiation of distinct experiences has not been a characteristic of writings on popular culture in Britain, and it seems to me that the immediate task is to indicate grounds

233

for taking popular culture, and in the specific context of this essay, the cinema, as commanding serious attention. Having indicated some of the grounds for supposing that art of a high order of excellence may be achieved in the popular cinema and having argued this contention through an elucidation of the qualities of a specific film, we may then go on to consider the ways in which a scheme of reference, larger than that of an individual director's, actor's or scriptwriter's work, may prove illuminating. The perspectives in which we may best achieve an understanding of 'The James Brothers' are those of the director's, Nicholas Ray's, other work, and that offered by other similar films of the genre. For example, it seems to me that much of the dramatic irony that is at work in the film and that informs an audience's response, at once provoking a deeper involvement in the course of events and a detachment enabling one to contemplate, order and comprehend events, is a matter of knowing from expectations formed in seeing both other films about the James gang and those about the problems posed by the disorientation of frontier life, the possible and likely end of their career. Just as the Jacobean revenge play offers a perspective that illuminates our understanding of *Hamlet*, so does the Western, its conventions and language, illuminate and inform a response to 'The James Brothers'.

Comment at considerable length on a single film may perhaps require justification in a general essay, but it seems to me that the only way in which cultural assumptions and evaluations may be subjected to empirical testing, and verified or discarded, is if they are supported by an account of individual works in some specificity. I hope that, having indicated some of my grounds for admiring one film, generalizations about the Western, the cinema, and popular culture may assume a firmer and more concrete definition than a more discursive procedure would admit. However the excellence of one film is no testament to the vitality and fruitfulness of a tradition, nor does it permit any generalizations about what I take to be the key concept for an understanding of popular cinema genre. I hope that my remarks will act as a provocation to explore the writings on the American cinema, some of which are indicated in the book list at the end of this chapter.

234

But some further comments about the function of genre may be in order. I referred earlier to Sam Peckinpah's film 'Guns in the Afternoon' offering a different account of the west to that of earlier Westerns. The theme of the past, of history, is the central concern of Westerns and Peckinpah's film is explicitly concerned with history, expressing the notion of temporal transition in personal terms through the two central characters played by Randolph Scott and Joel McRea. The two men have 'outlived their time'; the values by which they lived in their youth, in the heroic past of the frontier, in 'manifest destiny', have been displaced by the advent of technology and industrialization. The central concern of the film is how each comes to terms with this displacement and his own sense of incongruity.

A sense of the past pervades the whole film and is not only given through the actors' performances but determines the whole nature of the visual experience – the colours are on a narrow band of yellows, golds, browns and russets – predominantly autumnal; the pace of cutting is slow and shots of considerable length are juxtaposed. The pace is leisurely. But elements of dissonance and conflict are constantly introduced, a tone of assurance and repose constantly disrupted. The film opens with a slow evocation of a familiar townscape – the small western town populated by men wearing jeans, jackets and large hats, horses tethered, the kind of scene shown in many Westerns and which the cinema-goer has learnt to associate with the west. But our expectations, formed in seeing other films and alerted by the first familiar images, are disconcerted by the intrusion of a motor-car, a policeman in uniform and the familiar noble and self-assured figure of Randolph Scott clad as a ridiculous Buffalo Bill; the sense of incongruity is confirmed when we witness a race between horses and a camel.

Without a series of expectations formed by seeing other Westerns prior to 'Guns in the Afternoon', expectations that exclude cars, policemen and camels from the landscape of the west, much of the force of the early part of the film would be lost. Peckinpah is able to draw on the qualities of the genre, work against them and communicate a sense of unease, dissonance and insecurity in an economical, restrained and wholly realistic way.

The theme of the film, the nature of the experience of men who

235

have outlived their time, is given us in the most pertinent and resonant series of visual images, an achievement of the director made possible by the nature of convention, the stereotypes of genre and the popular cinema. As I. C. Jarvie says: 'The medium is a sophisticated and refined one which cannot be appreciated without a degree of involvement and learning'.

BOOKS

General

S. HALL and P. WHANNEL, *The Popular Arts*, Hutchinson Educational, 1964

S. HALLORAN, *Effects of Mass Communication*, Leicester University Press

R. HOGGART, *The Literary Imagination and the Study of Society*, Centre for Contemporary Cultural Studies, University of Birmingham

I. C. JARVIE, *Towards a Sociology of the Cinema*, Routledge

T. SEBEOK (ed.), *Myth: a Symposium*, Midland Books

R. WILLIAMS, *Communications*, Penguin Books, 1968

R. WILLIAMS, *Culture and Society*, Penguin Books, 1968

American Cinema and the Western

A. BAZIN, *Qu'est-ce que le cinema?*, Editions du Cerf, 1958

J. KITSES, *Horizons West*, Thames & Hudson, 1969

J. P. RIEUPEYROUT, *La grande aventure du Western*, Editions du Cerf

A. SARRIS, *The American Cinema*, Dutton, 1969

P. WOLLEN, *Signs and Meaning in the Cinema*, Secker & Warburg, 1969

The Industry

P. FRENCH, *The Movie Moguls*, Penguin Books, 1971

P. MAYERSBERG, *Hollywood the Haunted House*, Penguin Books, 1969

THE MONOPOLIES COMMISSION, *Films*, H.M.S.O

The British Film Industry (1952 and 1958), P.E.P

Much of the best British writing on the cinema is confined to journals:

MONOGRAM, 63 Old Compton Street, London W.1

MOVIE, 23 Emerald Street, London W.C.1

SCREEN, 63 Old Compton Street, London W.1

The British Film Institute Education Department has an excellent study unit on the Western for hire: it consists of an Anthony Mann feature film, film extracts and an abundance of documentation and slides.

The British Film Institute (81 Dean Street, London W.1; Education Officer, Douglas Lowndes) has done much to foster film study in Britain and is an invaluable source of help and advice for student and teacher. The study of the American cinema in British higher education is centred on the American Arts Documentation Centre at the University of Exeter. The Centre for Contemporary Cultural Studies at the University of Birmingham is concerned with general cultural issues and includes the cinema within its frame of reference.

Notes on Contributors

PHILIP ABRAMS is Professor of Sociology at the University of Durham. His interests include the sociology of culture and mass communication and political sociology. As a result of the publication of the first edition of *Discrimination and Popular Culture* he was involved in a number of radio and television broadcasts which powerfully confirmed his view of the problems these media face.

RICHARD COLLINS teaches film and communication studies. Born in London in 1946, he read English at the Universities of York and Warwick. He contributes to and helps to edit *Monogram* film magazine.

DAVID HOLBROOK's books on the teaching of English include *English for the Rejected*, and on the psychology of culture, *The Masks of Hate* and *Sex and Dehumanization*. Recent works: *Dylan Thomas: The Code of Night* and *Human Hope and the Death Instinct*, on psychological 'models' of human nature. He has published a novel, *Flesh Wounds*, and four volumes of poetry. Forthcoming works include *English in Australia Now* and *Sylvia Plath and the Problem of Existence*. He is at present working on a Humanities course under an Elmgrant Trust award.

DONALD J. HUGHES was educated at Brighton, Hove and Sussex G.S., where music – not being on the curriculum – became his absorbing interest. Later he took both a B.Sc. in Economics and a Doctorate in Music, and is now Principal Lecturer in the Music Department of the North-East Essex Technical College. He has been concerned with musical activity among all kinds of young people since the war, and is Chairman of 'Sing for Pleasure', an association of youth choirs. Publications include *Let's Have Some Music*.

FRED INGLIS is Lecturer in the Advanced Studies Division of

238

the School of Education, Bristol University. He is an active conservationist, a Parliamentary Labour Party candidate, and has taught in secondary schools and colleges of education in the U.S.A. and in this country. Previous books include *The Elizabethan Poets*, *The Englishness of English Teaching*, *Literature and Environment* and *The Imagery of Power*.

GRAHAM MARTIN is Reader in Literature at the Open University. His main interests are in twentieth-century and Romantic poetry, the interaction of 'high' and 'popular' culture, and the educational uses of radio and television. He has published essays in Volume 7 of the *Pelican Guide to English Literature* and has edited a symposium, *Eliot in Perspective*, and an anthology, *Industrialisation and Culture, 1830–1914*. He has written articles on Coleridge, whose poems he is currently editing, and books for Open University courses on D. H. Lawrence, Dickens, George Eliot and James Joyce.

FRANK WHITEHEAD, after lecturing in English at the University of London Institute of Education, is now senior lecturer in English and Education at the University of Sheffield. His publications include *The Disappearing Dais, Creative Experiment: Writing and the Teacher*, a contribution to Volume 5 of the *Pelican Guide to English Literature*, and a volume of selections from Crabbe's poetry.

239